This memoir is true to the best of my recollection.
The story, however, has been fictionalized so that the
reader could experience the events as I experienced them.
Many of the names have been changed to protect the identities
of the people involved so that no harm would come to
them as a result of my story.

* * *

All statements of fact, opinion, or analysis expressed are those of the author and do not reflect the official positions or views of the CIA or any other U.S. Government agency. Nothing in the contents should be construed as asserting or implying U.S. Government authentication or Agency endorsement of the author's views.

This material has been reviewed by the CIA to
prevent the disclosure of classified information.

Spies, Lies & Psychosis

To: Joan,
Live life passionately!
Joan Kopczynski

JOAN KOPCZYNSKI

Gray Dog Press

Gray Dog Press
Spokane, Washington
www.GrayDogPress.com

Spies, Lies & Psychosis

For information contact:
Gray Dog Press
2727 S. Mt. Vernon #4
Spokane, Washington 99223

Printed in the U.S.A.

ISBN-13: 978-1-936178-38-4

To the memory of Jack Trevanian Hashian
my mentor, my friend

As promised, I'm dedicating my first book to you. In all my travels, adventures and experiences, I never met a more decent human being than you, my dear friend. I've never met someone I wanted to be like—until you. I could never fill your shoes but you've made me a better Joan Kopczynski for having known you. Thank you for the memory.

Acknowledgements

First, I would like to thank five women who inspired and encouraged me to write this book: my three sisters, Connie Esser, Theresa Wessels and Karen Stubbs, and my friends, Eleanor Tolar and Lori Speight. When I felt like bagging it because it was too emotionally draining to relive past experiences, their reassurance that my story needed to be told provided incentive to keep going.

Secondly, I would like to thank my tutor, Mr. Robert Gover, for his expert advice, for teaching me the fundamentals of writing over the past ten years and for inspiring me to persist in honing my craft.

Thirdly, I would like to thank Sue Jostrom for the great love and compassion she showed in editing my manuscript and for encouraging me to improve.

Fourthly, I would like to thank the following three women (out of six people that I approached) who took the time to respond to my endorsement letters: (in the order that they responded) actress and mental health advocate, Glenn Close; the author, Danielle Steel and former First-Lady, Rosalynn Carter. Although they each declined for different reasons, their authentic and encouraging letters proved to give me greater motivation to share my story.

In addition, I would like to thank the following men for their encouragement and lending a supportive ear in my struggle with mental illness: my wise friend, Terry Stout, for his kind and steadfast emotional support; my cousin, Dave Reed, who told me "it takes fifteen years of hard work to become an overnight success;" my cousin, Chris Kopczynski, for inspiration to climb my own Mt. Everest; my psychiatrist, David Bot, M.D., a great listener and mental health advocate who never let me wallow in self-pity and Abe Ferris, also a great listener, who introduced me to a support group and helped me put my issues into perspective.

Special thanks to my great friend, Aunt Maxine Kopczynski, who stunned me by her concern and many questions about my illness and for offering to catch me if I needed financial help.

I would also like to thank Greg Wherry, editor of my hometown newspaper, for allowing me the opportunity to publish mental health articles in *The Cottonwood Chronicle* which started the ball rolling.

And, I'd like to express my gratitude to my writer friend, Betty Deuber, for her editorial comments on the manuscript and for taking me under her wing and introducing me to a writer's group and Writer's Workshop for Seniors in Spokane, an incredible and to-die-for experience.

Lastly, I would like to express my thanks to Russ Davis and his crew at Gray Dog Press for all their hard work in helping to make my dream of publishing come true.

Chapter 1

Danger lurked in friendly faces. After working for the CIA for five years, I resigned and in 1979 found myself living in San Francisco and dating Connor Eubanks, an FBI agent. It was easier to date someone from the military or intelligence services because they didn't treat you with contempt. Most of the San Francisco men I met hated the military-industrial-complex and anyone connected to it. An FBI agent wouldn't ask questions that I wasn't allowed to answer.

I was twenty-five and taking love where I found it. I found Connor in a singles bar in San Francisco. We both commented that you never meet someone nice in a singles bar. But, I could not possibly have foreseen the trouble to come.

One of the things I loved about Connor is that I could be honest with him about every aspect of my life.

"Come on. You can do it."

"No, I can't."

"Connor, you can if you want to."

"Joanie, I can't," he said, starting to smile.

"Yes, you can. I'm tired of men always giving me that excuse. You're being selfish. Now, just concentrate. Mmmmmmmm, that feels good!"

"I can't do it any longer. I'm sorry."

"Don't give up yet. Oh, please Sweetheart. Just a little while longer."

"I can't do this with just anyone, you know."

"Do what?"

"Stay up like this. This is the longest I've ever done it."

"Keep it up. Keep it up. We like it. We like it."

We both laughed. The laughter made him lose it, as he crashed to the queen-size, flower-covered bed.

"Were you ever a cheerleader?"

"No. I had a chance to be one in high school but I refused to try out. I thought it was too bourgeoisie."

"You'd make a great cheerleader. Joanie, are you interested in getting married? I don't mean to me necessarily, you are such a free spirit."

"I never really thought about it much but yes, I guess it interests me. That is, if it's to the right person." I kissed him tenderly on the lips. "Why do you ask?"

"I don't know. Remember that girl I told you about—the one I started seeing before my wife and I got divorced?"

"Wasn't she the one you found birth controls in her medicine cabinet and you'd had a mastectomy so you couldn't have any more kids?

He looked at me puzzled. "Do you know what you just said?"

"I think so. Why?"

"You said I had a mastectomy." He laughed as if I had just tickled him. "I had a vasectomy not a mastectomy."

"Oh, I get my *ectomies* mixed up sometimes. But what about the girl? Why did you bring her up?"

"Well, I thought she burned the thought of me ever marrying again. She made me distrustful of women. Actually I guess she just wanted to have a baby and since I couldn't . . . but now I'm feeling like I would like to get close to someone again. Would it matter to you that I can't ever have kids again?"

"If I was in love with someone, I mean really in love, whether I could have kids would definitely not matter. If I am honest, marriage and kids have not really been a motivating factor in my life. If I had wanted to be married and have kids, I had opportunities to do so before now. I want freedom more. Like you say, I guess I am a free spirit." I put my arms around him, ran my fingers through his hair and kissed him gently.

"You'd make a great hus . . ."

A knock at the door interrupted us. I lived on the third floor of a three-story apartment building on Clement Street which had a security buzzer downstairs near the main entrance. The building was an old converted Victorian mansion but with a little paint, wallpaper and designer furniture, I transformed my place into understated elegance like that found only in Pacific Heights.

The conversion of the mansion to apartments, however, had created an oddity—both the bedroom and the living room had an outside door to the hallway, which locked. The knocking that Connor and I heard came from the door to the living room.

"Just a minute . . ." I said as I slipped into my blue velour robe. A friend once told me I had the naiveté and wide-eyed innocence of the actress Goldie Hawn yet I was a tall, thin, intelligent brunette. My friend said it was my eyes that told the whole story. They were large, almond-shaped hazel eyes but it wasn't the color that struck him when he first met me. He said it was the purity of my child-like gaze.

Connor took my arm. "Wait to open the door until I tell you," he whispered. He grabbed his pants, zipped them up and then took his gun out of his holster. He never went anywhere without his "piece." Bureau training had made him feel insecure without it. Kneeling on one knee, he stretched out both arms before him and aimed the gun at the door.

"Connor, you're paranoid!" I said, smiling. "Besides, someone had to have a key to the downstairs door to get in."

"Just do it!"

"But, I *hate* guns," I whispered through clenched teeth.

"Joanie, trust me on this."

"But . . ."

"Do it!" he said sternly.

Connor's intensity scared me. "Ok, ok." *Maybe he was right,* I thought. *Maybe he knew better.*

"Ok, now!" he said.

With one quick jerk I simultaneously swung the door open and stepped to the side, freeing Connor's line of sight. There stood a frail, little lady with white hair whose name I could not pronounce. She was my White Russian neighbor, the one who lived closest to the outside bedroom door.

"Excuse me," she said in a frightened, broken-English voice, "did your lights go out?"

"What??" I replied, not understanding why the lady didn't see Connor or the gun.

"No, mine are ok. Are your lights out?"

"Mine are all out," replied the little old lady. "I'm worried. I've been having trouble with my eyesight lately and can't see very well. What should I do?" She threw her arms up in the air.

"Go ask the manager to check the breakers. It looks like the hall lights are out, too. Do you have a flashlight?"

"Yes, but I am afraid to go down the stairs in the dark."

"I'll go. Just give me your flashlight. You stay here while I go tell the manager. I closed the door to just a crack to give the old woman enough light.

The woman muttered something in Russian. *A thank-you,* I thought. Just yesterday this little old lady stopped me in the hallway and asked if Connor and I were married? I lied and said, "Yes," thinking it wasn't any of the busybody's business. I didn't care for nosey neighbors.

Connor became inquisitive as to who else lived in the building—the nosey, eccentric manager who had invited me on an outing in the harbor with older women; my reclusive next door neighbor, a reporter for *The San Francisco Chronicle*; and the lady directly beneath me, a currently unattached female, who walked a fat dachshund every day. The manager's husband was an invalid. The manager worked every day at the Presidio somewhere in shipping or something—I couldn't remember. *It didn't really matter anyway,* I thought.

The manager came to the door in her robe, thanked me for alerting her and told me it would be just five or ten minutes before the lights were on again. She had to go to the basement for the breaker box. I was halfway up the stairs when the lights came on again. The little Russian lady waited for me at the top of the stairs.

She muttered something in Russian again. I took it to be a thank you.

"No problem. Are you going to be ok now?"

"Yes, yes. At least I can see things now."

I opened the door to my apartment to see Connor still in the same squat position, putting away his .38.

"See. It wasn't anything. Just the old lady who lives next door."

"I can't take a chance. You can never tell when some flaky person might do something. Joanie, from now on . . ."

"Connor, you're paranoid. The lights just went out on my neighbor. That's all! End of story!!"

"I don't think so. I think those wacko spies you work for may have had something to do with it."

I rolled my eyes, shook my head as I walked toward the kitchen. Anyone connected to the "Company" was still family to me. My boss was Barry Lipman, a former CIA Case Officer and now the wealthy owner of Snoops, Inc., an international intelligence gathering company in Emeryville, across the East Bay from San Francisco. Barry recruited me from the CIA.

"My boss? Barry? You've gotta be kidding! You are really something, Connor. Another Bureau Agent who hates the CIA. Why should Barry have an interest in whether the lights go out on my neighbor?"

"Has he ever been here, Joanie?"

"Only once. He and his wife stopped by last week."

I knew he was mentally connecting the two events with Barry, thinking that even though I couldn't see the connection, *he* could.

"Connor, that has nothing to do with the lights going out. You are really paranoid."

"Maybe. But I don't think so. Now, listen. From now on when I leave from here I want you to be in the shower or at least running the shower water. Ok?"

"Connor!"

"Joanie, please!"

"Even when I'm going running or . . ."

"Just do as I say."

"Ok, just for you. I wouldn't do this for just anyone." *One of the hazards of dating an FBI agent,* I thought.

"Wham bam, thank you ma'am," Connor said matter-of-factly.

"Oh brother. I'll bet you Bureau guys are really like that, too. In one bed today and in another tomorrow and one female doesn't know about the others."

"Who knows what evil lurks in the hearts of men?" he said in an eerie, sadistic laugh. "The Shadow knows!"

"Are you leaving now?" I said as I watched him get dressed. I wondered whether he went home to shower and change or whether he went to work "as is." I dared not ask.

Connor stood in the living room putting on the clothes he had dropped there the night before—a pair of blue dress slacks, a light blue shirt and a burgundy, Pierre Cardin tie. His dark brown hair set off his almost blonde mustache, radiant blue eyes and long, coal black eyelashes. He finished putting on his dress boots and secured his gun.

"Yes. I am leaving now."

"Would you like me to walk you out to your car?"

"This isn't funny, Joanie."

"Ok, ok, I'll go get in the shower." I couldn't figure out what good it did to have the shower water running but the water was on for what seemed like five minutes when the door to my living room shut and I could hear Connor's footsteps down the stairs. I wondered if the water was supposed to somehow camouflage Connor's footsteps and I wondered if all FBI agents were this bizarre.

Chapter 2

A few weeks later I got up early, ran my normal five miles around the streets near my apartment in the Avenues by the golf course and came back and took a shower. I was blow-drying my shoulder-length hair, trying to feather back my bangs with a small round brush, when the phone rang.

"Hello," I said as I picked up the phone in my bra and pantyhose, getting dressed for work.

"Hi Joan, this is Michael."

"Michael O'Neill? I hardly recognize your voice. It's been awhile, hasn't it? Two months, I think?"

I met him, an Army Captain, at the Officer's Club in Berlin while visiting a girlfriend there when I lived overseas. I'll never forget that first night. He took me home to his apartment the inside of which resembled a city dump—clothes strewn everywhere, a bathroom that had not been cleaned since Vietnam and a kitchen that had mold growing on top of mold. While he lived in a pigpen, he astonishingly appeared to be of the classy, romantic sort. Fussy about his attire, his khaki uniforms had to be expertly pressed with creases just so and he had a clean cut look to him like he had just stepped out of the shower. Old Spice often wafted from his presence. But what I liked most was the romance and humor he offered me. He filled me up with his eccentric wit and sang love songs to me with his guitar on his rose-colored couch. I fell in love.

Now living in Dahlonega, Georgia, he kept in close touch with me except for the last two months during which I had written him off. He had upset me at Christmas by deciding at the last minute not to spend the holidays with my family and me. When I thought all hope was lost with Michael, I met Connor. I had not spoken to Michael since Christmas and he did not know about Connor.

"Yes, it has, Joan, and I'm sorry."

"And to what do I owe this honor?"

"Cut the sarcasm, Joan. I guess I really screwed up. I'm sorry. I miss you."

"What would you do if I told you I found someone else?"

"Probably die. Don't tell me that. Come on, Joan, quit clowning around. I told you I was sorry."

"I know you are, Michael, but you're good at apologies and I always seem to get soft and . . ."

"And you're good at accepting them."

"Did you like the lump of coal?"

"Well, I deserved it."

"You're right about that. You spoiled my Christmas. I bought all kinds of presents for you at that nice men's store on Chestnut Street and then had to go and take them all back. The Centurion storeowners weren't very happy with me. And then to top it off I had trouble cashing in those plane tickets I bought for you. I'm sure I angered almost all of the ticket agents at Delta Airlines, I was so mad.

"I'm sorry."

"So, why didn't you come? You never did tell me why."

"I had to work."

"That's not the reason. No one has to work on Christmas."

"Well . . . I couldn't afford it."

"That's not the reason, either. I was paying for the tickets, remember?"

"Oh, yeah. Well, I couldn't leave my troops."

Now bristling, I said, "You can come up with a better reason than that. Why not just tell me the truth. You're not a Company Commander any longer like you were in Berlin. You don't have to babysit those boys anymore."

"Well, I had to take care of my house."

"That's not the reason!" I said. "You have good neighbors who could look after it just fine."

"Well, you scared me."

"That's the reason! Now maybe we're getting at the real truth. Why did I scare you? You're bigger than me and I don't even own a gun. I scared YOU!" I started laughing.

"This is so hilarious," I said. Then in a more serious tone I continued, "Michael, I wasn't asking you to marry me or anything. I just wanted you to share Christmas with my family. I thought you really liked family. You always talk about yours."

"I do. I really screwed up. I'm sorry. Do you still love me?"

I wasn't sure. In all the time that I had known Michael the one thing that had stood out crystal clear in my mind was his fear of commitment. He would do or say almost anything to keep from making a commitment. *Do I still love a man who had stood me up for a long Christmas holiday together?*

"Do I still . . . ?"

"Do you?"

"I'm thinking. Are you still one of the most handsome, well-built men in the United States?"

"What do you mean one of the most handsome?"

"Are you still the *second* fastest runner, after me, in the San Francisco Bay Area?"

"Second fastest? Hey, I could kick your butt. I was just a little out of shape because we Georgia boys don't get to run outside all year long like you."

"It's warm in Georgia."

"Not where I am it's not. You know, though, Joan, you were really awesome running up those hills. You're really good at running hills—I'll never forget it."

"Coming from you that's quite a compliment."

"You deserve it. Say, Joan, listen, have you had any more problems with Barry since last Thanksgiving? Remember when he took you to lunch and told you he had sex with all those women at one time?"

"Yeah, I remember. He knew you were coming to visit and he saw how excited I was. I think he must have been jealous of you or jealous of my feelings for you. I just stared at him blankly as if I didn't hear what he said. It was so unlike him. Normally, he's such a family man. It just didn't fit so I ignored it."

"I'd watch it if I were you. Do you know what happened to me?"

"What?"

"I had a little accident when I got back. It may be just a coincidence but . . ."

"You think that Barry did it?"

"I don't know. He isn't connected to the Trilateral Commission, is he?"

"I don't know. What happened?"

"Oh, I hurt my foot. It was in a cast for a while. The thing is I believe it wasn't really an accident."

"What wasn't an accident? Tell me what happened."

"Well, the police stopped and said it was the other guy's fault. Said he was going too fast. Said it looked like he *meant* to hit me."

"Michael, are you serious? What happened? Why would someone be out to get *you*?"

"That's what I'd like to know. The police said the guy had a criminal record. Nothing major, but it certainly raised more questions than it answered. Do you know of anyone who would want to get rid of me because of you? Is there any possible connection between me and all those ex-spooks you work with?"

"Michael, that's preposterous. The only time you met Barry was at Thanksgiving." I had written Michael and told him what happened with my old boyfriend, Bill. Bill and I split after I came back from Germany. Michael could hardly contain his excitement. He wanted to come see me as soon as possible. He flew to San Francisco at Thanksgiving and Barry and his wife hosted us for Thanksgiving dinner in their home in Tiburon. Michael seemed impressed with my boss and I thought he was slowly coming around. He told me that weekend that even though he thought it would be ten years before he married, now he thought it would be less. It sounded to me like a half-assed marriage proposal.

"What did you and Barry talk about when we were at their house for Thanksgiving?"

"Oh, he talked about the Russians a little bit. That's about all I remember."

"So why would he try to hurt you?!"

"I don't know. Maybe it was a signal to stay away from you."

"Michael, he may be a little jealous of you, but I don't think he'd do anything to harm you. I don't think he'd harm anybody. I remember when you both met. You were so funny when you were getting ready to meet him. You wondered what kind of T-shirt he wore under his dress shirts – V neck or round." I laughed.

"Ok, so I'm vain. You know that song that Carly Simon wrote about me." He laughed, teasing me. "Barry wasn't much better. Look how much time he took getting dressed. He wasn't even ready when we arrived."

I mindlessly drifted off for a minute. I caught myself and glanced at my watch. "Michael, listen, I have to go right now. I'm late for work. I'll call you later."

"Ok, but if you get in over your head, let me know."

"I'm a big girl. I can handle it."

"I know you are and you can, but don't let your foolish pride come in the way of staying alive. Bye, Sweetheart."

"Bye. I'll call you soon. I still haven't forgiven you for Christmas so don't call me Sweetheart."

"I told you I was sorry."

"Well, this time sorry isn't going to get the job done. You owe me. I need something more from you than just 'I'm sorry.'"

Michael's call left me confused. I liked him—he was romantic, had perfect biceps and was great in bed but he was as paranoid as Connor. Barry purposely injuring him? Ridiculous.

I had met Connor a month ago and already I sensed he was as romantic as a wet fish (he gave me a smoke alarm for Valentine's Day) but he was fun in bed and he was a solid family man who seemed a more likely candidate for a long-term relationship.

Hmmmmnn . . . Connor or Michael? Should I sacrifice romance for a sure thing? Who should I choose?

Chapter 3

In the ensuing weeks, I put Michael in the back of my mind and focused on Connor. I never had luck with long distance relationships. But, because Connor and I met in a singles bar, I always felt a little insecure about our relationship, whether he might be out hustling other women when I wasn't with him since he was a good looking FBI agent with a quick wit. Women liked Connor.

One evening, Connor invited me to the retirement party for his boss. Before the party, we lingered at his place in San Ramon. His roommate, Frank, was away so we had the house to ourselves. Although we were already dressed to go out, Connor persuaded me to go upstairs to his bedroom and fool around. We had about an hour before we had to leave for dinner. He hurriedly undressed me. We made love. I quivered for hours, maybe days from the orgasm. I had never had an orgasm like this before. My body trembled, throbbed for Connor. I thought about it later. It was the first time I felt *he* wanted to have sex with *me*. I wasn't just another bump in the night, another one-night-stand. He really cared about *me*, cared about *pleasing* me. Connor told me he loved me and I believed him. I wanted nothing more than for us to be together.

I let my relationship with Michael slide, almost forgetting about him, deciding instead that I'd give up a relationship with him if I could be with Connor forever. I cared for Michael but a long distance relationship was not something I wanted to maintain. Connor took center stage. He spoke about getting married someday and I hoped it would be to me even though the commitment still scared me. I just needed to give it more time.

* * *

I got up early, put on a pair of royal blue running shorts, a skimpy white T-shirt, no makeup and my blue running shoes and drove to the

Marina Green, a playground for amateur athletes nestled in the harbor by the Bay. Located approximately mid-point between Ghirardelli Square and Ft. Point, the Marina Green drew outdoor enthusiasts from the whole Bay Area.

Many who came were addicted to the light-headedness the Marina Green encouraged them to experience, i.e., the runner's high. Some runners came to compete or to set new personal records. Others came just for the sake of exercise. And some came just for the pleasure of hanging out with the beautiful, physically fit people.

I glanced over at the children tugging multi-colored kites—dragons, lions, butterflies and monsters—but didn't find Connor. Neither was he by the stripe-shirted Latinos playing soccer.

I spotted him several feet away near the boats by Ft. Mason wearing maroon running shorts, a navy T-shirt and white running shoes. I watched as he bent over and touched his toes several times. Then he flexed his thigh and calve muscles by doing a half squat with one leg extended backwards.

Wasn't he one of the most handsome men I had ever met? How could I have been so lucky to meet him? I remembered meeting him at Happy Hour at The Holding Company, a singles bar in the Financial District in the Upper Level of the Embarcadero near the Salmagundi Restaurant and Bar. It was THE place in the Financial District then with its combination of ferns and wood as well as its reputation for serving excellent, gratis hors d'oeuvres at Happy Hour.

Two female friends and I went there early to get a good table. One of the young females, a CIA Case Officer on vacation from Washington, who barely knew me, spotted Connor and pointed him out to me. Tall, very dark and handsome, he came over to our table and laughed and joked with us but didn't hit on anyone, and suddenly he disappeared. I left early, too—a half hour later—to meet some other friends for dinner and there Connor stood outside the side entrance. He started talking to me nonstop, telling me, a perfect stranger, everything—he was a FBI agent, divorced, with bi-weekend custody of two children both over the age of ten. He loved skiing at Tahoe and was an avid runner.

I remembered looking at his gut. It was unusual to see a runner of any consequence with a gut like that. *He's a runner?* I thought. *I bet I could beat him, giving him a two block lead. He would certainly eat my dust up the gradual, diagonal climb from the Bay up to the Presidio.* I remembered Connor innocently inviting me to run with him, not knowing what he was getting into. Has it really been six months since we set eyes on each other?

Comfortable where I was, I motioned Connor to come over to the lawn where I was sitting, doing my stretching exercises.

"Connor! Over here!"

He ran over to me. And farted.

"Oh, a spider! Damn spiders!" Connor called farts spiders.

I laughed and then blushed.

"Oh, I suppose you never fart."

"Not in public if I can help it," I said laughing.

"Well, let's just check something." He grabbed a hold of my butt and squeezed one of my buns.

"I knew it."

"What?"

"You're a quart low. That's why. Maybe we should have chili tonight?"

"Maybe we should get going," I said, kissing him lightly on the cheek.

"You're on!" he said as he took off running. Connor was a fast runner. He could always outrun me except uphill where I normally caught up to him and usually managed to pass him.

We passed an older jogger, clad in a gray sweat suit, who puffed and groaned as we went by. He smiled as we passed but neither Connor nor I hardly caught a glimpse of his weather-beaten face before we politely said hello and were gone. I saw Connor who had sprinted ahead of me, stop and wait for me at Marina Green's answer to "hanging out at the pool" where scantily-clad sun worshippers staked out a piece of the Green to get a tan. Connor seemed to be enjoying himself when I stopped near him. Once I caught up, we were off running again.

"Slow down a bit, please," I said, trailing behind him.

"You can catch up," Connor said, smiling.

Once I got closer, Connor always sped up, thus forcing me to speed up, too, which both irritated and slightly amused me. I was a plodder.

Before I met Connor I ran nine-minute miles. Now I was down to less than seven minutes, although I preferred to run at a slower pace. With Connor by my side this became virtually impossible. He was constantly pushing me to exceed my goal.

"Connor, please slow down. I want to talk to you."

"I've heard that before."

"You're too fast. I can't keep up."

"That's what she said."

"In bed, I suppose."

"Where else? Now tell me what's up."

Connor slowed and I finally managed to keep abreast of him.

"Are you still breathing?"

"Yes, silly. I have great lungs."

"I'll say. That's not all you have that's great!" He winked at me.

"Connor!" I blushed.

"Ok, what's up?"

"It's just that we hardly get a chance to talk."

"Well, what do you want to know?" Connor turned his head around to see who was behind him. I looked at Connor.

"What are you looking at?"

"Just that old guy in the gray sweat suit."

"Well, why are you looking at him? Do you think he's following us?"

"Don't be silly. Now what was it you wanted to talk to me about?"

"Well, I was just wondering what happened between you and your ex-wife. Did you leave her or did she throw you out?"

"A little of both."

"Were you having an affair with someone?"

"You know, that's the one thing I regret. My wife is a nice lady and we get along fine now, to a point, but I wish I hadn't cheated on her. I've never forgiven myself for that. I guess I got what I deserved though."

"What do you mean?"

"I had to leave my kids. She got them. She got the house. She got everything. I ended up in a 'stinkin' apartment with no furniture, nothing."

"Were you alone?"

"Except for Tiffany, my girlfriend. She was the one I cheated on my wife for. She didn't live with me though. We were just boyfriend/girlfriend."

"How old was she?"

"Ten years younger than me. About the same age as you."

"Scary thought. How old are you?"

"I'll be thirty-six next January."

"What happened with her? Why aren't you married to her?"

"She wanted to have kids. Like I told you, I was in an accident several years ago. I fell off a building while I was working for the Bureau and had to have a vasectomy. Tiffany knew it, of course. She told me everything was cool but I once found contraceptives in her medicine cabinet. She lied and said they weren't hers. Two weeks later she married the guy."

"I'll bet you were devastated."

"I've never forgotten it. That's for sure."

"I'm glad you had a vasectomy."

"Why?"

"It means I can have as much sex as I want and never have to worry about a thing."

"You think so?"

"I know so. I'm totally safe with you."

"What? Totally? Even emotionally?"

"Yes, for sure. You'd never hurt anyone knowing what pain you went through yourself."

"Wait a minute, Joanie." Connor stopped.

"What?"

Connor turned around to look. "That guy is still there. We've slowed down and even stopped and he's still there. We've given him ample opportunity to pass us and yet he doesn't. What do you suppose he wants with us?"

"You're paranoid, Connor. It's nothing."

"I suppose you're right. Keep talking. Tell me something, Joanie, do you have a spare that you keep in your closet just in case something goes wrong with your current relationship?"

"What?"

"Another boyfriend from your past that you care about that you keep in reserve in case things don't work out in your current relationship? Someone you can turn to if the relationship turns sour?"

"Connor, what brought this on?"

"Well, do you?"

"Honestly?"

"Yes honestly. I have one."

"Who is it?"

"A stewardess named Val. She used to be married but she's not any more. She lives in Dallas. I rarely see her but I suppose she's there if I need her. So, who is yours?"

"A guy named Michael O'Neill. He lives in Georgia."

"Do you love him?"

"What kind of a question is that?"

"Well, do you?"

"Yes, I do. I will always love Michael. He's that type of a person. There are some types of people you meet in your life that you will always love no matter what. He is one of them."

"And what about me?"

"You? You are the man I am in love with. You're my main squeeze."

"There's a difference?"

"Yes, there's a difference."

"Tell me something, Joanie. This has been on my mind all day. Why did you get so quiet at the Bureau party the other night?"

"Well, for one thing, you and your friends are all ten years older than I am and all they talked about was buying a house and having children, two things I have never experienced yet."

"But, Joanie, you've been everywhere. You've traveled every inch of Europe; you've lived in Washington, DC, and traveled across the United States. You're far more cultured and sophisticated than any of them."

"I know. In my heart that's what I feel but in my head I think I should go back to school and do something more professional than secretarial work." I had been reluctant to ever tell Connor what I really did at Snoops, Inc.

"There's nothing wrong with secretarial work."

"I know. I know. I just want to do something different. I think I might take some courses at night to see if I like it. You know, sort of try it out. I've already got the school bulletins. Berkeley has a computer course I want to take and the University of San Francisco is offering an Accounting course which would fit into my schedule."

"Joanie, are you sure you want to do this?"

"Yes, Connor. I hated the way those women looked down on me because I didn't have a college degree."

"Well, what do you plan to get your degree in?"

"I don't know yet. I talked to a Counselor at Berkeley about a journalism degree but Berkeley doesn't even have an undergraduate degree in Journalism. Right now I'm just going to take some basic courses that will transfer to another school later."

Connor looked like he was far away.

"Connor, what's the matter?"

"Nothing. Look, here's that incline you like. Race you to the top!"

"You're on!"

Chapter 4

Life was never dull dating Connor. Several weeks passed with us going out to dinner frequently with one or two of his FBI friends and their dates.

"Did you like the Green Oaks?" Connor said, inviting approval as he walked past the bushes and unlocked his front door.

The two-bedroom house was partially owned by Connor and partially owned by Frank, Connor's straight housemate. For both, the convenient arrangement offered a way to build up equity until each married or split.

"Dinner was wonderful. I loved it. I love you," I said as I kissed him gently on the lips. I looked sporty in a pair of black Calvin Klein skin tight jeans, white skinny T-shirt with white embroidery in the front and cap sleeves, white short cable-knit sweater and black suede clogs. Connor had on dark blue Levi jeans, an off-white, button down, Oxford shirt, a khaki corduroy blazer and loafers.

"I've never been to Lafayette before. Where is it exactly?"

"It's near Walnut Creek. They're all burbs, running into each other. You can hardly tell where one city stops and the other starts. It's sort of like farting."

"Connor!" I blushed. "You must be anal retentive."

"I am not! I'm not fart retentive," he said, farting again. "That's for sure."

"Quiet. I think I hear somebody. Is Frank home?"

From outside the sliding glass doors into the dining room in the back of the house came Larry and Holly, Frank's friends. Frank had been there earlier but left for a date. Frank had promised Larry and Holly that they could use the hot tub later that evening—a hot tub which remained the pride and joy of Frank and Connor who were planning to build a gazebo around it.

"Gee, that's a great hot tub you have," said Larry, looking at Connor. "I'll bet it would fit almost eight people comfortably. Whose idea was it to build one?"

"Mine," Connor said. "It was a tax write-off."

"A tax write-off?" said Larry. "You've got to be kidding."

"Not at all. My doctor prescribed it for me for my back."

"It doesn't look like there's anything wrong with your back to me—wish I had a doctor like that. Say, you two can join us if you like. We don't mind. By the way, do you have some towels we could use?"

"Sure," Connor said. "Just a minute." He ran upstairs to get some.

"Oh, I hope it's not too cold outside," Holly said. "That warm hot tub ought to feel real good."

Connor came back with the towels. "Here you are."

"Thanks," Larry said. "Are you two coming?"

"I don't know yet," Connor said. "We'll think about it. You two go ahead."

"Ok," Larry said. "Come on, Holly, the water's getting cold."

"Ok, ok, I'm coming. Larry's never been in a hot tub before. I've been in one a couple of times so it's no big deal for me. He's like a little kid though. Look at him. On second thought . . ."

Larry, standing with his back toward his audience, stood next to the hot tub and suddenly dropped his towel.

Everyone laughed; Larry stood stark raving naked.

"Have fun!" Connor said as Holly walked out the door to the hot tub.

Connor came over beside me where I was sitting in a recliner. He bent down and said, "Let's wait a bit."

I felt relieved but found the courage to ask the inevitable question which had consumed me in the last few minutes.

"Connor," I said squirming in my chair, "uh . . . don't they . . . uh . . . wear swimsuits?"

"Nope," he said, matter-of-factly.

My face turned ghost white.

"Oh," I muttered somewhat embarrassed.

"Joanie, do you want to go in the hot tub?

"With them?"

"Yes, with them."

"Naked?"

"Yes, naked."

"Are they friends of yours?"

"No, they're Frank's friends. Does that bother you?"

"Well . . . I don't know."

"Joanie, do you want to go in the hot tub?"

"Do *you* want me to?

"No fair, I asked you first. It's ok if you don't. It's no big deal to me."

Squirming and feeling red in the face, I closed my eyes and slightly shook my head in embarrassment.

I felt nauseated. *How could I disappoint Connor like this?* I thought. *He must think I'm a real prude from the backwoods of Idaho.*

"I'd probably go if it were just you and me, but not with people I don't know."

"It's ok, Sweetheart. I love you just the way you are."

"Well, right now I'm cold. I know this is odd because I turned down your hot tub invitation, but would you mind if I took a warm bath?"

"No, go ahead."

I went up to the Master Bath in Connor's room and ran hot water in the tub. I was in the bathtub lathering myself when Connor suddenly appeared and flipped a switch by the light switch, turning on the Jacuzzi without me knowing it.

"Aaaaaaaaaaaaaaa!!!!!! I screamed with my powerful voice. Even the hot tub participants looked up to see what Connor and I were up to. Connor laughed.

"That's not funny! Turn this thing off!"

"Will you come to bed with me?"

I broke into a smile. "Yes, I will come to bed with you."

I dried off with a king-sized blue towel, put it around me and then went to join Connor in his queen-size bed. Slipping out of the towel and under the paisley comforter and sheets, I left the brass lamp on which sat on the bedside nightstand. As I snuggled up next to him, I smiled seductively at Connor to let him know that I wasn't ready for sleep just yet.

As I cuddled up to him, he whispered "I love you" in my ear.

I loved feeling his warm body next to mine. I loved holding him. I loved being held in his strong arms, smelling his scent, feeling like we were inseparable.

I whispered, "I love you" back several times.

My eyes closed, my face and body pressed against his, kissing him as I went, searching for his mouth and when finding it, letting him kiss me several times softly before he thrust his tongue inside. It was obvious Connor wasn't ready for sleep either.

I felt tingles run up my spine. I loved his tender kisses but French kissing with him evoked a sense of oneness in me. In the instant we shared the kiss, he made me feel content, happy, peaceful, like all my worries were gone forever.

We made love tenderly to each other. I never felt so loved in my whole life. I opened my eyes to get a better look at Connor, to see him kissing me, when all of a sudden I noticed something on his pillow.

I looked closer. I carefully took it in my fingers. I felt anger rising within me. I was coming to a full boil, but stopped before I let the rage that was building out. I had to make sure this thing was real before I let him have it. I pulled away from Connor and then slowly and deliberately sat up in bed.

"CONNOR!!!" I screamed.

"What?"

"Look at this!"

"Ok, so I see it's a hair. So, what?"

"Not just a hair. What color is it?"

"Blonde. So, what's the big deal?"

"The big deal is that I'm a brunette, you jerk!"

"So. I don't get it."

"You don't get it? You just told me you loved me. Whose is it? Tell me that. Maybe then you'll get it. Who have you slept with lately besides me?"

"It's Shelley's," he said, nonchalantly looking at me, slightly baffled.

"What is Shelley doing in your bed? Do you always sleep with your daughter?"

"She was up here laying on the bed talking to me while I put away the laundry," Connor stated, somewhat annoyed by this strange turn of events. "It's a simple enough explanation. What's the matter with you?"

Almost too simple, I thought. *Too cool. But maybe I overreacted. I've never caught him lying before.*

"You're right. I'm sorry. I overreacted. Can you forgive me? I love you and I really am sorry. Please forgive me. Connor, what do I need to do to get us back to where we were?"

Slowly he reached out to me and drew me close to him. "Joanie, you need to learn to trust me. I really do love you and I want you to know that."

I snuggled up against Connor but could feel the rigidity of his body next to mine. He may be saying he was forgiving me but his body was certainly telling me something else. In the next few minutes Connor seemed more relaxed but I looked at the expression of deep thought on his face.

Chapter 5

We spent every weekend together; we went running together, skiing at Tahoe and had sleepovers frequently during the week. Till I moved from my place on Clement Street to a larger apartment with a garage on Union Street which I shared with my roommate, Miriam. After I moved, Connor always seemed irritated when he came over because he had to drive around the block to find a parking space near Union Street. Friends had to fend for themselves on Union and Polk streets which had limited parking spaces.

A few weeks later, Barry and his wife asked me to housesit at their luxurious home on the top of the hill in Tiburon. I was thrilled. I figured Connor and I could live like kings for a weekend. I asked Connor to come with me but he said he had his kids that weekend. As it turned out, Barry came home early and figured he would finally get to meet this mysterious person I dated but I was there alone. I wondered why the two seemed to be so adept at missing each other.

In mid-June, I got sick with strep throat and Connor stayed away. I hardly saw him for two weeks. He called once but he didn't linger on the phone or make jokes like he usually did. He just said he had things to do with his kids. It was as if he couldn't get off the phone fast enough. Feeling neglected, I was so choked with emotion I could barely talk. Finally, I got over my strep throat. I worried about our relationship, the anxiety tying my stomach in knots. Normally we talked to each other every day. Suddenly he had stopped calling. *What was happening? Did it have anything to do with my boss, Barry? Was I just being paranoid?*

I left the next Friday for a weekend trip to Spokane to attend my brother's wedding June 30. Connor was planning on coming with me but at the last minute he told me he needed to stay home for Val, whose father had just died and needed a shoulder to cry on. Val was Connor's stewardess friend who he kept in his back pocket as his spare in case anything happened to his current relationship.

When I returned, it was back to work as usual at Snoops, Inc. The last time I had talked to Connor was when I was sick, two weeks earlier. After I returned from the weekend at Don's wedding, I didn't have the guts to call him. I was afraid he might tell me it was over between us and I could not imagine letting him go. I missed him, missed his nutty jokes, missed the feel of his lips kissing mine, even missed his paranoid antics. I decided that if I just remained positive, things would work out. All this worrying was probably for nothing. Many couples go two weeks without communicating, I decided. I was certain I was just being paranoid. After all, Connor was one of the most decent men I had ever met. Just look at the way he treated his kids. A man like that was hard to find.

Chapter 6

Soon after that, I chatted with Sonya Lackey, a paid consultant to the company, in the restroom.

"Hi Sonya," I said. In contrast to Sonya's style of frumpiness, I dressed in my smart looking navy crepe pant set and matching suede pumps. "Are you enjoying your stay here?"

For all of Sonya's importance to the two companies, in my mind she was just a "crazy lady."

"Yes, but I'm getting tired of all these meetings and dinners with everyone. What I wouldn't give for a quiet dinner somewhere without a lot of people."

"I know what you mean. I feel that way myself sometimes."

"Would you like to go out to dinner?"

"Well, I had planned to go out with some friends but since they just cancelled, yes, I would."

"Great. I should be finished around 7:30 p.m. What time do you usually leave?"

As we walked out of the restroom and into the office, I said, "Normally I leave at 5:00 p.m. but I can just hang around the office and wait for you. It seems silly to drive over to San Francisco and have to come right back."

My staying late drew a little suspicion from coworkers because I never stayed past 5:00 p.m. Herbert, a former Oakland cop who was Alice Sanborn's right arm at National Investigations, raised his eyebrows. His assistant, a heavy-set single woman with thick make-up, came up to Sonya.

"Would you like to go out to dinner with Kristine and me?"

"I'm sorry, I can't seem to remember everyone's name here. Who is Kristine?"

"Alice's personal secretary. The one who loaned you her car."

"Oh, yes. I remember now. Thank you for the offer of dinner but I have already made other plans."

I didn't understand Sonya's evasiveness but figured it was her business. The secretary glared suspiciously at me as if she had just caught me in some sort of wrongdoing, which I didn't understand because no one ever said anything about Sonya to me. Even though I thought she was a little crazy, she was nonetheless fascinating to talk to. She seemed to have been everywhere—Russia, the Orient, Europe, the Middle East. There was almost no place that you could talk about that Sonya hadn't either lived in or visited.

Sonya and I finally left the office around 7:30 and drove a half block to the nearby Holiday Inn so Sonya could freshen up. Sonya mentioned to me that she wanted to get in touch with her husband. Inside the hotel room, I excused myself to use the bathroom while Sonya made the call to her husband. She was just finishing as I came out of the bathroom.

"I thought I heard you speaking some other language. What language were you speaking?"

"Arabic."

"Your husband knows Arabic?" I asked, unbelieving.

"Yes." Sonya said curtly without comment, as she excused herself to use the bathroom. "I'll be just a minute."

On our way again, we turned left onto Powell St. and then a quick right towards the tollbooths for the Bay Bridge.

"Joan, did you have any restaurant in mind?"

Momentarily startled, I said, "Huh? Oh, I was thinking of eating either at Paprikas Fono or somewhere else in Ghirardelli, what do you think?"

"I don't really care, but I would like a quiet place where there aren't too many people."

"I know. How about the Russian Renaissance?"

"A real Russian restaurant? There are so few ethnic restaurants in Nashville; I like to take advantage of them as much as I am able when I travel. Let's eat there."

"You speak Russian, don't you?"

"Yes. This will give me an opportunity to practice. You know, Joan, I was very uneasy about coming out to work for National Investigations. I'm getting indications that Alice doesn't want me to come out and work anymore."

Sonya seemed to constantly change subjects and bring things up out of the blue. She was the hardest woman to stay with in a conversation that I had ever known. You couldn't stop paying attention for a moment. If you did, you'd be lost for an hour trying to find your way back in the conversation. *Interesting lady*, I thought, *but she is really strange.*

"Well, it's my impression that they think very highly of you."

"That's nice. I just feel that both Alice and I are very dominant women and I feel that Alice wants to supervise me too closely."

"How do you mean?"

"Well, I am in control of my own department at HEW . . ."

I assumed she meant the Department of Health, Education and Welfare in Nashville.

" . . . and I am pretty much free to do as I please. I don't get along well with my boss at HEW though. He always gives me a Black . . . excuse me, African-American . . . secretary which he thinks would bother me but it really doesn't. I have him under control though because of some photographs I have which could be very embarrassing if they ever got out."

Lost again momentarily in the conversation shifts of Sonya, I struggled to catch up.

"What are they of?"

"Joan, did I tell you that I asked Alice if I could have you as my secretary when I come out to work here?"

Reeling now from Sonya's evasiveness and shift in the conversation, I shook my head twice—once to clear my thoughts and once in total frustration.

"What did she say?" I said.

"Alice told me that I was supposed to have that older lady as my secretary. I think her name is Helen. Helen was supposed to work for both Joe Walsh and me. While I'm here, Joe Walsh and I are supposed to report to Alice."

"Sonya, what kind of work do you do for HEW? And what did you do before that?"

Sonya hesitated. "Oh, I had been a reporter and now I work for HEW."

I dropped the subject for the moment. Sonya gave me the impression I was prying.

We headed for the Russian Renaissance on Geary Street between 16th and 17th and arrived there around 8:30 p.m. A small square yellow and red neon light marked the entrance on tree-lined Geary. The restaurant had been here since 1959.

As we walked into the dark, L-shaped interior, we were greeted by the elderly owner, the granddaughter of the White Russian founder. Sonya haggled with her over whether we should sit in the back like the old woman suggested or the front as Sonya wanted. Sonya wanted to sit up front so that we could hear the music better. A violinist was playing *Ochy Cherneya*.

Sonya got her way and when we were seated she motioned to me, pointing to a table full of Russians who sat uncomfortably close to us. "Do you think they are spies?" she whispered.

"They could be relatives or friends of the owner."

The waitress came to take our drink orders.

"What are you going to have, Joan?"

"I don't know yet. Maybe a glass of white wine."

Sonya said something to the waitress in Russian. Within minutes the waitress brought over a three-tiered, red, white and blue drink.

"What's that?"

"They call it an Imperial Russian. Why don't you try one?"

"What's in it?"

"Could you tell her?" Sonya said to the waitress.

"Certainly. The white is Cointreau, the blue is Curacao and the red is Creme de Noyaux. It's named after the imperial Russian flag."

I thought for a moment, then reflecting on my current mental state said, "Sure, ok, I'll try one."

Sonya sat listening to the music, lost in time, back to the days when she lived in Moscow, I guessed.

"Were you a reporter in Moscow?"

"No."

"Did you work for the Agency there?"

"No, but another government agency."

"NSA?"

She nodded. "My parents both worked in intelligence."

"CIA or NSA?"

"Uh-huh," was all Sonya said evasively. "My mother helped me out of a predicament once in the Silkwood trial. I called my mother up to come and do some laundry and we met in the laundry room and exchanged baskets of wash, thereby getting rid of some incriminating material."

Sonya was referring to the Karen Silkwood trial. Karen, a former $4/hr. nuclear technician at Kerr-McGee was killed November 13, 1974 under suspicious circumstances when her car crashed off a two-lane road enroute to meet a *New York Times* reporter and an official from the OCAW (Oil, Chemical and Atomic Workers Union). Her trial ended May 18, 1979, three months prior to Sonya's visit at National Investigations.

Lost again momentarily, I asked innocently, "You mean you both worked in a laundry in Oklahoma?"

"No," she said slowly and deliberately, looking at me as though disbelieving my question. "My mother was retired then from intelligence and living in Dallas. I was living in an apartment that they set up for me in Tulsa. I was being asked to clean up the mess for one of the Agencies. It was one of those situations where I needed my mother's expertise."

After finishing two Imperial Russians and a heaping portion of *Chicken ala Kiev*, Sonya ordered another two Imperial Russians. As Sonya relaxed more and more from the effects of the drinks, she talked more freely.

"Lenny Carlson, an FBI Agent in Oklahoma, saved my ass on more than one occasion during the Silkwood trial—and more than once I saved his."

"I dated an Agent with the Bureau who had lived in Oklahoma or near there." *Do I sound like I'm bragging? I don't know Sonya very well though so why should I be sharing the intimate details of my love life with her?*

"Lenny would probably know him. What's his name?"

"Connor Eubanks."

"Maybe we could have dinner with him and some of his friends."

I was afraid you might want to get together with him. You sure are pushy. Now what should I say? I think I'll just tell you I'm not seeing him anymore. It's not really a lie. I haven't seen him for two weeks since I got sick. "Well, I'm not going out with him anymore. Some agents hang out at Liverpool Lil's once in awhile though."

"Oh, let's go there."

After finishing the third Imperial Russian and dinner, we left. It was late now and I was thinking of heading home.

"Yes," she persisted. "Come on. It'll be fun."

"I don't know," I said hesitatingly. "I don't want to run into Connor."

"He won't be there, c'mon."

"He might. I don't want to."

"I'll talk to him for you if he's there."

"No, I just don't want to see him right now!"

Liverpool Lil's sat in the bottom of a beige and brown Victorian at the east edge of the Presidio near Letterman Hospital. As we approached the bar, Sonya stopped, looked briefly up and down the street and then turned to me and said, "Oh, I recognize this place; it's only four or five blocks from the Russian Consulate on Green Street."

Confused again by Sonya's comments, I wondered why she would know the Russian Consulate was on Green Street.

"You go ahead. I'll wait here in the car for you."

Sonya went up to the door but it was closed. Once back in the car Sonya and I headed for Vlasta's on Lombard instead. Vlasta's was also closing as we pulled up but the bartender said we could have a drink.

A Japanese American and his girlfriend were at the bar. Sonya, now thoroughly drunk from the Imperial Russians, got into a game of Liar's Dice with the bartender.

I had never played Liar's Dice but had heard about it. I knew that you bet with articles of clothing or jewelry. If you lost, you had to take off something you were wearing. As I watched Sonya and the bartender play, I felt my heart race, my face flush and my mouth go dry. A wave of fear came over me in a flash, a fear of losing all my clothes in public. I quickly grabbed Sonya by the arm and dragged her out the door to the car.

"Wait a minute," Sonya said, "I'm just getting started."

"I think you've had too much to drink."

"No, I haven't. Where are you taking me?"

"Home."

"I don't want to go back yet. I promise I'll be ok. Just one more drink somewhere. Come on, Joan. I never get to go out at home. My husband doesn't like to drink and, of course, I have to take care of the kids."

"Ok, but only one."

We left then and went to a Middle Eastern place on Columbus Ave. When it closed up, Sonya wanted to go to my apartment.

"I only have gin and tonic."

"That's ok."

After one drink, I took her back to the hotel.

"Let's go to dinner again tomorrow night," Sonya said.

"No, I can't," I said.

"Why not?"

"I just can't. I'll call you."

Chapter 7

The next day, Saturday, the phone rang.

"Hello," I said.

It was Sonya.

"Yes, I could be ready by 7:00 p.m.," I said hating myself for wimping out, not standing up to her and doing what I wanted instead. I didn't really want to take Sonya out to dinner again but I felt sorry for her since she didn't know anyone in San Francisco and everyone at the office didn't seem very friendly towards her lately. I didn't know why.

I wore a pair of casual dark navy pants and a sky blue silk flowered blouse which tied in a large bow in front. The weather was cold as San Francisco summers always are, so I threw on a sweater.

I got into the car and headed for the East Bay to the Holiday Inn. Sonya was ready this time. She was dressed very conservatively. We drove back to San Francisco and ate in Ghiradelli Square at Paprikas Fono.

"You know," Sonya said, "I have real misgivings about National Investigations. I think I'd prefer to work for Barry rather than Alice. Actually, what I'd really like to do is work for the CIA."

"I really liked working for them. I think they have a recruiter in the Bay area. He's in the phone book."

"Do you know his home phone number?" Sonya asked.

Looking a little puzzled, I wondered what was going on. I understood that Sonya currently worked for one of the government Agencies. So why was she telling me she wanted to work for the CIA? *Was something else going on here?*

"No, I don't know his home phone number and besides, he's out of town a lot anyway from what my Agency friends tell me," I said. I knew the recruiter from my days with the CIA.

"Could you give him a call and get an application for me?" Sonya asked. "I had a job offer from the PLO in Geneva recently for a public relations job, but I wasn't really interested. Being in the Middle East would have brought me closer to my husband but the job would have taken me further away from my kids."

I just stared at her. *Was this woman for real? A job with the CIA? The PLO? What was with her?*

"My husband had to leave me because of all the publicity of the Silkwood trial and return to the Middle East. I lost my job as a reporter when my editor found out that I was moonlighting for one of the Agencies. After all of this happened, I got a job as a secretary for HEW and finally worked my way back up the ladder.

"The Judge in the current case I am involved in had formerly worked for the FBI so I am somewhat confident of the outcome. I wouldn't divulge the names of my FBI sources but I didn't want to go to jail either. The FBI has a complete file with a whole new identity for me. All I have to do is pick it up and leave."

Sonya was being more vague than usual. "Well, what about your children? What about your husband? Are they going to be with you? Will they get new identities, too? Where do you think they would send you?"

"I like San Francisco and think it would be easy enough to get lost here. I think I could easily get a job here and just sort of hide out while things cool down."

"What about your kids? Wouldn't you miss them?"

Sonya changed the subject again. Either she didn't have any concern about leaving her children, which I felt was odd, or her concern about Alice was greater.

"The only thing I'm wondering is whether Alice and I would clash. I mean, she's a very dominant woman and so am I."

I had to agree. I had only seen Alice's self-confidence wane once, just prior to one of her "big meetings." I had seen Barry totally monopolize her though. Alice controlled the money but *he* sometimes controlled her.

"You two would be quite the match. I don't think it would work. You are extremely independent and Alice likes to have a great deal of control over her employees. She once cautioned me that you've never dealt with the Mafia until you've met her Irish Mafia. She's of Irish descent. I think she was kidding but it sounded to me like she'd let you have it if you didn't do as she said or didn't please her."

"She said that?"

"In so many words. Sonya, you are both very driven, intelligent women. I get the impression you would do almost anything to get what you want. You would destroy each other. It would never work. Not in my lifetime."

"This is none of my business but you know Alice seems to spend most of her time at the office. Who takes care of her kids?"

"She spends enormous time there. Barry does too, but *she* stays all night a lot."

"Does Barry stay with her?"

"What are you getting at?"

"Are they an item?"

"Are you ready for another drink?" I caught the waiter's eye. He came over to the table.

"Yes, make mine a double this time," Sonya said.

"I'll just have another glass of white wine."

"So, tell me, Joan, do you think Alice and Barry are seeing each other?"

I was determined not to let my true feelings for Barry show, how I felt he deceived me when I initially took the job because he failed to disclose certain aspects of his relationship with National Investigations that I might have found distasteful and the fact that he was continuing his connections to his old spy networks which the CIA forbid. This wasn't the proper time to be pouring out my emotions and I felt Sonya was only interested in office gossip anyway.

"I don't know if they are. It's not really any of my business."

Sonya seemed disappointed at my answer. Obviously she hoped for more. She changed the subject. "Hey, what do you say we go to Liverpool Lil's again?"

"You really like that place?"

"Well, I'm hoping we might run into some of your FBI friends."

I relented. We left the restaurant and went there. Liverpool Lil's catered to the would-be jock set, was a well known FBI agents' hangout, and stewardesses came there as well. The bar had a Liverpool, England ambiance. Being a small bar/restaurant, it had the effect of looking like there was a crowd inside even if there were only three or four people at the bar. Its amber lights gave the atmosphere a golden effect.

Sonya and I didn't meet anyone interesting so we had a couple of drinks and left.

"What are you doing Sunday?" Sonya asked.

"I'm going up to Muir Woods with two girlfriends."

"Gee, that sounds nice."

"Would you like to join us?"

"Yes, I would but I'd have to clear it with Alice first. I'll call you around 10 o'clock to tell you whether I am able to go."

I thought that was odd but I felt Sonya was odd and that she was just using it as an excuse. Maybe she really didn't want to go. "See you later."

"I'll call you."

Chapter 8

On Sunday, Sonya called me at 10 o'clock, telling me that she couldn't make it but that she'd call me later on. She called again at 8:30 p.m.

"How did you like Muir Woods?"

"We had a great time. You would have loved it."

"I'm sorry I couldn't join you. I talked to Alice. She was upset but I talked her into letting me stay one more day."

I didn't know if Sonya was planning on leaving, if that was why she couldn't go to Muir Woods. "That's great."

"By the way, were you able to get in touch with that CIA recruiter?"

"No. I think he has an unlisted number but I think I can get it from my friend Eleanor in Virginia."

"Would you mind calling your friend in the morning?"

"I'll try her then. Hopefully she'll be home."

"I'm leaving Tuesday morning but I am telling National Investigations people that I'm leaving Monday night. I want to check into that hotel close to your apartment, *The Vagabond*. Only trouble is I have this new dress I'd like to wear and I need an iron."

"Sonya, you can stay with me. I have an iron you can use."

"That's a terrific idea. Thank you. That's really nice of you. I've gotta run now but I'll see you at work tomorrow."

I called Eleanor early the next morning to get the number of the recruiter.

"Hi, this is Joan Kopczynski. You may remember me from the CIA.

"Joan, who?"

"Kopczynski. Joan Kopczynski. You worked one floor above me in Personnel. I worked for "Stinky." You remember him, don't you?"

"Oh, yeah, Joan, how are you?"

"I'm fine. I hope you don't mind, I got your number from Eleanor. Say, do you miss overseas as much as I do?"

"All the time, but it's fun here, too. What are you up to?"

"I know a lady who wants to apply with the government and I was wondering what the chances are of her getting hired."

"What's her salary range?"

"Approximately $30,000."

"Joan, it would be a waste of time to apply."

"But she knows several languages."

"How old is she?"

"40, I think."

"Don't bother. She's way overpriced for us. We usually get college grads and pay them in the 20's. We like to get them young because they aren't set in their ways yet."

"Well, is there any hope at all? Either in your division or any other division?"

"No, my best advice is to just drop it. However, if she insists, she can always put in an application, but I can tell you unequivocally for certain it's not going to go anywhere."

"Well, thanks anyway. It's been nice talkin' to ya. I've gotta run. See ya in the trenches."

"It's been good talking to you. Say hi to Eleanor next time you talk to her."

"I will."

* * *

Herbert walked past Sonya's door and looked in where Sonya and I were sitting. A big burly ex-cop with a receding hairline and a bald spot in the back, Herbert had dark eyebrows, a large pointy nose, large hands, a protruding gut and a mean look.

"Sonya, when are you leaving?"

"I don't really know yet. Why?"

"Well, I'd like to give you a ride to the airport."

"That won't be necessary."

"Is someone else taking you?"

"No one in particular."

"Sonya, who is the 'no one in particular?' Joan, are you taking Sonya to the airport?"

Before I could answer, Sonya said, "Don't worry, Herbert. It's all taken care of. It's been arranged."

"I do worry about you, Sonya. I worry you're not leaving this place," Herbert said tersely.

I guessed that Herbert had been assigned by Alice to be Sonya's control person while she was at National Investigations. He needed to know all the details on Sonya at all times. Any deviation from Company policy put Herbert on edge and made him a little more anxious than normal. Herbert didn't like loose ends. Twenty years with the Oakland Police Department taught Herbert to be suspicious of loose ends. Sonya was one enormous loose end and Herbert didn't like it. Not one bit.

"I am leaving. You can put your mind at ease."

"So, why won't you tell me who is taking you? Is it Joan?"

"All right, if you must know. She is. Satisfied?"

"Very." He stomped out.

* * *

Sonya told me she would be ready by 5:30 p.m. When I drove to the side entrance to the Holiday Inn, she was waiting.

We stopped for gas then went straight to my apartment. Sonya put her suitcase and other things in the living room.

"Would you like a drink?"

"I'd love one."

As I went into the kitchen to make the drinks, Sonya opened her suitcase and hunted for something. When she found what she was looking for she waited patiently for me to come back with her drink.

"I hope gin and tonic is ok."

"It's fine. I brought along some news clippings I thought you might like to see. These are from *The Tennessean*. They're about the trial."

Another oddity, that this woman packed these news clippings around with her. None of them had dates on them. *Who else did she show them to?*

I felt a deep concern for Sonya and said, "Gee, that must have been awful. How did you handle all that? Who did you have to talk to when your husband left you?"

Sonya, diverting her eyes and not answering the questions, immediately turned the conversation back to me. "Do you talk to your roommate?"

"About some things but not much about my past or present employment. Why do you ask?"

"What about your friends?"

"I don't tell them either," I said, getting a little irritated with the direction of the conversation. *This woman can be really exasperating. One minute I want to cry for her and the next minute I want to slap her.* Returning from my thoughts I said, "Most of them are liberal, too. I didn't even tell Connor much. We never talked about National Investigations or Barry and Snoops, Inc. or what they did. I could have told him, I guess. But it is sort of a holdover from my Agency days when we were *encouraged* not to talk shop outside the office."

"Did any of these people know that you worked for the Agency?"

"Barry, Joe Walsh and the rest of the people at National Investigations and Snoops, Inc. of course knew, and Connor also knew."

"What type of work did you say Connor does for the FBI?"

"I didn't say but he works on bank robberies."

"And you said he's married?"

"No, he's divorced."

"Any kids?"

"Yes, two."

"Boys?"

"A girl and a boy."

"Do they go to school in San Francisco?"

"No, they live in San Ramon. Hey, why all the questions about Connor all of a sudden?"

"Just curious. Does anyone else know of your Agency affiliation?"

"My Agency friends know, of course. But for the rest of them, no. It never came up. They would probably have a fit. I told you they are real liberal. They're far left of center and National Investigations and Barry are extreme right."

"And where are you?"

"Right in the middle where I belong. I'm a middle-class, middle child, middle-of-the-roader."

"It's amazing what opposing sides think, isn't it? I mean the Soviets think we are planning war on them and we think they are planning to wage war on us. Each side believes God is on its side. It's enough to drive you bananas if you let it. Have you ever read a book called, "Armageddon?"

"No, but it sounds religious."

"It is sort of. They talk about the coming of the end of the world. But they also talk about powerful people."

"Sonya, you told Herbert that I was taking you to the airport, didn't you?"

"No, why?" Sonya asked, diverting her eyes again. She was lying. I was there when she told him.

"Then why was everyone at National Investigations giving me dirty looks as I was leaving? Herbert and company want to make sure you get on the plane and that you don't see anyone or do anything suspicious before you leave."

"Oh, I guess I did say you were taking me. Say, why don't you call your friend Connor and invite him to dinner? I bet I know him or know somebody he knows. I really think highly of guys in the Bureau."

"Noooo, I don't think so," I said, emphatically.

"Oh, come on. It will be fun. Where is your iron?"

"Here it is. The ironing board is all set up."

"Connor's probably sitting there wondering whether to call you right now. Come on, give him a call."

I took another sip of my drink.

"I think he's busy. He probably has to comfort his friend Val," I said sarcastically.

"How will you know unless you call?"

"I don't want to know."

"Why not?"

"I just don't. That's all. End of conversation. Why are you so interested in FBI agents?"

"Would you mind if I made a long distance call to my husband? I'll make it collect."

She changed the subject again. I went with the flow. "Sure. No problem."

I wondered whether she really intended to call her husband or whether it was someone else.

Maybe Connor was sitting around waiting for me to call. I hadn't heard from him since before last weekend, before Don's wedding. With Sonya's encouragement, I decided to call. I went to the bedroom, picked up the phone and dialed Connor's number. I got his roommate.

"Hi Frank, how are you?"

"I'm fine, Joan. I haven't heard from you in awhile."

"I know. I know. I've been up in Spokane at my brother's wedding. Where's Connor?"

"Uh . . . he moved."

"What?? Where did he move to?"

"A place called Claremont and . . . uh . . . he's married."

"Married??" I was shocked. I turned pale. My fingers felt cold and they were trembling. "Who did he marry—Val?"

"No, a girl named Helga."

"Helga? Is she German?"

"I think she speaks German."

"How did he know her?"

"She lived nearby."

"How long did he know her?"

"A couple of months. Listen, Joan, I don't want to be telling you all this over the phone. Why don't you call Connor at the office tomorrow?"

"I will. Thanks, Frank."

"Bye."

Damn. Sonya would have to be here when this happened. I wish she'd go away. I'll have to give her some plausible explanation for my suddenly powder white complexion. I stood stone-faced. I was still in shock.

"Sonya, I'm sorry but I just learned that my boyfriend ran off and married someone else when I was away on vacation. I'm so shocked." What I really felt was rage, like I could claw Connor's face with my long painted nails if I were near him right now.

"I'm sorry. Is there anything I can do?"

"No, really, I'm fine. Just give me a minute. Have you decided where you'd like to go to dinner?"

"I think I'm partial to the Russian Renaissance."

"No. That's out of the question. Once was enough for me. Pick another place. I know a good Italian restaurant down at the Wharf. How about that?"

"I can get Italian food in Nashville. You know, my husband doesn't drink and never goes out so when I'm out of town that's the only time I get to go to a real ethnic restaurant like the Russian Renaissance. Come on. It will be my treat."

"Ok."

We arrived at the Russian Renaissance and were treated royally by the same waitress who gave Sonya such a hard time before. She sat us in front.

"Could we have an Imperial Russian?"

"No, I'm sorry Madame. We only serve those on weekends."

Sonya said something to her in Russian and the waitress disappeared and reappeared moments later with two Imperial Russian drinks on a tray. I didn't think about why the lady decided to bring the drinks or anything else. My mind was still reeling from the conversation with Frank about Connor's marriage.

Trying to make small talk, I blurted out, "You told me earlier that you went to the Russian Consulate. What did you do there?"

"I am editing a book about sports medicine for Barry's father-in-law and I wanted to get some pictures of Olga Korbut for it." She laughed. "I went there in Alice's secretary's car. I know the FBI watches the entrance to see who comes and goes." She grinned. "They'll trace Kristine's car."

"How did you get involved in doing this for Barry?"

"I had lunch with Barry and his father-in-law one day and Alice rode with us to San Francisco but she didn't know about the book. Barry had kidded me, saying, 'See if you can get some pictures from your KGB friends.'"

"Did you get them?"

"Yes, of course. I plan to mail them from Tennessee."

"Did you know any Russians at the Consulate?"

"No, but I didn't tell Alice and Barry that. At first the Russians weren't receptive to me but later when I began speaking in Russian they were more responsive to my request for the photographs. While I was there a guy from Venezuela came in and asked for asylum. He wanted to study in the Soviet Union. And, you'll love this, an Avon lady came in to sell them something."

Sonya laughed flamboyantly at the incongruity of an Avon lady and the guy from Venezuela. I just laughed politely, my thoughts still clinging to Connor. My heart numb with the thoughts of him married to someone else.

* * *

We left the restaurant early. Sonya wanted to go to Liverpool Lil's to hopefully run into some FBI agents and talk about the Silkwood case. As we entered Lil's, I saw Willie, an undercover FBI agent, a friend of Connor's.

I waived to him, remembering I once told Connor that of all his friends, I liked Willie the most. I didn't know why I ever told Connor that because Willie wasn't the jock type or the intellectual type, he was just friendly and nice. Tall with lightning blue eyes that looked straight through you, he usually wore Hells Angels clothing and sported a beard and reddish-blonde, shoulder length hair. Connor told me Willie was about to close a very hush-hush case on organized crime in Sacramento.

"What are *you* doing here, Willie?" I said loudly as he walked over to our table. *Wasn't he supposed to be up in Sacramento?*

"Me? How about you?" He sat down next to Sonya. His dirty cowboy boots barely fit under the small, round wooden table.

"I brought a friend. Sonya Lackey, this is Willie. Willie meet Sonya."

"My pleasure," Willie said in his husky voice.

"Likewise," Sonya said.

"Hey Willie, did you hear about Connor? I'm so shocked. I just heard."

"Why yes, I called him up the other day to see if he wanted to go dancing and he said, 'I don't think my wife would like it.' Well, I said, who'd you marry? Joan? The last time I saw him he was with you. I'm sorry, Joan. Truly sorry."

"Well, I'm not. I think he's a flake. He did it to his first wife, he did it to me and he'll most likely do it to her if he gets a chance. A repeat offender, that's what I'd call him. His wife didn't get no prize. She's the loser. I'm better off without him."

Willie's balding friend came over to the table, bringing his drink—straight coke.

"And who are these two lovely ladies?"

There was an awkward silence. I was lost in thought. Sonya spoke up.

"Hi, I'm Sonya and this is my friend, Joan."

"Nice to meet you. My name is Conrad. Can I buy you all a drink? What are you drinking, Joan?"

"Make mine a Black Russian," I said, sitting there dazed, going over in my mind what had happened to me. Angry thoughts kept replaying in my mind as if the mechanism to stop them were stuck. *Connor married? He married Helga not Val? Who was Helga? Was she blonde? Did she own the blonde hair I found in his bed? Why did they get married while I was on vacation? Why is my life so messed up? Why did this happen to me? And why did crazy Sonya have to be here when I found out?*

"How about you, Sonya? What will you have?"

"I'm still not finished with mine. I've been too busy talking to Willie here. She looked at Willie. "I heard you're an undercover agent."

"Who said that?"

"Joan."

"Oh. Well, maybe I am. What of it?"

"Do you know Lenny Carlson in Oklahoma?"

"I've heard of him, yes. He's with the Bureau. I know that."

"Well, he saved my ass on more than one occasion."

"What case were you working on?"

"Silkwood."

"Ah, now I get the picture. You're the person that caused so much trouble there—FBI agent, FBI informant, CIA agent—which one were you anyway?"

"I was just a writer, trying to get my story." She grinned.

"Did you get it—the story, I mean?"

"Yes, but it cost me a lot. I lost my job. My husband left me."

I was listening to the conversation. *If her husband left her, who did she call from my apartment?*

"Where do you work now?"

"For HEW in Nashville."

"Well, at least it's all over with."

"No, I have a hearing coming up soon with the Dingell Committee."

"The Dingell Committee?"

"Congressman John Dingell's Subcommittee on Energy and the Environment."

"Oh. Well, you'll survive it. Don't worry."

Conrad and I sat there sipping our drinks and listening to Willie and Sonya's conversation. All of a sudden Conrad broke the ice.

"I heard about Connor, Joan. I'm sorry."

"Are you a friend of his?"

"We know each other but no, we're not friends. The Bureau is a big place."

"You agents are all the same. I know you stick together. Just like the Agency, you're family to each other."

"No, really. I don't know him very well. In fact, we've only met once."

"Yeah, sure. You'll probably tell him everything I say tonight."

"I promise I won't. I'm not like that. I know how you feel. I've had it done to me before. It isn't fun getting over it. Hey, did you hear that?"

"What?"

"Your friend just asked Willie to go to bed with her."

"I don't care."

"Would you like to leave?"

"With you? No. But I would like to leave. Sonya, are you ready to go or are you staying with . . .?"

"I'm coming."

"I'll call you," Conrad said.

"You don't have my phone number."

"What is it?"

I hesitated and then wrote it on a napkin. I was so woozy I didn't care whom I gave it to. I could always say no when he called.

Sonya and I left then and quickly returned to my apartment.

"I'm sorry for being such a party-pooper, but I just don't feel like company right now. Did you like Willie?"

"Yes, he was very interesting," Sonya said, closing the door. "Did you like Conrad?"

"No. I'm afraid Bureau agents aren't my cup of tea right now. Sonya, are you ok? You look like you're about ready to . . ."

Sonya started crying. "It's just that I'm so afraid of this damn trial and everything and my boss at HEW," she sniffed, dabbing her eyes with her sleeve, "and I won't give up my FBI sources but I don't want to go to jail either. If they are going to put me in jail, then I will leave for the Soviet Union. I already got three visas, just in case, when I went to the Soviet Consulate."

"Sonya, you don't have to worry. You've got everyone on your side. Everything will be alright."

I wished I wasn't drunk. I knew my words were slurred.

"You don't know what it's like to be fired, have your husband leave you, your kids taken away from you . . . Really, the other guys, (the Russians), are just as nice once you get to know them."

"No, they're not!" I screamed. "Don't do it, Sonya! They'll only lie to you to get what information they want out of you and then they'll discard you. Would you like to live in a dacha in Moscow the rest of your life? They don't have nice shopping malls over there." The beginnings of a smile crinkled Sonya's face.

"Let's get to bed. We are both too drunk to be talking about this."

Chapter 9

On Tuesday, I got up early, ran five miles, showered and put on a dusty rose colored over-the-knee skirt with a pleat down the middle and a matching jacket over a satiny pale pink blouse with a peter pan collar. My older sister made the suit for me. It wasn't my favorite but it was the first thing I grabbed from my closet that morning. I quickly blow-dried my hair, put my mind on automatic pilot and went through the motions of putting on my makeup. All I could think of was Connor. *How could he do this to me? How could he hurt me like this? When will the pain go away?*

I took Sonya to meet the plane at 7:00 a.m. I stopped at the Gate to let Sonya off with her bags.

"I hope everything works out well for you."

"I think it was probably just all the stress of the trial coming to a head. Thank you, Joan, for letting me stay with you and for taking me around."

"Call me, ok? If you don't call me, I'll call you. I just want to make sure you're all right."

"Ok. I will. Bye."

"Bye. Good luck."

* * *

I arrived at my office before 8:00 a.m. and kept busy absently shuffling papers on my desk until 8:15 a.m. when the FBI office opened in Hayward. I waited another fifteen minutes to be sure he'd be there and then dialed.

"Hello Connor," I said icily.

"Hi, Joanie. Frank told me you called. Listen, I can explain . . ."

"I just want you to know I think you're a flake."

He laughed. "No, I'm not a flake. Joanie, I can explain . . ."

"Does your wife let you out for lunch?" I said with a bite in my voice.

"Yeah, I can meet you for lunch. Where?"

"Denny's. Emeryville. 11 o'clock."

"I'll be there."

I had a difficult time concentrating on my work and little did I realize I was making minor mistakes, which didn't go unnoticed by Barry.

"Are you alright, Joan?" Barry said.

"I'm fine," I said tersely. "Why?"

"Oh, nothing. I was just wondering."

I spent the rest of the morning rehearsing over and over in my mind exactly what I wanted to say to Connor.

Denny's, open 24 hours, was located on Powell Street near Christie Avenue and the Baybridge Office Plaza which housed First Interstate Bank—just on the other side of the underpass near my office. Connor and I met there frequently because of its easy access to the freeway.

When I walked in, Connor sat in a two-person booth near the counter and cash register in the middle of the restaurant. I sat down and put my "praying" hands on the table. An African-American waiter came by to take our order.

"What are you going to have?"

I wanted something simple and light but I was too upset to study the menu.

"I'll have a Patty Melt. And ice tea."

"And I'll have The Works Burger. And milk. Thank you." He gave the waiter back the menus.

"So, how are the kids doing?" I said, politely.

"The kids are fine. I had lunch with them at their school last week."

"Gee, you have lunch with them a lot, don't you?" I said, waiting for the opportune time to go in for the kill.

"Not as much as I'd like. They're growing up so fast. I talked to Marvin's teacher yesterday. She said Marvin *never* takes his baseball cap off. Ever. He wears it during class, during recess and all through lunch. He'd sleep with it on if I'd let him. He wants to be a pro baseball player."

"I wonder where he got that from." I tried to withhold my anger a little while longer. "So, what about Shelley?"

"Shelley's at that awkward age between being a child and an adult. I never know whether I should cuddle her in my lap like a little girl or leave her alone to work out her problems herself like an adult. She gets her braces off soon."

"That's nice. Listen, Connor, I didn't ask you to come here to tell me about your kids." I conveniently forgot that I was the one to bring them up.

"Joanie, I can explain . . ."

"Would you mind telling me why the hell you didn't have the decency to tell me?" My voice rose and carried automatically whenever I was excited, upset or angry. Several people looked up and over at us.

Connor looked like a mouse being scared by a pussycat. He blushed, his neck turned beet red and he fidgeted uncomfortably in his seat. I observed guilt choking him.

"I tried once to tell you but I just couldn't. You were at home sick with strep throat and you sounded like you were dying. I tried to tell you then but you were sick so I decided to tell you later when you were better but by the time you were better you were already gone to your brother's wedding."

Even though I wasn't dying you "thought" maybe I was dying and what did you do? You left me alone to die. There were obviously two kinds of cowards in the world—one who lacks physical courage and the other who lacks emotional courage. Connor was definitely an emotional coward. My heart was racing.

"Oh, I see. I only gave you one chance to tell me. Well, tell me now. Where did she come from? How did you meet her?"

"I met her at a local Neighborhood Watch Organization meeting. She lived in my development."

I glared at him. "How convenient! I bet she went in your hot tub with you." I'd been too conservative to go in his hot tub with a bunch of naked strangers.

Silence.

"How old is she? Helga sounds like an old person's name."

"She's a few years younger than me but she's older than you. It was just better for the kids to have someone older around. For Chrissake, you're only ten years older than my daughter."

"So this is what it was all about? Finding a surrogate mother for your kids? Those kids have a mother."

"Joanie, I know that but . . ."

"But what?"

"Do you remember the blue paper book for kids I had in my car that one time? You asked me about it."

"Yes. What about it?"

"Helga's a writer. She wrote it." Connor looked pleased with himself.

I felt a tinge of jealousy. Imagine that! We were both creative. I had talked to Connor before about going back to school and getting a journalism degree. I guess Helga was a little further along in her career. "I see. How long did you know her?"

"A few weeks."

"A few weeks? Frank said a couple of months. Which is it?"

"It doesn't matter."

"It does to me." My voice rose again. "How do you think I feel? I'll never be able to trust anyone again, Connor, because of you."

"I'm sorry. I loved you, Joanie. I really did."

"I don't believe that. I was just a bump to you, as you say all the stewardesses are."

"Joanie, just last week I was in the kitchen and I turned around to Helga and called her Joanie by mistake." He smiled.

His small attempt to make me feel better bombed. I ignored it.

"Are you going to tell your wife about us having lunch?"

"Should I?"

"If *you* don't, I will."

"I will. I will. Only kidding."

"I'm not hungry." I had only eaten two bites. "Let's get out of here."

Connor walked me back to my car over by First Interstate Bank. He resorted to his old trick of faking a bump into me, letting me know he wanted to hug me.

"Cut it out, Connor."

"Joanie . . . Look, I was afraid I'd never get to see you again."

"You think you'll see me again now?"

"Well, I'd like to. Would you mind if I called you sometime?"

Oh, so I was better in bed, is that it? "Ask your wife if it's ok with her."

"OK," he said, as I shut the car door and drove off.

Chapter 10

I lived in a nice apartment building on Union Street with my Jewish roommate, Miriam. I wondered if maybe Connor had decided on Helga because he could never find a parking space on Union Street. I was thinking all kinds of crazy thoughts, imagining that she was better looking, older, more mature, better able to handle his two kids—and did the kids like her better?

After I got over the initial shock, I stayed home, bawling my eyes out for weeks. I'd take a bag of Toll House Morsels from the kitchen cupboard and spend the rest of the evening locked in my room. The chocolate helped to satisfy me. The pain never seemed to go away. Losing Connor made me feel worthless. No more running along the Bay and the Presidio with him. No more dinners out with him and his other agent friends to restaurants in the Bay area. No more snuggling up to him at night or wild orgasms that left me quivering. No more intimate conversations with him about how my day went or what was on his mind.

I hadn't cried so much since I was five. Tears would well up in my eyes at the thought of Connor. I'd wipe my eyes and then eat some chocolate chips. It wasn't too long before I'd start thinking about Connor again and I'd start sobbing. I sobbed so hard I could feel a throbbing pain behind my eyes and my upper body would shake in unison with the sobs. My red, swollen eyes hurt to the touch. I couldn't sleep. I never knew it could hurt so much to have someone you loved taken away from you. I felt like the life in me had been taken away. I couldn't charge Connor with murder, couldn't put him away behind bars where I thought he belonged. Instead I wrote a poem.

BLOODY MURDER

Death brags
Of its accomplices,
The physical blow
And its competitor
The emotional blow.

And whether one dies
By failure of a heart
To go on beating
Or by failure of a heart
To go on loving,
Which is more cruel?

* * *

I was dying inside but seemed to be functioning normally on the outside. At home, however, I stayed locked up in my bedroom. Even Miriam couldn't get me to unlock my door.

"Joan, let me in. I want to talk to you."

"Go away. I want to be alone."

"But, Joan, I need to talk to you."

"What about?"

"Please open the door. I can't talk to you like this."

"Leave me alone, please. I just want to be left alone."

"Ok, if that's how you want it."

"I do."

* * *

The crying would stop; it always had before. My family home had bedrooms on each floor but only one bathroom on the main floor. We never turned the lights on to go to the bathroom at night but rather would feel our way down the stairs from the outside light coming in the kitchen window. One night, when I was five, I crept slowly down the stairs and stopped outside Mom and Dad's bedroom door when I heard Mom say my name. I cracked the door open a bit and listened quietly. They were having an argument about me.

"Joanie cries all the time," Mom said. "Over nothing. I can't stand it anymore. I don't know what to do with her."

"She's only five years old. Maybe there's something wrong with her. Why don't we take her to see a doctor?"

I ran into the bathroom. I shivered at the word doctor. *Dad, no! I'll be good. I promise. I'm not sick. I don't need to be taken to no doctor. Doctors give you shots. There isn't anything wrong with me.*

I stopped my crying. I didn't want to see a doctor.

* * *

I called my parents after the Fourth of July and let them know what had happened, looking for support and solace.

"Mom, what did you guys do for the Fourth?"

"We went to the breakfast at Greencreek and then to the Grangeville Park and then we watched the Grangeville parade."

"Was the whole family there?"

"No, Don and Melissa were busy putting away their wedding gifts. Theresa, Marilyn and Connie came. Karen had other plans."

"Where did Don and Melissa go on their honeymoon?"

"Well, they spent the night at the Coeur d' Alene Hotel Resort and then the next day everybody went to their place and they opened up all their gifts. Their place is tiny."

"Where's it at?"

"It's over by Washington Water Power. Don just started working there so he didn't have any leave. What did you do over the Fourth?"

"Nothing. I just found out Connor married someone else while I was at Don and Melissa's wedding."

"Oh?"

"I found out from his roommate. I guess it's good I didn't end up marrying such a flake."

"Say, you have to see the cute baby quilt Carole made. It's one of her best ones. She embroidered the white blocks with nursery rhyme pictures on it and then put it together with blue cotton. I'm surprised she can do such good embroidery work with only one eye. You'll just have to see it."

"Maybe another time, Mom. I gotta go. Bye."

"Bye."

It was clear that this heartache was something I had to get over myself.

* * *

Although I inherited a susceptibility to my disorder, being jilted by this FBI agent was the first traumatic episode that triggered the onset of my illness. It's as if some of the chemicals in my brain (serotonin and dopamine) were depleted or imbalanced due to the prolonged stress or trauma. Not everyone who inherits the susceptibility develops the illness. Triggers (the loss of a loved one) help the illness surface. I learned that onset is normally between 25-30 years of age and it often takes just such a traumatic event or trigger to jump-start the symptoms of the disorder.

I also learned that my depression at this time, although severe, was not biological, i.e., it did not all of a sudden surge within me without warning. Instead it was situational depression caused by traumatic events in my life. Nevertheless, the trauma radically altered my life. There would be other triggers or traumatic episodes to follow.

Chapter 11

My life quieted down on the job, but Barry and Uncle Joe Walsh, another retired Case Officer from the CIA (affectionately called Uncle because it was a term of endearment often used for superiors at the CIA) who I worked with continued to do "dirty tricks" and spying, as they had done at the CIA. Whenever Barry and Alice traveled, they wore disguises. I was not privy to a lot of what they did but they did tell me they were able to get to a furniture dealer inside a high security fence in Cuba, something the Agency could never do. Barry bragged that they were the only ones able to do something because, as he said, the CIA had their hands tied. Barry had been pink-slipped by Jimmie Carter's CIA head, Stansfield Turner.

Uncle Joe Walsh was not pink-slipped by Turner and didn't brag like Barry. He didn't work for Barry. He worked for Alice. Uncle Joe was a brilliant man. He just quietly retreated to his windowless office and wrote voraciously about Nicaragua. He had once planted a story in the foreign press and it showed up in the FBIS microfiche. (Foreign Broadcast Information Service.) The CIA has been accused of doing this before and, like I said, Barry and Uncle Joe continued on with spying and "dirty tricks" as they had done at the Agency. I saw documents Barry had written for distribution to certain high-up Republicans but at the time it meant nothing to me because I didn't know who they were and didn't know they were about to become major players in the Reagan Administration. Although I have no evidence, it would not surprise me to learn that the idea for the Nicaraguan Contras came out of that office.

Barry had me, a twenty-five-year-old who lacked a college education, writing country studies for international investors (read multinational corporations). I wrote a report on the Philippines. I took information from country files they had put together. There were articles from magazines in that file; there were publications from various political organizations; there were flyers and pamphlets secretly obtained from leftist groups. I loved the job. I didn't have to know much about politics to realize Barry and Alice were extremely conservative in their political views. Most of the information I used came from John Birch Society documents. They loved my reports and ended up giving me a big office.

I had a high regard for Barry, Uncle Joe and Alice. We were saving the world from communists and I felt very patriotic and righteous. I didn't like their "we are kings and queens" attitude and "you are our lowly subjects" but I didn't have the education or experience to look elsewhere for a job and I was starting to ease myself into going back to college. They frowned on me going back to college, especially to the liberal colleges in the Bay Area. I wondered what they were afraid of—that I might discover the truth and not have such a high regard for them? Alice's kids all went to extremely right-wing colleges that I had never heard of. I later realized this was so they wouldn't be tainted with a liberal view.

I said nothing about all of this to my parents, partly because of my days working for the CIA when I never told them anything about my work and partly because I felt they wouldn't understand it anyway. And I knew how to keep a secret from my days with the Agency. Besides, I was only following orders from Barry and Uncle Joe. I didn't really understand what they were doing.

* * *

I thought I looked classy in an off-white silk knit turtleneck underneath a soft, bright navy blue, over-the-knee, empire-waisted dress with a patterned red, navy and green yoke bodice. The dress offset my dark brown hair, hazel eyes and ruby red lips and nails. I wore navy hose and black T-strap shoes with a thick 2" heel. The clothes and shoes were European—part of a collection I bought while I was passing through London on my way back to the States from overseas. I thought I looked smart and felt smart, too.

It was early morning when I bumped into Barry getting coffee in the lunchroom. I was ready to leave Snoops, Inc. and had been looking for another job, combing the want ads, but nothing had materialized yet. Sometimes Alice and Barry couldn't meet their payroll on time even though the office was furnished to the hilt. I wondered if they were going under. I thought I'd get out while the getting was still good. I was still merely toying with the idea of going back to school. After writing that report on the Phillippines I knew I needed more education. But I didn't know how I could afford it.

Barry looked like a Wall Street executive in a Brooks Brothers navy suit with his signature thick red suspenders over a blue-and-white striped shirt and red Italian tie. He commented on my outfit.

"Joan, you look terrific. New clothes?"

"No, I bought this in London on my way back to the States," I said matter-of-factly. "I've worn it before."

"Say, could you bring your report on the Philippines and come to my office."

"Well, I'm not finished with it, yet." I panicked. I felt I really didn't know what I was doing writing reports about countries I had never even visited.

"That's ok. I just want you to give me an update."

Barry didn't really want an update on the Philippines report. The client didn't need the report for six months. He just wanted to know what was going on in my life.

I got my report and sat down on one of the leather chairs in Barry's office. He sat behind his desk, lighting up a cigarette.

"Ok, shoot."

"Well, from what I've read so far in the file Alice keeps, Marcos has some heavy opposition. This opposition includes four groups: the Moro National Liberation Front, the Muslims in the south—they want to increase their number and their power; the oligarchy which includes former Senator Benigno Aquino—these are former landowners whose land and power was taken away from them by the Marcos regime and they obviously want things back the way they once were; the New People's Army, the communist group . . ."

"I knew there were communists in on this. How many are there?"

"I don't know. None of what I read gave me a figure."

"You see. You see. Our work is more important than ever. The CIA can't do it anymore. The CIA is handicapped by all these Congressional mandates, oversight committees and all those good people they let go. I am the only one who can do anything."

How could a tiny operation called Snoops, Inc. have more of an effect on a country like the Philippines than a zillion-man operation of the multi-billion dollar business of the CIA? Who was really handicapped here?

"Oh, by the way," I continued, "there is strong sentiment over in the Philippines and members of Philippine organizations within the United States to get the U.S. bases out of the Philippines or at least have them controlled by the Philippine government."

"Joan . . ."

"Yes."

"I heard you went out with Sonya."

"So? I am allowed to, I think." *Now, you're trying to control my life, too.*

"Well, did anything unusual happen?"

"Unusual?"

"Did she do anything strange?"

"Sonya *is* strange. She's a bananas lady."

"Joan, she's a KGB agent."

"What?? Are you sure?" *I don't know whether to believe him.*

"I know what I'm talking about. Talk to Alice."

"Why should I talk to Alice? What has she got to do with it? Sonya told me she'd rather work for you than Alice."

"Just talk to Alice."

I walked out, turned the corner and went to Alice's office. I found the patriot alone in her office.

"Alice, Barry asked me to come and see you. It's about Sonya."

"Oh, did you get it, too?"

"Get what?"

"Her sob story about defecting."

"You mean she did that to someone else, too?"

"She singled out several people in the office and after getting them boozed up, she pulls this stunt about defecting on them. She doesn't need to defect. The trial was over with May 18. Why is she still worried about it three months later?"

"She's just a really crazy lady. Barry thinks she's a KGB agent. I don't think she is, do you?"

"We don't know what to think. I wouldn't continue any contact with her though if I were you."

"Why?"

"I just wouldn't. She took Ron out one night and his small car suddenly flipped over. Sonya had grabbed for the wheel. She's dangerous. We've got Herbert assigned to her now. Her only contact with the office will be through him."

"Oh, I see. Ok. You know, I really liked her though. She was a journalist and I really admire that in her. I know she was bananas but you might have to be bananas in that job."

"Just remember, Joan. No contact!"

"I hear ya."

Chapter 12

Work continued uneventful until Dash (his nickname), the Soviet defector hired by National Investigations, invited the whole office to a party at his nearby Watergate Condo, named after the Watergate Apartments in Washington, DC. They were converted from apartments into condominiums in 1979, and Dash bought his that year with the money he received from the United States government for "telling all." Rumor had it that he was offered a million dollars but he refused it, saying he didn't defect for the money.

I never trusted him completely—the slight man with dark brown hair and thin brown mustache who always looked sloppy because his American clothes didn't fit his Russian body. I found it difficult to believe he could leave his wife and children behind and jump sides like he claimed he did. Besides, I knew that the only way the Soviets could penetrate National Investigations was by sending one of their own in. Security was tighter than Calvin Klein jeans on a 300 lb. woman.

I got tired of waiting around at the office for everyone to leave so I asked Herbert's secretary for the address and directions and then left. Dash had left an hour ago.

I drove down Powell Street past Admiral Drive and turned right on Commodore Drive. Sandwiched between a gorgeous marina on one side and the skyline of San Francisco on the other, the grounds surrounding the condominiums were kept beautiful by landscaping crews.

I parked outside the condominium complex because only residents with a Watergate decal on their car were allowed to park in the underneath garage. I walked over to the lobby outside of the garage and rang Dash's condo. He answered and pushed the button to let me in.

I rode up in the elevator and walked down a long hallway to his condo and knocked on his door. He smiled and asked me to come in. I was the first to arrive. As I sat down on the couch I listened to Russian music playing in the background. *So, he didn't completely hate his country after all,* I thought.

"That's pretty music," I said, politely.

"From Russia," he said, smiling.

"Are you getting settled here?" I asked, speaking slowly and deliberately. "Do you like it here so far?"

"Yes, I like it here very much," he said in broken English. "What would you like to drink?"

"Do you have wine?"

"No, just liquor."

"Then I'd like a gin and tonic. Do you know it?"

"Yes, I know it."

"You have a nice place."

"Yes, I like it." He handed me the drink and a napkin.

Just then Herbert, his Assistant and Alice's secretary buzzed the intercom and Dash walked over to buzz them in. Dash and I could hear Herbert's loud boisterous voice coming down the hallway. When they entered, Herbert immediately noticed the music.

"What's that horseshit you've got on the stereo? Why don't you play something good like the Star Spangled Banner?"

Dash apologized and went to put on some other music. Herbert and company helped themselves to drinks.

"We had one before we left the office," Herbert bragged. Then the intercom buzzer went crazy.

"It must be everybody else," Dash said.

They all came in at once—Barry, Alice, Barry's secretary, the Accountant, Uncle Joe Walsh and his wife, Sancho, the researchers, the news clippers, the file clerks and the token black chauffeur. They filled the small kitchen and living room with excited conversation and laughter.

"Joan," someone said. The voice belonged to Barry. "You look like you need a refill."

"I guess I do. I hadn't noticed."

Dash, Herbert's Assistant and Barry were all in the kitchen busily getting people drinks.

"What are you drinking?" Barry said.

"Gin and tonic."

Herbert's Assistant brought it over to me.

"There you go."

"Thank you."

I chatted with several people and took three big sips of my drink. All of a sudden I felt woozy, like I needed to lie down and rest for a while. Someone had slipped me a Mickey. My brain signaled that it was time to leave.

"I've gotta go," was all I said to anyone. No one seemed to notice how drunk I was. Feeling dizzy, I rushed out of the door and out of the condominium complex, barely able to remember my way to the elevator or where I was parked.

Later I would not remember getting into my car, driving onto Interstate 80, driving past the trashy artwork of Emeryville Mud Flats, paying the 75 cent toll at the toll booth, waiting for the on-ramp car meter light to turn green, merging with five lanes of traffic, driving across the Bridge, getting off at Freemont Street, turning left at Pine, right at Polk and left at Union, activating the garage door opener, parking in my designated spot, riding up the elevator or walking down a long hallway to my apartment. It would all be a blur. The only thing I would remember was wanting badly to go home and how much Connor had hurt me.

I never remembered being this drunk except for one time overseas when my best friend Eleanor and I were invited over to her boss's house for dinner. Booze flowed freely as it always did overseas because of the cheap price. Eleanor and I were drinking wine when all of a sudden the drinks were changed to Schnapps and then after-dinner brandies. The combination made us both sick and we ended up at Eleanor's apartment which was closest, puking our guts out in the bathroom.

I remembered this occasion and also remembered a nasty habit that Eleanor and I had overseas—calling our boyfriends in the States long distance late at night. Not knowing who did this to me, who made me this drunk and still hurting from the jilt from Connor, I picked up the phone and dialed.

Chapter 13

I never thought of calling my parents. There was no comfort or support there so I called my "spare," the boyfriend or lover I carried in my back pocket in case anything happened to my current relationship. I called Michael.

The oldest in a military family, he quickly learned to be a Mama's boy in Texas when his father, who was also in the Army, left for Vietnam for a number of years. I imagined his mother confided in her oldest son a lot, telling him what women really wanted out of a relationship. The son obviously wanted to please his mother, and was motivated to please women ever since. The one he chose as "his woman" would receive his undying attention. He would treat her with the reverence he would treat his mother. However, getting him to choose one woman seemed virtually impossible.

The alarm clock flashed 1:15.

"Hello."

"Michael, it's me—I." I was drunk and hurting badly, turning to the only friend I felt I had left in the world. I needed another person I cared about, an old familiar face, someone I could fall back on, someone I could count on to be nice to me. Michael was it. My speech was slurred and slow.

"I just went to this party at this defector's place and someone put something in my drink. I don't know who did it. It could have been Barry. It could have been Dash. It could have been Herbert's Assistant. I don't know why someone would do that to me. I think they were trying to get information out of me. But, I don't talk—not even with booze—except to my friends."

I was having difficulty putting all the pieces of the puzzle together. It was as if I thought that by telling Michael, things would suddenly fall into place. Michael could make it all better. Michael listened with interest but had difficulty understanding me because my speech was so slurred and my thoughts so disjointed.

"There was this KGB agent at work—well, Barry said she was a KGB agent—and she asked me out to dinner. We went to the Russian Renaissance a couple of times. Sonya Lackey was supposed to be coming to work for Alice but everyone in the office was mean to her. I don't know why. She was crazy. She was vague about her past. She talked about defecting to the Soviet Union, defecting from her job as a newspaper reporter or at HEW. She didn't make sense."

Being the gentleman that he was, Michael politely didn't interrupt.

"But, she talked me into inviting Connor for drinks at Liverpool Lil's one night. Connor was an FBI agent I dated for the past six months. I called Connor's house to talk to him but his roommate answered and told me Connor didn't live there anymore and that he was married. He married while I was on vacation going to my brother's wedding in Spokane." I started crying.

I would later realize Michael was perturbed at finding out about another man in my life—the rule was to never tell the other, to pretend that there never was anyone else. Michael, nevertheless let me run my batteries out.

"You know, once Connor asked if I had any spares in my closet, meaning old boyfriends I kept on reserve, and I told him about you." I was desperate for his friendship, desperate to be loved, hugged and cuddled. The booze made the pain of rejection all the more acute. I believed I could count on Michael to say he loved me. He would make things better.

"I . . . I haven't heard from you in awhile. I thought . . ." Michael tried to interject several times to gently let me down easy but I seemed incapable of listening. I was like a stuck CD player.

"Michael, I said that I would always love you. I told Connor that."

"Joan, it's no good . . ."

"I do love you, Michael!"

This was embarrassing for Michael. It was late and I was getting on his nerves. I was drunk and had awakened him in the wee hours. Nevertheless, being the gentleman that he was, he just said, "Shhhhh, Joan, you don't know what you're saying. You need to get some sleep." He sounded like he hoped I'd get off the phone.

"No, Michael. I do love you." I was argumentative in my drunken stupor.

Michael couldn't stand it anymore. Finally he shouted, "I DON'T LOVE YOU!"

I stopped rambling. All of a sudden I didn't feel drunk anymore. I was silent for a minute.

"You don't . . ." I said in disbelief. Then I suddenly passed out. In the morning my phone was still off the hook.

Chapter 14

When I came to my senses, I was determined to go for a run. I hadn't slept well and I was feeling stressed. It seemed only yesterday that Connor and I ran together—he six-minute miles and me about seven or eight. I ran five miles a day usually in the Presidio or down by the Bay. I believed a good run would lift my mood.

No one was in the hallway. The small elevator arrived quickly. The garage was empty, too. I climbed into my yellow Volkswagen Bug and drove up to the NRAA Overlook near the tollbooths on the Golden Gate Bridge. Connor and I considered this a favorite running spot because the view was so spectacular. On a clear day we could see Alcatraz.

Today the only other car that could be found at the viewpoint was an old green Ford sedan which seemed to have lost its owner—at least he or she was nowhere in sight. I parked my car and dragged myself out to stretch. I touched my toes several times, and then squatted in a half split to stretch my back tendons. When my body loosened up, I pulled my hair back, took a deep breath and leaped into a long stride toward the bridge.

The air was crisp, no trace of fog could be found. It had rained several hours ago but the morning sun was beginning to warm the surrounding hills, brightening up an otherwise gloomy day as I pounded the pavement. Across the bridge and back was almost three miles. Certainly no ordeal for me.

I ran hard that morning on the wide sidewalks, trying to release the tension I felt inside. My body was tight, tense. My breathing was shallow and hard. I made it almost halfway across the bridge when suddenly I felt a lump in my throat as I remembered running the bridge with Connor. It was hard to be without him, hard to be alone. The ache inside never seemed to go away. My body craved his touch and like a hurt child writhed with a desire to be held.

Why did Connor do this to me? What will I do without him? No one loves me. No one cares. Oh God, why does it hurt so badly? I feel like someone stuck a knife in my heart, twisting it over and over again. The pain is so terrible! Please, somebody, make it go away!

Tears welled up in my eyes. I refused to succumb. I stopped briefly to quickly wipe my eyes with my hands then took off running again, consumed by my thoughts.

Oh my God, it's so hopeless. There isn't any way out. There just isn't any way out.

As I neared the middle of the bridge, I could feel the ache inside me building but could no longer hold back the wrenching sobs which overpowered me. I wiped my eyes and nose and resolved to keep running, resolved to get Connor out of my mind, resolved to be strong. I picked up the pace a little bit and ran more purposeful. My feet felt heavier. I tried hard to block everything out but the tears came again. I slowed down and sauntered to the side, grabbed hold of the rail and looked out across the Bay, then down at the water, my sobs overtaking me. I tried to compose myself, wiped my eyes and brushed my hair away from my face. My forehead was moist as were my hands, which were trembling. I folded my arms in front of me and glanced down the left side of the bridge and then to the right. No one was in close proximity. I paused and sighed heavily, my chest still heaving. I bit my lower lip as if I were weighing an important decision and stared blankly into space, fixating my eyes on a minuscule bolt in the railing. *Should I?* I thought, impulsively. *Here is my way out. Who would care? What would be the difference? Nothing mattered anymore. Not Connor, certainly. Not anybody. Not anything. Nothing mattered. Even life itself seemed an irritation, a nuisance to be avoided.*

I felt beaten, downtrodden, powerless. I couldn't sort anything out.

I lifted my leg up the first rung on the bridge's edge. It looked like a red ladder turned on its side. I held onto the red, horizontal rope-like cables made of steel suspended from the top of the bridge. These cables appeared every few feet and aided anyone climbing up. Hanging onto the cables, I managed to climb to the top of the "ladder on its side." I stood up, my palms sweating, holding onto the red ropes. I looked down and felt dizzy.

Just then a car full of kids drove by.

I turned around to see the intruders as they sped off towards Marin. Half smiling, I shook my head slightly in disbelief, climbed down from the "ladder" and walked away from the bridge's edge. I inhaled deeply, wiped my red, swollen eyes once more and in a moment was off running again.

* * *

I never ran again.

Chapter 15

It was awhile before I tried dating again. I couldn't remember exactly how long it had been because I was still numb but the weeks drifted into months. Conrad, Willie's friend whom I met at Liverpool Lil's with Sonya, had called several times but I always begged off, saying I wasn't over Connor yet. Conrad was always polite and said he understood and that he cared very much for me and would give me as much time as I needed. Over time I slowly began to go out of my mind from the loneliness. Conrad was not my first choice but he offered me an escape from my problems and my loneliness.

"Joan, the phone is for you."

"Hello. This is Joan."

"Hi, Joan. This is Conrad. How are you doing?"

"I'm still kind of depressed. How are you?"

"Well, I'm great. I'm up in the high country. Can you hear me ok? This phone system hasn't been working well."

"I can hear you fine. Are you up at Tahoe?"

"Yeah, in the general area. Listen, I am going to be down this weekend and I'm staying with Willie. I was wondering if you would like to have dinner with me in Marin. No strings attached, of course."

"Which day?"

"Saturday, if you're free."

"I'm free. But, Conrad, I don't really want to date one of Connor's friends."

"We weren't really friends. We just knew each other in passing. The Bureau out here is really a small place so everyone knows everyone else."

"I don't know, I don't even want to date another FBI agent. You know, you get burned once, you don't go back for seconds."

"Joan, believe me, what Connor did to you was atrocious. He should be shot. He should have at least had the decency to break up with you before he married the witch. I promise you, Joan that will never happen with me."

"That's because I won't let it happen."

"Joan, it's not like I'm asking you to marry me or anything. It's only one dinner. What do you say?"

"Well, ok. What time?"

"I'm embarrassed to ask, but do you think you could swing by Willie's place and pick me up? You see, I won't have any wheels."

I laughed. "So, you go for the liberal-type woman, do you?"

"No, actually I go for any type." He laughed.

"I see. What time would you like your subservient chauffeur to arrive, Monsieur?"

"Seven would be fine. Let's dodge the crowds.

"I think I'll need an address."

"He lives near The Chart House Valhalla restaurant in Sausalito. I'll call you with the address later. I've gotta go now. Bye Hon."

"Bye."

I was amused. I couldn't see myself with balding, bearded Conrad with a sea worn face who was an inch shy of being able to look me straight in the eye. He looked like Zero Mostel, playing Tevye in "Fiddler on the Roof." I almost expected him to break out in song, "If I were a rich man . . ." No, he was too old for me. But, it was something to do, someone to talk to and I had felt cooped up long enough.

We had dinner that Saturday at Flynn's Landing on the corner of Johnson Street and Bridgeway, a restaurant known for its mouth-watering seafood as well as a magnificent view of Sausalito Yacht Harbor where hundreds of pleasure boats anchor a few feet in front of the restaurant's waterfront windows.

Conrad, dressed all in black, took my arm and led me out towards Bridgeway. I had on a pair of loafers and a pair of navy gabardine pants and blazer and a navy-blue-and-lighter-blue tiny striped cowl turtleneck from London. I found Conrad easy to be with. He was a very good listener and so attentive. It was as if every minute detail of my life was important to him. And he wasn't pushy about sex either like most guys I'd met. It never came up.

We strolled down Bridgeway and sat on a bench near the fountain by one of the two elephants in Vina Del Mar Park in downtown

Sausalito. We faced each other and he took my hand in his and occasionally caressed it and sometimes just squeezed it slightly to let me know he cared. I found the attention comforting. I found in the strength of his hands something unexpected. I relaxed and began opening up to him.

"Conrad, you can't imagine how hurt I was by what Connor did."

"I know, dear. That bastard should be hung for what he did to you. Why do you think he did that, anyway?"

"I don't know why he did it but I think it had something to do with Barry." I had been mulling it over in my head now for days before I came to this awareness. I even argued with myself over it. The pieces of the puzzle were starting to fall into place. Barry was obviously responsible.

"Who?"

"Barry. Barry Lipman. My boss at Snoops, Inc."

"What is Snoops, Inc.?"

"It's a company that does research and writes studies about countries for overseas investors."

"You mean multinational corporations?"

"Yes, companies that do business in more than one country."

"So, what kind of studies do they do?"

"They do economic, political and intelligence studies for their clients."

"What?"

"If a multinational corporation like ABC Corporation sells pineapples and they grow those pineapples in a country like the Philippines, then they have an interest in the political and economic developments in the Philippines because if the economic climate is favorable under a certain regime and that regime suddenly gets ousted, then ABC Corporation might find itself booted out of the country and its assets seized. So, we watch the political and economic developments and report them to our clients."

"So, what you're really saying is that they do some of the same stuff as the CIA."

"Well, sort of. Very similar."

"You mean he does black bag jobs and all?"

"He is a former Case Officer with the CIA."

"So?"

"So, he is out to get revenge because they pink-slipped him. He thinks the CIA is handicapped because they lost their best people and he is the only one with the power to do something."

"Like what?"

I hesitated. It was unlike me to go telling company secrets. After all I didn't know Conrad very well. But . . . he was a good listener and I felt he could keep a confidence. Besides, isn't that what went wrong with my relationship with Connor? I never told Connor anything about Barry. I was sorry now that I hadn't. Now here was my chance to correct that mistake.

"Like overthrow a government or maybe overthrow those in power in the U.S. government."

"How do you know this?"

"I found some documents."

"You have proof?"

"Well, not exactly. Barry has the documents. I've only seen them."

"Who does he want to overthrow?"

"Well, I don't know for sure but it looks like anyone who is not Republican or right-wing. Jimmy Carter for sure. The Soviet Union. Castro if he could. Any leftist government is a candidate."

"How do you know it isn't just 'we' against 'them' politics as usual?"

"Normally it would be but he has been trained by the CIA to overthrow governments. It's one thing when they were foreign governments but now he's trying to overthrow our own U.S. government. He's not allowed to do that. The rules say so."

"But, how do you figure into all this? Why would Barry have anything to do with you and Connor?"

"Barry invited me to housesit one weekend. I invited Connor but he had other plans or so he said. I think Connor knew about Barry."

"Why do you say that? Did you ever talk about him?"

"I never ever discussed Barry with Connor but he always seemed to be avoiding him." *That's right,* I thought, *I never ever discussed Barry with Connor. I never discussed anything of importance with him, so why am I doing it now with Conrad?*

I just sat, looking straight ahead, not looking at Conrad, deep in my own thoughts. I didn't know whether to be afraid or not about what I just said to Conrad. This much information in the wrong hands could certainly get me in deep, deep trouble. Why in the world did I tell Conrad all of this stuff about Barry and the Company? *I told him because I want to make things right this time. What Barry's doing worries me. I want to tell an FBI agent about Barry. Conrad is an FBI agent. He will listen to me. He will help me.*

I thought long and hard about Conrad for a moment. What was it about this man that made me open up so much? Certainly he was a great listener and really empathetic. I really believed him when he told me how disgusted he was with Connor and the things he had done. That was it. I just really believed him. He was a very believable guy and easy to talk to.

Snapping out of my thoughts, I continued, "Barry never wanted me to have contact with Connor. He always felt like I was giving away secrets to the FBI and you know the CIA and FBI have always hated each other. And at the time I thought either Barry or the FBI arranged for Connor to meet Helga so he'd dump me."

"Isn't that a little far fetched?"

"Is it? I've thought about this a lot. Blonde, little Helga suddenly appeared out of nowhere. I'll just bet Barry or the FBI had something to do with it. Besides, Barry has gone after every guy I've dated since."

"How so? He's never gone after me."

"This is our first date. Anyway, a friend of mine, an insurance salesman for Levinson Brothers, found all four tires flat when he tried to leave the morning after he went out to the movies with me. I saw Connor's friend, Mickey, at the movie theater, which was odd because I think he lived in the suburbs. Another guy I dated was a San Francisco cop and someone hit him with ice on the forehead which cut him while we were walking to my place. I never heard from either of them again. They never returned my calls. I imagine Barry or the FBI scared them off."

"But, what about me?"

"Either Barry doesn't know about you yet or he probably won't touch you because you're with the FBI. He will try to break up our relationship. I guarantee it."

"Why is he so hot on you?"

"I'm his favorite employee. That's what he tells everyone. I guess he just thinks he's looking out for my best interests and he doesn't want any secrets to get out."

"It's probably the latter. What's this company that you work for? Tell me more about Snoops, Inc . . ."

"Well, it's connected to this detective agency called National Investigations. It is owned by Alice Sanborn. She's the only one who really pays everybody. She and Barry operate like partners even though they swear the companies are separate.

"National Investigations is kind of like the FBI and Snoops, Inc. operates like the CIA. I told you Barry was a former Case Officer. Another former Case Officer works there, too. His name is Joe Walsh and his wife works as a secretary there as well. The Walshes work for Alice which is strange but Joe told me he knew Barry back at the CIA Headquarters and said he would not work for him."

Conrad caressed my hand. What does Joe do?"

"He sits in an office that he designed with no windows and writes voraciously about Nicaragua."

"What about it?"

"I don't really know. I've never read anything he's written on Nicaragua and I don't know the country anyway so it probably wouldn't make much sense. I have read other reports he's written and he's a good writer. The only thing is he kind of does things he's not supposed to do."

"Like what?"

"Like he wrote this political article on what was happening in Nicaragua and had it planted in *La Prensa*, a foreign newspaper in Latin America. Then the FBIS picked it up like it was a genuine article, as if it were true. It was fabricated."

"What is FBIS?"

"Foreign Broadcast Information Service. They excerpt all kinds of foreign newspapers. It's a good source to find out what's happening in a certain country. Can you imagine? The CIA people read all about what's happening in Nicaragua and the story was fabricated by a former Case Officer. I guess ol' Joe pulled a fast one over on the CIA."

Conrad laughed. "You're with a bunch of crazies. What other fruitcakes do you have working there?"

I suddenly became withdrawn. I suddenly realized that I had said far too much to someone I barely knew. Cold chills ran up my back. "Say, do you mind if we go back now?" I got up to leave.

"Not at all. I hope it wasn't something I said." Conrad could see that I needed my own space so he never tried to put his arm around me or hold my hand.

"It's nothing. I just feel like leaving. Conrad, what did you think of Sonya?"

"Sonya?" Conrad was taken aback at the abrupt change in subject.

"Willie seemed to know her. Did he say anything about her?"

"I don't really know. I only met her that one night. She sure was aggressive, wasn't she?"

"Aggressive isn't a strong enough word. She came back to my place and was crying about defecting to the Soviet Union because of some trial she was involved in. I found out later that her trial had already been over with. Three months previous. I don't know why she did that other than to feel me out about defecting. I told her no, I could never defect to the Soviet Union because they didn't have good shopping malls there."

Conrad's deep voice roared with laughter. "I can't believe you said that."

"I can't believe I did either. I was very drunk. But, that's what I said. You know, Conrad, my office is the strangest office I've ever been in. Sonya would have fit in well. None of those people ever go out to lunch. I've invited them to but they always decline. They won't talk to anyone outside the office and God forbid if they find out someone's a liberal. They're suspicious of everyone. It's really like a prison. Even the Agency wasn't this bad."

"So, what do you want to do?"

"I don't know. I want to go out to lunch. I want to know all kinds of people. And I want to have all kinds of friends. I want to be open and honest about everything. I want to be normal again."

Conrad bit his lower lip to keep from laughing. "But, what are you going to do about your situation?"

"Well, I wrote to a girlfriend overseas. She's a Case Officer and she knows Barry real well. She told me to get the hell out of here as soon as possible. I guess I'm just waiting for the opportune time. I'll make him mad if I leave him before the time is right. Barry always has to be the one in control. I'm afraid of what he might do to me. But, like I said, I'm just waiting for the right moment."

"I have full confidence in you that you'll do the right thing, you sound like you have such a grand sense of the right and wrong. Oh, look. We're here. Did you want to stop for a nightcap somewhere? Where I don't know because everything in Marin is closed at this hour."

"No, I think I'll just take you home and then go. I hope you don't mind."

"Not at all. I've enjoyed a marvelous evening with you tonight. Look, I'm not going to be in town much but I promise I will call you again soon."

"Conrad, you are so sweet. But, like I said before, I don't really want to date another FBI agent. Don't call me, please."

"How about just to say hi, to see how you're doing. It's going to take you awhile to get over this. You might need a friend."

"Well, I guess that would be ok. I need lots of friends."

Conrad leaned over and kissed me lightly on the lips.

"Bye."

Chapter 16

Conrad called frequently but never made noises about the two of us getting together. He always politely listened to whatever was going on in my life. I found his friendship addictive. I almost waited for his calls. He was the most caring friend I could have wanted.

One day, out of the blue, he called and told me he was in Los Angeles and he invited me down for the weekend, saying how nice it would be for me to get away from everything that reminded me of Connor. Besides, what could it hurt? It was only a weekend. We could visit a couple of museums, take in a few movies, eat out, poop around, and just relax. He said he'd pay for everything, including my airfare.

The idea of getting away from everything appealed to me. I said yes. On such short notice I selected a light brown pair of Liz Claiborne tapered cord jeans and a flannel plaid shirt to match. They weren't my best color or my favorites but they were clean. I'd wear the jeans on the plane with a T-shirt and pack the flannel shirt as a spare. I also packed an off-white linen casual jacket and pants and a silky navy blouse with rounded collar and tiny white stars all over it.

I thought about taking my "knock 'em dead" black dress, the one I wore when I met Conrad. The Tracy below-the-knee crepe dress had off-white, yellow, purple and red flowers all over its blouson top and free-flowing skirt. The off-white against the stark black background picked up contrasts in my newly streaked hair. I put the dress in my suitcase at first but then threw it out because Conrad had already seen me in it once.

I packed light, deciding that I wouldn't need many clothes if we were just going to poop around together. I couldn't see a need for a dress either. Conrad didn't strike me as the type of person who spent a lot of time getting dressed up.

I got off the plane looking very casual, wearing my cord jeans, T-shirt and light-brown cord jacket. Conrad dressed casual, too, in blue jeans, light blue shirt and a navy jacket. His beard was closely cropped and meticulously trimmed.

"Hi Hon, how are you feeling today?"

"Wonderful. Conrad, this was the best idea. Thank you."

"Did you have a good flight?"

"Yes. Thank you, I did." I kissed him on the cheek.

"Let's get your luggage and then I know a quiet place where we can get a bite to eat, a cup of coffee and just talk. Does that sound good to you? Have you eaten?"

"No. I couldn't stomach the airline food. It sounds great."

We went to a nearby bistro. I was amazed and pleased Conrad didn't take me to his hotel and immediately attack me. He was my friend, after all. We sat in the tiny restaurant talking and eventually the conversation drifted toward Barry and his operation. I trusted him completely. I felt comfortable in telling him anything and in answering any of his questions.

"They had an FBI agent passing them intelligence information and a CIA analyst who did the same. I met both of them. They were introduced to me as people who were gallantly breaking the rules to save our country."

"Oh, Jesus! To save our country from what—the liberals?"

"There's more. National Investigations has an unwritten reciprocal agreement with the police to exchange information. They helped in the Patty Hearst kidnapping. Of course, they can't charge for the information and time spent in researching it; otherwise, it would be breaking the law. But, no law says anything about freebies."

"Did you tell Connor any of this or report it?"

"I was afraid to tell Connor and so I never did. Connor hardly ever talked about his work. I never talked to him about mine. Once I did try to tell him about the documents but then Helga suddenly appeared. I spoke to a Security Officer at the CIA and I contacted a friend and Case Officer overseas about Barry. I already told you what she said. You know something, I just thought of something else."

"Which is?"

"Barry came in one day with his cohorts and they were all smiling and bragging because he was signing papers which made him the head of a small nation somewhere."

"Do you remember where?"

"It was a difficult name and I had never heard of the country. It was tiny. I think it was either in Africa or South America somewhere."

"That means he's more than a registered agent for another country. He is *the* head of the country."

"It also means he is doing politics as usual with his agents from his CIA days and his former colleagues in the CIA and no one knows about him working for another government."

"Gee, this guy needs to be reeled in."

"Conrad, you are so easy for me to talk to. Thank you."

Conrad grinned. He wasn't a macho man by any means. Rather, he was someone who listened intently to everyone's problems and in the process became their best friend.

"Joan, it's such a pleasure to have you here. You've really brightened up my day. Are you through here? Let's go get settled in the hotel."

"I'd love that. Maybe I could freshen up."

"By the way, tonight we're going for dinner and drinks with my friend James Kaufman and his girlfriend Marcia."

"Really? I thought it would be just the two of us this weekend. Oh well." I was flexible. After all, Conrad was paying for the weekend.

"You'll like them. I know you will."

Conrad took me to the Wilshire Orange Hotel on West 8th Street, which was only a fifteen-minute drive to Beverly Hills. Located in a residential area, rates were cheaper than in Beverly Hills.

Conrad's room, #20, was located in the front of the building and had a balcony. Each room had its own set of entry door keys and there were complimentary magazines and daily newspapers to be read on the veranda.

In the room, I kissed Conrad on his semi-bald head.

"Thank you for inviting me down here. I really needed to get away. How can I ever return your kindness?"

"You don't need to. That's just how I am."

"You're wonderful." I kissed him hard on the lips.

Conrad pulled me onto the bed and began peeling off my clothes. I helped him and undressed him down to his bright blue jockey underwear. I took off his last vestige of clothing and threw the underwear to the side of the bed. I couldn't believe the transformation in Conrad. His face looked old and shriveled but he had the body of a twenty-year-old. He was trim and fit—no paunch—and I detected no wrinkles except in his face. His skin was well lubricated, not dry like someone well beyond my age might have been. I wasn't sure exactly how old he was but I knew he'd outlived me by more than a few years.

I also found it hard to believe he had no difficulty getting it up or keeping it up. *So, what's all this fuss about sleeping with an old man?* I thought. We made love one time, mechanically, as if that was in his prearranged schedule. He climaxed on cue but I never came. *I thought maybe there should have been more foreplay. It didn't matter for I was starting to care for Conrad. I was surprised about feeling this way so soon after Connor's stunt.*

"You don't have an inhibited bone in your body, do you?"

"Does that surprise you?"

"Yes, because you're not like that outside of bed."

"I'm inhibited because my parents raised me that way. I'm not inhibited when it comes to sex because they had no control over that part of my life."

"Look Hon, we'd better get dressed. I think James is picking us up here."

"Aren't we going to shower?"

"We'll have to hurry."

"I'll hurry but I need a shower."

I showered first and was buttoning up my silky navy blouse when Conrad stepped out of the shower.

"Did you bring that dress?"

"Which dress?"

"The one I saw you in when I first met you."

"You really liked that dress, didn't you?"

"You looked gorgeous in it."

"Well, I thought about bringing it but I didn't."

He looked crestfallen.

"I'm sorry, Conrad. I wish you had told me. I thought it was going to be just you and me for the weekend and we would just poop around."

"I guess I should have told you. Oh, well. Did you bring so: nice to wear?"

"I thought I'd wear this casual suit. Where are we going, by the way?"

"We're going to the Polo Lounge first and I'm not sure where we'll go for dinner."

"What is the Polo Lounge?"

"It's a bar. You'll like it."

"Are my clothes ok?"

"They're fine."

Conrad picked up the phone and dialed a number.

"Yes? Is this 007?"

Silence.

"This is Boris. Rendezvous point will be at the Wilshire at 1830. You know the address. Defector? Yes, sitting tight."

Conrad laughed and then hung up the phone.

"What was that all about?"

"It was James. Sometimes we play spy."

* * *

The Polo Lounge, a famous bar inside the Beverly Hills Hotel, attracted celebrities, movie producers, directors, other famous people and some not-so-famous.

A waiter dressed in a white coat took our orders.

"What would you like, Madame?" he said, looking at Marcia.

Marcia was James's blonde, elegant tail. She followed him everywhere. She adored James, always smiled attentively into his face and hardly ever left his side if she could help it. A natural beauty with large, notice-everything-eyes, full lips and a smile that seemed to stay no matter how many times you wiped it away. She treated me with the politeness and warmth reserved for close friends. Divorced and the mother of a young son, she was currently taking lessons to convert to Judaism which pleased James who was of the Kosher persuasion himself.

"I'll have a Vodka martini."

"And you, Madame? he said, smiling at me.

"I think I'll have a Black Russian."

"Very good, Madame. And you, sir?"

Conrad looked like he was studying the drink menu.

"Make mine a Coke."

I stared at Conrad but didn't say anything.

"And you, sir?"

James, sitting there in a pale blue, thinly striped shirt and a pair of khakis, took his time ordering. He rubbed his cleanly shaven face with both hands from his ear to his chin.

"Give me Scotch, Glenfiddich if you have it. If you don't, Chivas is fine."

"Very good, Sir."

James looked at me and let go a healthy, athletic smile. I found myself mesmerized by the GQ look, a man who looked more like a former model than a former FBI agent. His shiny black hair cropped close to the neck offset serious eyes of ice blue hue with long, dark eyelashes. Any woman would kill to sit next to such a gem.

"Joan used to date Connor Eubanks. You remember Connor, don't you, James?"

"Yes, I do. How is he?"

"He's fine."

"James is a runner, Joan."

"Yes, I run six miles every day."

"Up hills or around a track?"

"Around a track, I'm afraid."

"Joan runs too, don't you, Joan?"

"I used to."

"You stopped running?"

"For awhile."

"Why did you stop?"

"Oh, I just did."

The waiter brought our drinks.

"So, what are we doing tonight? Anyone want to see a movie?"

"What's on?"

"*China Syndrome*, starring Jane Fonda."

"I love Jane Fonda."

"But, I heard the movie is depressing."

"So?"

"So, I feel like being cheered up."

"Yeah, I agree."

"Me, too."

"So, what else is on?"

"*All That Jazz, Apocalypse Now, Kramer vs. Kramer, The Rose* . . ."

"Are we going to dinner, too? We won't have time for a movie."

"He's right. Anybody got an idea for dinner?"

"How about Chinese?"

"No, we don't want Chinese. C'mon, Conrad, quit being so economical."

"I'm not being economical. I'm being reasonable. I love Chinese food."

"I know. Let's go to Balboa Island."

"Where's Balboa Island?"

"That's too far. Joan, it's near Newport Beach—about an hour's drive away. My stomach won't hear of it. It is growling already."

"How does Matteos sound?

"Sounds close. That's a possibility."

"Joan, do you like Italian food?"

"I love it."

"That settles it. Matteos it is."

We finished our drinks and then drove to Matteos on Westwood Blvd. Inside, high, red leather booths offered grandstand viewing of tuxedoed waiters while Sinatra music played in the background and the smell of Saltimbocca or Veal Parmesean permeated the air.

I excused myself to go to the Ladies' Room while James, Marcia and Conrad immediately sat down in one of the red booths. When I returned, the only available seat was next to James who sat opposite Marcia. Conrad sat across from me and for the moment was sidling up to someone the others seemed to know but I hadn't been introduced to. Conrad was kissing her. James caught my jealous glance.

"Joan, this is my sister, Marcia."

"But, I thought your friend . . . I thought her name was Marcia."

"It is. What a coincidence! Now, I suppose you're going to tell me your middle name is Marcia."

"It is."

They all laughed. Conrad hugged Marcia and James's sister left.

"What should we do tomorrow? Joan, you'll be here tomorrow, won't you?"

"My plane leaves in the afternoon."

"Why don't you stay another night?"

"My boss would kill me."

"Oh, come on. Just tell him you missed your flight."

"He doesn't even know I'm in L.A."

"Tell him we're taking good care of you."

James and Conrad laughed.

"An FBI agent—oh, he'd love that. I'll think about it."

"Why don't we go to the Beverly Hills Hotel tomorrow for brunch? Joan, have you ever been there before?"

"No, I haven't." *I thought of the dress I left at home.* I smiled at Marcia, feeling very uncomfortable. I was so preoccupied with my thoughts that I never even heard James say, "Oh, you must go. Brunch will be at 9:00. I'll pick you up at 8:30."

"No, I'll drive. It will be out of your way."

"Well, ok. If you say so."

James and Conrad began playing spy.

"Boris, defectors only talk if you torture them."

"Not so. You can get more information with honey than with vinegar."

"James, what is all this defector stuff? Who is a defector?"

"It's nothing really. We're just playing. Joan, Conrad tells me you used to work for the CIA."

"Yes."

"Did you know I used to work for the Bureau?"

"I think Conrad mentioned it. Why?"

"Well, I wouldn't mind doing a little extra curricular work for the Agency if they asked me."

"I can't help you. I don't have the power to hire you."

"I thought maybe you might know someone."

"All I can do is mention your name as someone willing to help."

"Well, if it would help . . ."

Is that what this is all about? I thought. *I wondered how much Conrad had told James. It had felt so right to confide in him. I thought what I had told Conrad was in confidence. Now it seemed as if he had told an ex-FBI agent everything. I began to see Conrad in a different light. And was this ex-Agent being up front with me or was he trying to catch me appearing more powerful than I really was?* I was confused.

"Stories are what we want. Do you know any good stories, Joan?"

"Stories? Let me think. Well, there was this grossly overweight girl who worked for the Agency. She had to be 6-700 lbs. easy. She lived in DC. One of my friends told me she saw her one day trying to get out of a seat in the bus. She was stuck and the bus driver tried his hardest to pry her loose. They had to call the Fire Department. Poor girl! It must have been embarrassing.

"Anyway, this girl worked on the British desk and we used to think she had a gland problem, she was so heavy. That is until we saw her go down to the Cafeteria about 10 o'clock for breakfast. She'd come back with four strips of bacon, two sausage patties, four eggs and three doughnuts. After that, she'd dig in her large purse and come up with several candy bars and a Twinkie for a snack. Then she'd wear these dark sunglasses. We could never figure out the sunglasses until we went by her desk one day and could hear her snoring. She'd sit straight up snoring and use the sunglasses to hide the fact that her eyes were closed. She never did much work between meals. Then around noon she'd be back down at the cafeteria loading up with two hamburgers, three hot dogs, a large bag of chips and a large soda.

"She told one of my friends about her fantasy of wearing sexy lingerie. Can you imagine? She was really a sad case. The manager at her apartment building banned her from the pool. The Agency tried to get rid of her but it wasn't easy. I guess it's hard to fire any civil servant but it must be really hard to fire someone just because they're fat. Honest to God, they have some real characters working there."

Everyone was laughing except James. He didn't seem amused. *Perhaps he wanted true tales of espionage,* I thought. I knew better than to give away company secrets.

They ate and kept filling my glass when it was barely empty. I stayed sociable but sober and didn't talk about my CIA experiences or Barry the rest of the evening. When Conrad and I got back to our hotel, I didn't want to be with him anymore. I felt he had broken a confidence. I now realized I couldn't trust him to keep a secret and I thought he was too old for me but I made the best of things and acted like I was still interested. The last thing I wanted was to be stranded in L.A. We kissed goodnight and slept, and I awoke wondering what in the world I would wear to the Beverly Hills Hotel.

Chapter 17

Conrad rose early to get a cup of coffee and read the newspaper out on the veranda. I immediately rolled over for a few more minutes of sleep. My watch had stopped but I assumed Conrad would come back and wake me up.

Conrad came back to the room at 8:30 a.m.

"Joan, aren't you up?"

"No, I've been waiting for you. What time is brunch?"

"You heard James yesterday. He said 9:00 a.m."

"I'd forgotten. What time is it now?"

"8:30 a.m."

"What???"

"You heard me. 8:30."

"But, Conrad, I still have to shower. There's no way I'll be ready."

"They have reservations for 9:00 a.m. We're not going to disappoint them."

"You go without me. Conrad, why didn't you tell me we would be going to this place? I never brought a dress. I don't have anything to wear. My hair looks terrible. I could just scream. Aren't you going to shower?"

"We don't have time. Come on, Joan, just throw something on. We're going to be late. I hate keeping James waiting."

"I can't possibly go. My hair still smells like alcohol and smoke from last night. I look terrible and I feel worse."

"It's only one brunch. You may never see these people again."

"You're right. After today, they'll never want to be seen in public with me again. Please, just a shower. I won't even put on makeup. But, please let me shower."

"We don't have time. You should have thought of a shower while you were lying in bed."

"My watch stopped. I didn't know what time it was. Conrad, I don't even have decent clothes to wear but I will feel like shit if you don't let me shower."

"The Beverly Hills Hotel caters to all kinds of people. You won't even be noticed. Come on, you only have 10 minutes."

I grabbed my Gloria Vanderbilt cord jeans and threw my plaid flannel shirt on. Brown was definitely not my color and today it made me look worse than usual. I took my European leather clutch purse and left with Conrad.

Conrad drove me over to the Pink Palace in his jeep. I felt a death by cancer would be kinder. There were all sorts of important people hovering outside underneath the long, *porte cochere* who were dressed in casual elegance and who, I assumed, had all showered.

The jeep pulled up and Conrad and I hopped out. *How utterly appropriate,* I thought. *A carriage fit for a raunchy, filthy Cinderella like me.*

We ate in The Loggia, a restaurant inside the hotel, which overlooked the Polo Patio. Marcia and James were already seated at a table. Marcia looked stunning in a two-piece St. John Knit suit, Gucci bag, hat and heels. Perfect hair, perfect teeth, perfect makeup, wearing expensive perfume. I wanted to die. I looked like a bag lady by comparison. I sat down at an angle across the table from Marcia by Conrad. *How long will we have to be here?* I thought. *I am going to kill Conrad when I get the chance.*

"Did you all sleep well?" James asked.

"Yes," I said, mumbling under my breath.

I yawned. I was hardly awake for this early brunch. To make matters worse, now I had to suffer through most of the conversation which I thought was dull, boring small talk. I perked up, however, when James started talking about the Agency. He wanted to be an Asset, someone who would wine and dine potential spies in order to recruit them. I told him I didn't have any power over hiring, but I said I still had friends at the Agency and I would pass it along that he was interested.

Two hours later I was worn out with all the small talk. When I couldn't stand it any longer I stood up and said, "Conrad, could you take me to the airport, please?"

"But I thought you were staying an extra day," Conrad said, smiling, indulging in wishful thinking.

I hadn't bargained for a rebuttal. I just wanted to go home. Immediately!

"No, I've gotta go. My boss is expecting me to go to work tomorrow and I have a lot of things I have to do before then. Could we go now?"

"Why don't you call your boss from here and ask him if it would be alright if you stayed another day?"

"No, really, I have to go."

"Oh, c'mon Joan. Be a good sport."

"Don't make a scene, Conrad. I said I have to go. Now, let's go," I said vehemently.

"Ok. Ok. You win. I'll ask the doorman to bring the jeep around."

I said goodbye to James and Marcia. I decided the probability of ever seeing them again was nil.

Conrad and I walked out to the *porte cochere* where soon Conrad's jeep arrived. I hopped in. At last, I would be leaving the sight of my humiliation. I didn't care how I was getting to the airport, only that the means of escape wasn't fast enough.

There was one thing though that was bothering me. Conrad had told me he'd pay for my trip and so far he hadn't been forthcoming with the money. *Should I ask him for it? Will he give it to me now that I turned him down for another day here? What should I say? How should I say it? Maybe I should just forget the whole thing. No, I can't do that. I have less than $10 in my checking account and I need the money for lunch next week, not to mention my parking at the airport.*

I waited until we got out at the airport to ask Conrad.

"Conrad, you said you'd pay my way down here," I said, sheepishly. I looked at him straight in the eye.

"I'm sorry," he said, wincing. "I forgot. Here." He reached in his pocket, took out a wad of bills and handed me a couple hundred dollars.

"Thank you," I said, as I kissed him lightly on the cheek. "I've had a great time," I lied.

Conrad looked a little disgruntled but managed a smile. Conrad had redeemed himself in my eyes. It wasn't really his fault I didn't get up early enough to shower. Anyway, his friends were nice and he did keep his side of the bargain.

"Are you doing anything for Thanksgiving?" I asked, innocently.

"No."

"Why don't you come to San Francisco," I said, politely. "I hate spending holidays alone."

"Me, too. That sounds like a wonderful idea. Why don't you call me? By the way, would you mind making reservations for me? I'm just not good at stuff like that. I need a personal secretary."

"I'd be happy to but only because you're so cute."

"Flattery will get you everywhere. Did you want diamonds, gold or my jeep?"

"The jeep, you silly goose." I kissed him tenderly on the lips. "I'd better be going. My flight will be here any minute. Conrad, thanks again for everything. I hope I didn't embarrass you too much in front of your friends." Conrad took my suitcase out of the jeep.

"Not at all. I told you they would understand. You'd better go now. I'm really looking forward to seeing you in San Francisco at Thanksgiving. Don't forget to call me."

"I won't, Sweetheart. Take care. I love you." The "I love you" sounded as though I didn't really mean it. I said it as though I was just being polite. Conrad answered back with equal politeness.

"I love you, too. Bye." He waived his hand goodbye.

Chapter 18

Back at work I never uttered a word to Joe Walsh about the weekend. I didn't feel my personal life was anyone's business.

When I thought about switching jobs though, I wasn't completely convinced that this was the best thing to do. The CIA was family to me. I still had the habit of calling Joe Walsh "uncle." Barry and Joe were retired Case Officers from the CIA and thus I didn't have to explain myself to them or anyone else at work. Some people thought I was a celebrity for having worked at the CIA but many more in the liberal Bay Area thought it was a negative. I didn't like fielding questions about my work with the Agency. Besides, it seemed my patriotic duty to stay and find out more about Barry's illegal wrongdoings in order to nail him. *Yes, I think I should just stay put.*

But, then again, I didn't like Barry's and Alice's arrogant air. They acted as if they were King and Queen and they looked down on everyone else who they considered peasants. Lunch always had to be served to them on special china with meals from the finest restaurants in the Bay area while the other employees ate from brown bags. They always flew first class and stayed at expensive hotels yet they couldn't always meet their payroll. I hated getting my paycheck late but there wasn't much I could do about it if I continued working there. Or was there?

"I'm going to take one of these $400 chairs home and sell it. I need to pay rent." I laughed, mischievously.

One of the Sanborn boys, the company Accountant, was in my office and had a quick comeback. "Don't sweat it, you have a five-day grace period to pay rent."

"I don't care. I like to pay all my bills on the first of the month. I like to pay on time."

"Chill out, Joan."

"What about food? I don't have enough money to buy groceries."

"I can lend you five dollars till we get paid."

"That's not the point. We shouldn't have to do that. When are Barry and Alice coming back?"

He shrugged his shoulders. "I don't know."

"Where did they go?"

"Somewhere East."

"I hate this. This is the third time we haven't been paid on time. We don't know where they are or when they'll be back. This sucks."

"Buck it up, Joan. We all have to make sacrifices."

"For what? What on earth am I making sacrifices for?"

"For the cause."

"What cause? What exactly is the cause? What are we fighting for? Is it to get the Republicans elected? Or is it for Barry and Alice to increase the net worth of this company while we suffer with continued low wages and unprofessional treatment? Or maybe it is to make the world a safer place for right-wing people? Which is it?"

Silence. He glared at me and then walked out.

* * *

Two days later Barry and Alice came home and I ran into her as she was coming out of her bedroom at work. She had a bedroom built in the executive suite in the new office.

She looked tired. There were bags under her puffy eyes and her normally perfect hairdo looked like she had slept on it. And she had on a pair of wrinkled gray sweats.

"Hi Alice. Getting over jet lag?"

"Hi Joan. Yes, these trips really take their toll."

"How was it?"

"Fine."

"Did you get any money?" I couldn't help being blunt.

"Not this trip. Maybe the next."

I wondered if the two companies were going under. If they were, I didn't want to be the last to know. I wanted to get out now. Talking to Alice was always a bit unnerving. If I wanted to know anything, I had to ask questions. Her answers, however, told me nothing. They were purposely vague. Still, I thought, if I could get her talking, maybe she'd tell me something she shouldn't. I tried a different tack.

"Didn't you tell me once that Barry's view of the future . . ."

"I don't think I said it was Barry's."

"Whose was it then? Didn't you say that America would experience great periods of creativity and the world would be different than we now know it?"

"Did I?"

"I think you did. You also said that a lot of people in the United States would have to change jobs in order for the global economy to work efficiently. When will this come about?"

I wondered where Barry and Alice got this global view of the world. I thought it had something to do with the roundtable she talked about but I knew better than to ask her such a direct question. I also wondered who was included in the roundtable. From what she had said previously she and Barry were in bed with multinational corporation heads, government heads and military commanders. But I wanted to know, were they only Republicans or were Democrats included? And who else was included? And, why and how did these people decide the fate of middle class America?

"Joan, you know, only a few people care about what's coming. The rest prefer to remain ignorant. It's just like the U.S. elections. Not very many people care about campaign promises. Most people vote on little things like whether they like the way a candidate looks or talks or whether they like the way the candidate's wife looks or dresses. Like I said, they prefer to remain dumb about the rest."

I was appalled but didn't say anything. I followed the candidates in the primaries, watched all the convention speeches and stayed tuned in for the debates. I didn't think "most" people voted for stupid things. Some did, sure, but they weren't the majority.

Why had I regarded Barry and Alice so highly when it was all such a sham? I'm not sure I'm on the right side anymore. There is no security in working for Barry. If something bad happened, I or one of his other employees could be expendable. I wonder what would happen if the liberals found out how National Investigations and Snoops, Inc. collected information on them for their information bank. When the shit hit the fan, it would be us, the employees, who were the fall guys and went to jail for their crimes. Management would remain untouched. Or, am I just being paranoid? I didn't know.

I didn't have many contacts on the "outside." I had a friend who worked for Levi Strauss but the clothing industry was so different from espionage and writing country studies. I didn't know if I could be as passionate about that kind of work or even if I would get hired but it was time to do something.

Chapter 19

Sunday, November 18, 1979

"Room 20, please."

"Hello."

"Hi Conrad, how are you?"

"Fine. Joan?"

"Yes. I wanted to talk to you about Thanksgiving. You're still coming, aren't you? I'm so glad you're coming. I told you, I hate spending holidays alone. Shall I fix us something to eat or do you want to eat out?"

"Eat out. I'm sure Masons at the Fairmont has a nice Thanksgiving feast. Have you made airline reservations?"

"Not yet, but I think I found you a flight. I didn't know when you wanted to leave but I thought Wednesday, the 21st would be a good day. Western Airlines has a flight leaving L.A. at 12:25 noon on that day."

"What time does it arrive in San Francisco?"

"1:32 p.m."

"What about the flight back to L.A.?"

"Well, you did say you wanted to leave Saturday, didn't you?

"Yes."

"There is a flight that leaves San Francisco on Saturday, the 24th at 2:40 p.m. and arrives in L.A. at 3:44 p.m. I figured you'd want to leave early afternoon, is that ok?"

"Listen, Joan, those times and flights look good. Tell them I'll pick up the tickets and pay for them at the counter. Now, I've got to run. I love you."

I answered back politely, "I love you, too, Conrad."

"Bye.

Monday, November 19, 1979

John Sinclair, a Manager in Distribution at Levi Strauss called to ask if I had plans for Thanksgiving. I had met him through my friend, Becky. He knew my parents lived in the Northwest and he was from Tennessee so he thought I might like to spend the holiday with him if I didn't have other plans. I turned him down. I had made arrangements with Conrad over a month ago and I was determined to do the honorable thing no matter how I felt about him. I told John I'd be in touch.

Wednesday, November 21, 1979

Conrad never called me again before his flight. He was due in at 1:32 p.m. Should I drive to the airport and pick him up or wait and let him call me from the airport? I wasn't sure. I tried his hotel.

"Ma'am, he checked out of the hotel last week."

"Last week? Did he leave a forwarding address?"

"Ma'am, we're not allowed to give out that information."

"Please. It's very important." I was desperate. I had no other way of contacting Conrad other than the hotel. "I'm his natural born sister, I lied, and we've never met. I've been trying to locate him for ten years. I've come so far to try and find him. Please tell me where he's gone."

"Very well. He said he was going to Hotel Del Sloeres."

"Do you have a number for that hotel?"

"Yes, just a minute. Here it is. She gave me the number."

I didn't waste any time in trying to contact him. It was now eleven and his flight would leave at 12:25. I still had enough time to catch him before he left. I dialed the number.

"Hotel Del Sloeres. Good morning. May I help you?"

"I'd like to speak to Conrad Simms, please."

"Do you know which room he is in?"

"No. I'm sorry."

"No problem. Here he is. One moment."

She waited.

"I'm sorry, Ma'am. There is no answer."

"Thank you."

I called again in 15 minutes but still no answer. Then I called the airlines.

"Western Airlines. May I help you?"

"Could you please check to see if a passenger picked up his tickets?"

"We don't normally . . ."

"Please. This is urgent." *Well it worked before,* I thought. "My husband is a doctor and he needs to be in San Francisco for an important seminar he's giving. His flight leaves Los Angeles at 12:25. He's so forgetful, I'm afraid he might have forgotten that he had to pick up the tickets. Could you check for me, please."

"One moment. I don't see them. Oh, here they are. No, they have not been picked up yet."

"That man. What am I going to do with him? Thank you for your kindness. You've been very helpful."

I realized I had probably been stood up and *how could he do this to me?* My head ached. My thoughts raced. I was outraged. When Conrad finally got around to calling at 11:30 that night, I was steaming.

"Hi Joan. Look, I'm sorry but I won't be able to make Thanksgiving dinner. I, uh . . ."

"I know, Conrad. I checked with the airlines. You never picked up your tickets." I held my rage in check.

"I meant to. Did you cancel them?"

"No." I spoke in a deliberate tone. "Conrad, you did this on purpose. No one calls me at 11:30 p.m. the night before Thanksgiving to cancel without it being premeditated." My voice rose. "I think you planned this. You did it because you wanted me to stay an extra day and I refused. You knew holidays were important to me. You knew I hated to be alone then. Conrad, you're disgusting."

"Joan, you're wrong. I'll make it up to you."

"Do you really think I'll give you a shot at Christmas?"

"This wasn't such a big deal."

"To you maybe."

"I know you're hurt Joan, but please give me another chance."

"No, Conrad. You hurt me intentionally. I don't trust you. You are yesterday's bad dream. Don't ever call me again. I never want to see you again."

"Joan, you're being harsh."

"Am I? I don't think so. You were the one who was cruel. Do you really think I'll sit home on Thanksgiving with nothing to do?"

"Well . . ."

"Not hardly, Conrad. I already have a date. I don't need you and I don't want you to ever call me again."

"But, Joan . . ."

"Goodbye, Conrad."

"Goodbye."

Thursday, November 22, 1979

The next morning, Thanksgiving Day, I thought about what happened and decided not to sit around and mope. I swallowed my pride, picked up the phone and dialed.

"Hello John?"

"Yes."

"This is Joan."

"Joan, what a nice surprise. I didn't expect to hear from you so soon."

"I hope I haven't called too early."

"No, no. It's fine."

"Well, things have changed. You know that guy from L.A. I told you about?"

"Yes."

"Well, he turned out to be a flake, too, or maybe just a jerk."

"What happened?"

"It's a long story. I'll tell you later."

"Maybe you ought to send him a dead fish in the mail."

"That's a good one," I said. "I never thought of that. Anyway, right now I am wondering whether your offer for Thanksgiving dinner still holds?"

"The invitation is still open."

"Well, I have reservations for two at the Fairmont at noon. Would you like to join me?"

"I'd love to. Will you be picking me up or shall I bring my chariot around to your castle?"

"Where do you live?"

"In Marin."

"It would be easier if you picked me up. My apartment is simple to find. I'm on Union Street between Van Ness and Polk."

"Ok, I'll pick you up about 11:30 a.m. We should allow some time to find parking at the Fairmont."

"See you then."

"Bye, Joan. I'm glad you called."

"So am I. Bye."

Friday, November 23, 1979

I was angry and upset with Conrad. I needed to talk to someone. The only one I could think of to talk to was Connor. But he was married now. I couldn't call him, or could I? This wasn't social after all. I just needed some answers. I dialed his office number in Hayward.

"Connor? Hi this is Joan. This isn't a social call."

"I gathered that. Where are you?"

"At the office. Could you meet me for lunch today?"

"Where?"

"Denny's in Emeryville."

"I can be there at 11:30."

"Ok, I'll see you then."

At exactly 11:30 a.m., dressed in my blue gabardine suit from London and a blue-and-white striped shirt with red tie, I sat in booth #11 at Denny's across the table from Connor. I was so uptight I told the waitress it would be a good while before we ordered. The waitress brought us the menus and ice water and then left.

"Connor, thanks for meeting with me on such short notice."

"No problem. What's up? Did you have a nice Thanksgiving?"

"That's what I wanted to talk to you about. Remember your friend, Conrad?"

Connor looked puzzled. "I don't have a friend, Conrad."

"Well, he works with you."

"We don't have anybody named Conrad."

"Well, he's an agent. He's with the Bureau . . ."

"We don't have anyone by the name of Conrad in the San Francisco Field Office. Where did you meet this person?"

"I met him at Liverpool Lil's. He's a friend of Willie's, your friend who is an undercover FBI agent in Sacramento."

"Oh, I know who you're talking about. He's kind of balding?"

"Yes. He stood me up at Thanksgiving."

"If it's the person I'm thinking of his name isn't Conrad and he isn't an FBI agent."

"What??" I felt sick. I had a flashback of all I told Conrad about Barry and the Company. All that information running loose in San Francisco and Los Angeles was enough to make anyone feel sick.

"Yes he is. He said he was. Are you sure?"

"Positive. He used to own a bar in San Francisco but he drank himself into bankruptcy."

"That explains it."

"What?"

"I saw a book from Alcoholics Anonymous on his dresser in L.A. and he always ordered straight cokes."

"What were you doing in L.A.?"

"Conrad asked me down there to pal around with his friend James. Is James really an FBI agent?"

"What are you doing with such an old guy?"

"That's my business. He's not so old."

"He's too old. Joanie . . ."

"Connor, I didn't ask you to lunch to be chastised for dating someone you think is too old for me."

"Ok, ok."

"You didn't answer my question. Is James really an FBI agent?"

"Yeah, he worked for the Bureau but he quit a year or two ago. He's real wealthy. Doesn't need to work. Where did you go while you were down there? Where did you eat?"

"An Italian restaurant called Matteos, the Polo Lounge and the Beverly Hills Hotel."

Connor looked impressed. "Did James ever marry?"

"He's dating someone named Marcia. She's gorgeous."

"Is she Jewish?"

"She's taking lessons to convert. Connor, what's wrong with me? Is it something I do that makes men treat me this way? I can change. Just tell me what it is."

"Joanie, don't look so sad. It's not you."

"Are you sure?"

"Positive. So, did you end up spending Thanksgiving alone?"

"No, I asked a friend at the last minute. We had dinner at Masons in the Fairmont."

"Well, if I were you, I would just drop contact with the guy you call Conrad."

"Ok, your Highness." The waitress came back to get our orders.

"Now, should we eat?" I said. "I'm buying lunch."

"No, you're not."

"Yes, I am, Connor."

"You are not, Joanie."

"I am, too."

"We'll see."

Chapter 20

I was through with men for a while. Conrad, who wasn't really Conrad, was the last man I would let in my life. I enrolled at City College in San Francisco. One day I was sitting in my economics class flipping through Milton Friedman's paperback "Free to Choose," waiting for Professor Luigi to begin. I had chosen City College because tuition was free to California residents and it had a reputation for being a pretty decent two-year school. Filled with 90 percent Asian-American students, the school was known as a commuter's school where the majority of students juggled part time jobs with academia, a drawback since hardly anyone had a chance to get to know each other. There were a lot of older students though, so I halfway felt I fit in.

As I waited for class to begin, I suddenly realized I had forgotten my Blue Book, a notebook to write homework assignments and tests in. I left the classroom to get it. As I was running up the sidewalk, I noticed a woman I had seen last semester in one of my other classes. Coal black hair, the tall manly looking woman wore tinted glasses which hid her large brown eyes. Although I had not so much as said hello to her previously, I nevertheless felt comfortable asking her to save a seat for me in class. The woman said nothing but nodded and continued on her way.

I retrieved the Blue Book from the backseat floor of my car. I grabbed it and rushed back to the classroom and found a vacant seat next to the woman near one end in the front row. I sat down, thanked my anonymous friend and waited two minutes until Professor Luigi started class.

"How are you today on this fine September morning? . . . this beautiful September morning?"

Bushy haired Professor Luigi with his large, bugged-out eyes, Jimmy Durante nose, colossal mustache and powerful voice began taking roll call. I had him for Econ 101, the study of Macroeconomics, last semester, and Econ 5, the current class I was taking from him in

Elementary Statistics. Typically he'd call roll every day at 8:00 a.m. in the square, concrete block, boxy Arts Building Extension on the corner of Cloud Circle and Phelan Avenue.

"Mr. Barclay. Are you here Mr. Barclay? Yes, there you are. I see you. Miss Chin. Where is Miss Chin?" He ran down the full alphabet until finally he'd say, "Mr. Ziebarth. How are you today, Mr. Ziebarth? Very well."

Class began. He taught Macro out of Milton Spencer's Third Edition of *Contemporary Economics*. Particularly fond of Thorstein Veblen's famous idea of conspicuous consumption, he argued that people may sometimes buy a higher priced good, e.g., Mercedes, than a lower priced good, e.g., Pinto, in order to impress others.

"Both are cars, you see. We believe, however, there is more value in the car with the higher price."

He always had a story to go along with a theory. One time he had a product to go along with the story. He sold students books about *Prevention*-type health and nutrition from the trunk of his car. One might have gotten the impression that grades were raised by buying one of his books but he never publicly admitted it.

Today in Econ 5, he spoke about population statistics and the 92nd percentile. Definitely a snooze. I sat upright towards the end of the class when I saw him coming toward me. He bent down, looked me straight in the eye, his nose an inch from mine, and put his hands on my desk.

"And I've been back to Washington, DC and I know that this is inscribed on the outside of the building of the CIA . . ."

I never told anyone at City College of my affiliation with the CIA. *Why was this ugly man, with his large nose only an inch from mine, ranting about an inscription on the outside of the CIA building? Does he know something about me or is he just guessing? What's going on here or is anything going on? Why was I being singled out . . . or was I?*

". . . and on that building the inscription reads, 'The Truth Shall Set You Free!' Isn't that right, Miss Joan?" he said, sarcastically.

All I could think in this particular instance was, "*You ugly son-of-a-bitch, how in the world would you know what it says on the side of the CIA building? You incompetent bastard, you couldn't even get an interview with the CIA.*" But, with my jaw set and looking him directly in the eyes, all I did was stare back at him. Thinking to myself, *the insignia on the building wasn't "The Truth Shall Set You Free." That was the inscription over the side of Science Hall, which faces Phelan Avenue at City College. The insignia he was referring to was part of a biblical inscription inside the front lobby of the CIA Headquarters Building over by the Memorial Stars. It read, "And you shall know the truth and the truth shall set you free. John VIII-XXXII."*

I knew he just told a lie but he was a Professor and I knew the class would believe him rather than me. Besides, an answer might have revealed the fact that I had worked for the Agency. No one at school knew of my CIA affiliation. I had resigned three years ago. So why did he single me out? I had been told liberal colleges hate the CIA. Is that why he was doing this?

I walked outside after class and there waiting a few feet ahead of me was the woman.

"How do you like your old Professor now?" she sneered.

"He's ok," I said, never letting on how much this upset me. *Was this girl siding with the Professor? Did she expect me to crawl to her for protection? I'm not afraid of her or Professor Luigi but it looks like I'll have to sit next to her every day from now on.* Seating arrangements were set after the first day so I continued to sit in the front row next to the woman.

* * *

The following day Professor Luigi quieted the class down and began discussing economics. I was a little apprehensive about being there after what happened yesterday but I tried to chalk it up to coincidence. *After all, hadn't Professor Luigi given me an A in Macroeconomics? We were almost pals. He'd never do anything to harm me, I decided.*

Professor Luigi started the class off by passing out corrected homework. He had given us four rather lengthy statistical problems to work and write out in our Blue Books. He went over each one in class. I noticed a discrepancy and saw a way to put some embarrassment in Professor Luigi's corner.

"Professor Luigi?"

"Yes."

"What is the answer to Number 2?"

"The average woman had one child, according to the mean. And then you get two points if you could write the equation correctly."

"I confused this with the median. Did everyone get this marked wrong who wrote the median instead of the mean?"

"Yes, everyone did," he said, mocking me.

"She didn't," I said, pointing to my unknown woman friend beside me. The class laughed.

"She has the same answer I do and I got it marked wrong and she has it correct."

"Let me see this. Let's see here." He took both Blue Books and studied the answers.

"How many other students thought it was the median?"

Half the hands went up.

"You're all wrong," he said kidding, waiving his arms to the entire class. "You've got to pay attention to what I ask for." Then looking directly at me, he said, "I have someone grade my papers for me. My teaching assistant occasionally makes a mistake." He quickly scribbled a grade change in my Blue Book and handed it back to me. "There, are you satisfied now?"

He finished class up by speaking about public opinion polls, how they influenced people's opinions or buying habits.

"If a person perceives a thing to be more expensive, then the price of that item will skyrocket. Which do you think is more expensive? A Mercedes or a Cadillac?"

"Mercedes."

"You're wrong. It depends on the model. That's what opinion polls will do for you. Speaking of public opinion polls, there was this famous study done. The Kinsey study. You've all heard of it. Yes, I know you've heard of it."

He looked straight at me. I tried to avert my eyes but he wouldn't let go of the eye contact. He was glued to me.

"Now, Miss Joan, what if I asked you how many times a day you orgasm, what would you say?"

The class laughed. So did I, quietly and nervously, but I didn't say anything. *I'm going to kill him.*

"No, really," he continued, "what if I asked you how many times a day you orgasm?"

I sat there, blankly staring at him. I was afraid to answer. I was afraid not to answer. Either way I would lose. The hate I felt for him at that particular moment consumed me. It stressed me to the point I thought of fleeing.

"I'm serious." Professor Luigi wouldn't let me go. He seemed determined to embarrass me. "How many times a day do you orgasm?"

Furious inside, I tried not to let it show. I returned his question with an icy stare. He moved on to one of his pet students.

"Mary, how many times a day do *you* orgasm?"

"100."

"So, here we have a 100," he said, "and here we have a 0."

The class roared with laughter. I died inside. How could I face anyone after this class? They would all call me a Zero. Professor Luigi got what he was after—humiliation. But, *I still couldn't figure out why Professor Luigi had picked on me. I had liked him before taking this class but now we were worst enemies. How had I displeased him? I got an A in Macroeconomics from him. What made him turn against me? I remembered him saying in class that two federal I.R.S. agents had visited him the day before, allegedly because he didn't pay his taxes. Did this have something to do with me? Was he taking it out on me because he found out I had worked for the CIA? Or, was it just another of the FBI's dirty tricks?*

* * *

The high level of stress caused my brain to do weird things like be overly suspicious or distrustful. This tendency is not normal but rather it is part of the illness I suffered from. I hadn't yet realized that I didn't know the difference between normal paranoia and schizophrenic paranoia.

* * *

My feelings were hurt and I felt deeply wounded and I kept replaying in my mind the incidents with Professor Luigi. I rehearsed over and over in my mind his comments and what I should have said to him. When he asked me how many times a day I orgasmed, I should have said, "Do you mean the median or the mean?"

When I've been hurt, I call people for advice. Instinctively, I knew my decision-making process was impaired so I relied on others to help. I never thought to call my parents because I thought they wouldn't understand. The first person I called was Uncle Joe Walsh. He had become a father figure to me and I respected his judgment and friendship. I was so paranoid, I called him from a phone booth so that the call couldn't be traced. Who was it that I thought would trace it? I didn't know. Stress was doing strange things to my mind.

Uncle Joe told me to get a lawyer and sue him for harassment if he didn't stop. I didn't know any lawyers. Besides, I didn't want to spread it all over town that I had worked for the Central Intelligence Agency.

With my last quarter I called ol' heartbreaker Connor. I knew he would help me if I ever got into a bind.

"Connor, this is Joan. How are you?"

"I know this isn't a courtesy call. What's up?"

"Connor, I need your help." I didn't know where else to turn. "I'm sorry, I don't mean to bother you."

"It's ok, Joanie. Are you all right? Where are you?"

"I'm in a phone booth."

"What's the matter?"

"I'm ok. I'm just upset. One of the professors at school has been giving me a hard time. It seems he has found out I used to work for the Agency and he's embarrassed me a couple of times in front of class."

"Like what."

"Well, today he started talking about the Kinsey Study. I don't really even know what that is but I know it has something to do with sex. Anyway, he asks me point blank how many times a day I orgasm."

"What?? Oh, Joanie, you could sue him for sexual harassment."

"I don't know any lawyers and I don't want to go spreading the word around town that I used to work for the Central Intelligence Agency. Just when I thought things had quieted down. I just want to go to school and get a degree. What should I do?"

"Go to your advisor. Go to the President or the Governing Board. You shouldn't have to take that."

"Thanks Connor. I'll try that. Thanks for the advice. I knew I could count on you. Bye."

"Bye."

Chapter 21

At the Cliff House in October, with its breathtaking view of the ocean and beach, waves lapping against the shore amid crystal blue water and nearby distant seals, Janie persuaded me to have a drink. Janie Mower and her husband Doug were visiting from Clarkston, Washington, in town for a CAT Scan/MRI Conference. Janie told me the drink was on Roy, my brother-in-law and her boss. I hadn't eaten all day and the drink made me woozy, not exactly drunk, but I wondered how I was going to drive. And my paranoia about Barry and his misdeeds was increasing.

I stood up to leave but Janie excused herself, saying she needed to make a phone call. "I'll wait for you here," I told her. *I wondered who Janie could be calling. After all, she didn't live in San Francisco and supposedly didn't know anyone here. What's going on? Am I paranoid? These people couldn't possibly be linked to Barry or the KGB.*

I am so paranoid; I think everything is related to Barry or the KGB. I don't feel safe anywhere or with anyone. It's as if there is danger everywhere I look.

Stop it! These people live in a small town. She's a lumber broker, for God's sake. It's just inconceivable that she could be connected to Barry for any reason. Yet, why do I smell something suspicious going on here? Why was she pushing me to have that drink?

Janie and Doug were back at the table with me still deep in thought.

"Are you ready?"

"Yes."

"Joan, will you be going straight home after you take us back to the hotel?"

I thought the question was odd since it was really none of her business. *Why would a lumber broker be interested in my schedule?*

"I'm going to visit a friend out in the Avenues. She lives on 14th. I promised her I'd stop by. Why?"

"No reason. I was just curious. Could you wait one more minute? I just remembered I need to make another phone call. Doug, do you have a quarter?" *Now, who was she calling?*

"Sure."

Five minutes passed and Janie was finally ready. I took them back to the Hilton Hotel. From the Cliff House, I drove down Geary which split into O'Farrell going one way east and Geary going one way west. The Hilton was located near Union Square on O'Farrell between Mason and Taylor. I dropped them off and said goodbye.

From the Hilton I took Geary to the Avenues to visit my friend. I couldn't turn left on Presidio Blvd. also known as Highway 1 so I crossed over it, turning left on 15th and then headed south on Anza. I stopped for a few seconds at the stop sign on Anza and quickly looked to the left to see if any cars were coming.

I was really feeling the effects of the alcohol now. My reaction time had slowed. I proceeded slowly across the intersection.

Suddenly out of nowhere a white car which looked to me like a Subaru came barreling at me from my left and a dark colored older car, maybe a Chevy, came from the right. I heard a loud crash and the sound of metal scraping against metal. The three cars collided and I felt my body lunge forward and then backwards against the headrest. Luckily I had my seatbelt on. I was stunned and suddenly very alert as if I had returned to consciousness from a daydream.

A Chinese-American woman with dark hair and glasses jumped out of the Chevy and started jumping up and down and screaming at the top of her voice.

"She didn't stop. She didn't stop. I saw her. She didn't stop. It's all her fault."

I wasn't sure whether I had stopped at the stop sign but I thought I had. Then they asked me what insurance I had. I was in trouble. I didn't have any. The Chinese-American screamed again.

"She doesn't have insurance! She doesn't have insurance! She did it and she doesn't have insurance!"

I wasn't going to lie to them. The bill for my insurance had been mislaid so I forgot to pay it and then they cancelled my policy.

"I promise I'll cover this if it turns out to be my fault." A young policeman came on the scene. I went back to my car, sat down and closed the door. I hoped no one would find out I had been drinking. I sat in my car alone for quite awhile, eating a breath mint, hoping the policeman wouldn't smell alcohol on my breath.

The driver of the white Subaru walked over and asked if I was all right. "Yes, I am," I said. *Now please go away,* I thought. He must've read my mind because he left shortly thereafter. *Damn Janie and Doug! Did they set me up? Why all the questions about whether I was going straight home? But why would a lumber broker who worked for my brother-in-law, Roy, set me up? It doesn't make any sense.*

The young police officer who came on the scene talked to the other drivers first. I felt I was dead for sure. I could see the Chinese-American vehemently explaining her side of the story to the cop. How in the world would I ever get out of this one?

Suddenly an older police officer arrived and he talked to the drivers, surveyed the scene and then came and talked to me. I rolled my window down and asked, "Did I do it?"

"No."

"How do you know?"

"The tread marks on the road. He was going too fast."

"Then he must've intended to hit me."

"Looks that way. Are you all right?"

"Yeah, I'm fine."

"Well, I am going to have to cite you for not having insurance. May I see your driver's license please?"

"Here you are." I breathed a sigh of relief as I handed him my license.

"Do you still live at this address?"

"Yes."

He finished writing the ticket and handed it to me.

"Be sure you take care of this right away."

"I will, Sir. Thank you, Sir."

"Is your vehicle drivable?"

"I think so. It just scraped the tire a little."

"Let me see if I can pull that fender out from the tire."

"It's ok. I don't live too far from here. I'll have someone pull it out in the morning."

"Ok. Do you need anything else, Ma'am?"

"No, Sir. That's it. Thank you."

"Be careful."

"I will, Sir. Thank you, Sir. Bye."

Chapter 22

"Hi Dad, I had an accident."

"Is that you, Joanie?"

"Yeah, it's me, Dad."

"So, what happened? You had an accident? When? Were you hurt?"

"Yesterday. No, I'm all right. I'm just shook up. The police said it looked like the other car meant to hit me."

"Joanie, you'd better come home. Your baby sister, Maureen, had an accident yesterday, too."

"What? Where? What happened? Was she hurt?"

"Out past John Willenborg's place in Cottonwood. She's in the hospital. She had a small cut on her face, bad bruises on her head and she is suffering from a concussion."

My mind raced with paranoid thoughts. Who hit her? I took this news as someone was out to get not just me but my family, too, and I didn't know who. *Was it Barry and Alice because I had spilled too much about Snoops, Inc. and National Investigations? Was it Conrad because I had gone back to Connor and found out the truth? Was it the FBI trying to intimidate me into telling all I knew about Barry and his cohorts? Was it Professor Luigi?* My fear and paranoia were nearly out of control but I had no one to talk to about it. I kept it all inside.

"You'd better come home, Joanie."

"I can't come, Dad. What would I do with all my stuff?"

"Roy can come down and help you pack. He has his own business so he can take off whenever he wants."

Roy Wessels was my brother-in-law, married to my oldest sister, Theresa. "Ok, Dad, I think you're right. I think I'd better get the hell out of here while I still can."

"I'll call Roy and let him know."

"Thanks, Dad. Bye."

"Bye."

* * *

On Tuesday, October 14, Roy, gave commands in a voice from his days in the National Guard. In Oakland, he rented a 20 ft. Ryder moving truck. Roy and I drove down to Los Gatos that evening to pick up some furniture I had lent my friend, Becky, and her husband, Mike.

Before they loaded the furniture, Roy insisted that they put my small yellow Volkswagen in the front of the truck bed nearest the cab. He asked Mike if he had any two-by-fours they could use to make a ramp so that they could drive the car up into the truck. I didn't like his idea.

"Why do we need to put my car into the truck? I can drive it."

"I don't want you driving it."

"Why not?"

"You've been through too much and besides, for all we know, some wacko might still be out after you."

"I'm fine and if they haven't got me yet, it's too late now. Besides, won't it cost more to transport it that way than if I just drive it up myself?"

"It shouldn't cost any more."

"But, you won't be able to fit it into the truck."

"It will fit."

"How can you possibly drive the car up there on those two-by-fours? Won't they snap in two?"

"Watch me."

"Roy, I can drive the car. This is silly."

"You're not driving it. Period."

"I am, too."

"You are not."

"Yes, I am."

"Joanie, I said no."

"I'm not listening, Roy."

"You will do what I say."

"Make me."

Little did I know, it was illegal to put an automobile inside the Ryder truck because of internal combustion. Besides, no insurance company would cover it. Something might ignite the gas tank and the explosion would ruin the truck, not to mention all my belongings inside. Roy didn't care. He was adamant about me riding in the cab beside him. I was too tired to put up much of a fight.

I watched them load the car. Roy started driving the little Volkswagen Bug up the two-by-fours and made it about halfway when all of a sudden the car wouldn't move any farther. It looked like the car was going to break the boards.

Roy got out of the car, surveyed the situation and told Mike who was trying to keep the boards straight to keep holding. Roy gunned the motor, then suddenly as if it had changed its mind, the car lunged forward and they were able to load it into the truck. After that, they loaded the furniture I had stored at Becky and Mike's house—a sofa bed and chair, coffee table, carpet and end tables.

When it was all in the truck we headed to San Francisco. The next morning we loaded the rest of my furniture and tried to get an early start on the long trip awaiting us. Roy parked the truck near the house on 14th Avenue. It took up several spaces.

I was both emotionally drained and physically exhausted from moving. Roy was pretty tired, too. We got up early, packed the rest of my furniture and belongings and headed out over the Oakland Bay Bridge.

* * *

As we drove on Wednesday, October 15, I began to feel an inner sense of peace. I was going home. No more fruits, nuts or flakes. Hopefully no more weird bosses or unfaithful lovers or mean Professors. Just Northwest conservatives, Mom, Dad and the family. It felt good to be leaving California. California had not been good to me. I finally felt safe. Roy would take me home. I felt a sense of relief that he was by my side. We were driving across the Oakland Bay Bridge without saying a word to each other when suddenly Roy broke the silence.

"Were those people you worked for in the East Bay connected to the Trilateral Commission?" he asked, turning his head slightly and looking me straight in the eye.

"What?" I was startled. "What is the Trilateral Commission?" A question like that was odd enough but coming from a small town hick like my brother-in-law, it was enough to send me through the ceiling. I remembered Barry's contact with his former German spy. I wasn't about to tell Roy, though. He knew nothing about intelligence matters.

"It's a powerful group of men and women who are trying to control the world. I don't really know that much about it but they describe it in this book I'm reading."

Roy reading a book? I don't think so. Not in my lifetime.

"What's the book?"

"Armageddon."

I don't believe it! What a coincidence! That's the same book Sonya, the KGB agent or FBI informant, mentioned. Hmmmn, both of them asked me about the same book. That must mean the KGB or FBI has gotten to my brother-in-law, too.

I'll bet the connection is that girl who works in his office. What's her name—Janie, I think. She and her husband Doug were the ones who took me for a drink before "the accident."

The puzzle pieces are starting to fit together. Well, Uncle Joe Walsh warned me that these spies might have gotten to my family. These KGB agents—they're everywhere. I rolled my eyes and turned my face toward the window and put my head on the headrest and went to sleep.

After driving half an hour, Roy pulled over to the side of the road and walked across the street to the gas station to use the phone.

Meanwhile, the stress and lack of sleep made my paranoia surface again.

He said he was going to call Theresa, his wife. Now why would he do that? The puzzle pieces weren't fitting together as nicely as I had earlier thought.

Suddenly it dawned on me that maybe Roy wasn't working for the KGB. Maybe he was calling the FBI. After all, I had phoned Connor before I left to say goodbye and he had asked if Roy was flying into Oakland or San Francisco and what they were doing with my car. Coincidence, maybe, but all of a sudden things seemed a little too coincidental.

Maybe Connor met Roy at the Naval Base outside San Francisco. There was a pass slip in the cab of the truck from the Base. It was dated

Tuesday, October 14, 15:32 which was yesterday afternoon. When I asked Roy about it, he told me it was nothing.

Roy crossed the road again and climbed in the cab of the truck. He waited for traffic to pass and then signaled and turned onto the freeway. I waited patiently for the right moment.

"Were you talking to the FBI?"

"What?"

"Just now. Who did you call?"

"That's none of your business."

"If you won't tell, it means you have something to hide."

"For your information I called Theresa."

"You're trying to tell me that a call to your wife was so urgent it couldn't wait till we stop for lunch."

"I wasn't talking to no FBI."

"Then who were you talking to?"

"I told you. I was talking to Theresa."

"I don't believe you. A call to Theresa could have waited. So, who were you talking to, Roy?"

"I told you," he said, exasperated.

"I don't believe you."

I clammed up. I would not say a word to Roy though he tried unsuccessfully several times to get me to talk. Finally, he let me have it.

"You drive!"

"What? I can't drive this thing." The 20 ft. truck was loaded with everything I owned—my car, my furniture, my clothes. I was scared shitless to drive it. Roy refused to be persuaded.

"But I've never driven anything this big."

"You'll learn."

"Just because I wouldn't talk to you."

"Uh-huh."

"I'll show you. I can drive this thing. Where's the first gear?"

"Over there. Now give it some gas."

"Piece of cake." The engine stopped.

"You need to give it a little more gas."

At least this will keep my mind off my other troubles.

I gripped the wheel tightly. I couldn't tell if I was shaking because of the truck vibrations or because I was scared, nervous and upset. And paranoid.

Then to my astonishment Roy fell asleep. I could hear him snoring lightly. Now what was I going to do? *What if something happens? What if I can't handle driving the truck? Have I been too harsh on him? Was my silence cruel? Will I have to drive the whole way to Cottonwood myself?*

After an hour Roy woke up and switched driving with me even though I still wasn't speaking to him. As we headed toward Reno, Roy scouted for a certain place to stop and have lunch. He found what he was after—a trucker's restaurant in the middle of nowhere. He obviously had gotten directions from someone because it wasn't located right next to the highway. He drove through quite a maze of back roads to get to it.

"Did someone tell you to go here?"

He didn't answer. He drove past the construction near the entrance to the restaurant.

"Who, Roy?"

"A friend."

"A friend—who?"

"You won't tell me about your friends and I won't tell you about mine."

"I'm not talking to you."

"Fine, but you'd better come in and eat something. It will be a long time before we stop again."

I wasn't prepared for what I found. My eyes bugged out. I couldn't stop staring. I was speechless. Inside the khaki colored, one-story, building were men who looked like they were FBI agents or cops, all with two-way radios on their belts. Short-haired men with polyester pants and short-sleeve cotton shirts open at the collar with white undershirts underneath; they walked gingerly around inside the small restaurant. I half expected for them to have jackets which spelled the letters F.B.I. on the back. I wondered what they were doing in such an out-of-the-way place.

I sat down near the middle of the restaurant on a vinyl seat in a booth. I took a menu and pretended to study it while I surveyed the restaurant. I counted the FBI Agents. There were six of them. *What in the devil are they doing out here in the middle of nowhere unless there's some kind of a stakeout? Maybe they are after me.*

Roy came and sat across from me in the small booth. We ate our burgers in silence. Roy futilely tried to make conversation with me, but I stuck to my guns and kept my mouth shut the whole time. Roy finished before me, got up, and said he was going to the restroom. He left enough money on the table for our meals.

He disappeared through the door nearest the Cashier. I finished eating and sat alone holding the check. I waited and waited but Roy never came back from the restroom. I waited 10 minutes more. I got up, went over to the Cashier and paid the check. I sat down again and waited. Then I got up again and headed for the restroom. The waitress behind the counter had a look of fear in her face like she was from another planet.

"Ma'am, may I help you?"

"No, that's ok. I'm only going to the restroom." I headed for the doorway I had seen Roy go through.

"I'm sorry but you can't go back there."

"Why not? The restrooms are back there."

"The restrooms are over there," she said, pointing to the opposite direction near the front door.

As I stood there puzzled and counting the FBI agents left in the restaurant, Roy suddenly appeared from the opposite direction and faked a bump into me like Connor used to do.

"Where have you been?" I said, angrily. "Roy, the restrooms are over there," I said, pointing to somewhere near the front door. In my anger, I had momentarily forgotten that I wasn't speaking to Roy.

"Don't tell anyone but I'm 007," he whispered as he looked in back of him and back and forth across the restaurant as if he were afraid someone might overhear his conversation. I had to laugh. A small town hick playing spy. It got the better of me. I cracked a smile for the first time in days.

"Who were you talking to?"

"Try not to take this so seriously."

"This is serious. You're not being honest with me."

"Who are those people you worked with in Emeryville?"

"Who wants to know?"

"No more answering a question with a question."

"Oh, we have rules now. Have you been talking to Connor? Where is he? I want to see him."

"I'm not telling."

"Then, I'm not talking to you."

"Fine."

Roy was as mad as if he had just found out his spouse had cheated on him. It enraged him but he couldn't do a thing about it. When I decided I wouldn't talk, I wouldn't talk—not to him, not to anyone.

I was upset. *Why is Roy secretly meeting with someone? It has to be the FBI but what does the FBI want with me? I don't know any secrets or at least I don't think I do except for the classified documents that Barry has. But, Alice, Joe Walsh, Herbert and others know about them as well. Why didn't the FBI go after them?*

"Joanie, we're not fooling around anymore. I'm tired of messing with you. Who are those people you worked with?"

I wouldn't tell him. I clammed up. Didn't say another word but just climbed into the cab of the truck. If I didn't want to talk, there was no one that could make me.

Chapter 23

We rode for hours in silence. The sun went down behind a mountain blanketing the interstate in a quiet darkness. I put on a sweater at Winnemucca where we saw signs for Highway 95. Highway 95 would take us to this side of Boise and up north through Homedale, Weiser, New Meadows, Riggins, and finally Cottonwood where we would store my belongings at my folks' house and then return the truck to Lewiston.

We came to a tiny town on the Idaho/Oregon border named Jordan Valley whose only claim-to-fame was a speed trap on the north side of the city which was manned by one of the highest paid policemen in the nation. Roy chose to stop here for the night.

Before he got to the speed trap Roy pulled the truck into the parking lot of a small motel, got out of the cab and motioned for me to go with him. I reluctantly followed. He went in the office and rented a double room in the sleazy motel.

"You need your suitcase," he told me.

"I do not."

"You do, too. Now would you please go back and get it."

"You can't make me."

"Fine. If you want to sleep in your clothes, be my guest."

I was exhausted. I was tired of fighting. I plopped down on one of the beds. A nightgown was the last thing on my mind. I hated sharing the room with Roy. *What will Theresa think? Why didn't he get two rooms? He doesn't trust me.*

Still, I can't figure him out. Why has he turned on me? Was he a KGB agent like Sonya? Or are they both FBI informants or sources? I will gladly give them any information they want if they'll just be upfront with me about it. I don't like giving out information to just anybody, not knowing who they are or what their affiliation is. My Agency training never allows me such a grievous mistake. I reserve my secrets for those on the same side as me.

Suddenly Roy came into the room.

"Have a drink of this." He shoved a small silver flask in front of me.

"What is it?"

"Whiskey."

"Ugh. I don't want it."

"It will help you relax."

"I don't need it. I need some answers."

He threw his head back and laughed. "*You* need answers? I'm the one who needs answers."

"Roy, I told you, I don't know anything."

"Come on, Joanie, you worked with these people and you don't even know who they are?"

"Who do you think they are?"

"Well, this book called *Armageddon* talks about them. Let me get it." He walked over to his suitcase, rummaged around and pulled out the book. "Here it is." He had a page marked. "Basically it says they are a group of powerful people who are trying to control the world."

"Give me that." I took the book and read the part about the Trilateral Commission.

"So?"

"It doesn't fit. This book says they owe no allegiance to any country. The people I worked for are very patriotic. They are conservatives who love America. In fact, I would guess that most or all of them are Republicans."

Roy seemed satisfied. *I wondered why I was protecting Barry. Didn't I catch him with classified documents and using moles inside the FBI and CIA and continuing operational contact with an agent of the CIA? Didn't he deserve to be handed over to the Feds? If only I could be sure who Roy is talking to. I don't want the information to end up in the wrong hands. What if he is talking to a terrorist group? I could never forgive myself if something bad happened because I've said something or did something wrong. What if he's talking to the liberals? Weren't they in favor of terrorist activity to effect change? It was all so confusing. No, I am better off keeping my mouth shut about National Investigations and Snoops, Inc.*

I got up, washed my face and took out my contacts. Roy had already drifted off to sleep. My thoughts ricocheted like racquetball. *Where do my loyalties lie? Family has always been important to me but should my loyalties lie with Roy? I don't trust him. Or should my loyalties lie with a former boss who is mixed up in the Trilateral Commission? I don't trust him either.*

But, should I look the other way when it comes to wrongdoing and keep in mind only one thing: the Cause (the Cause being taking control from the Liberals in American politics and bringing back the importance of family in the U.S.)? No, I can't live like that. It's black or white, right or wrong, there's no situational ethics here. I have to be sure who I'm talking to and what I'm saying.

Roy acted like I had done something wrong. I felt like I had been convicted and guilty but I didn't know what my crime was. If only he would just tell me who he was talking to. The whole problem could then be solved. I was sure it was a misunderstanding. All he needed to do was talk to me.

I finally fell asleep. I woke up an hour later when someone knocked lightly on the door. Roy was sound asleep. He didn't even hear it. I wasn't about to open the door. I heard a deep voice say something but he mumbled the first part of it, "Mmmmmdy. Mmmmmdy. Mmmmmdy, are you in there?" He knocked again softly.

I got up, walked over to the door and said, "She's not in here, whoever you're looking for." I thought the guy was looking for a prostitute.

Roy didn't even stir. *Some protector he is,* I thought. The man mumbled an apology and then I heard him walk away.

* * *

Roy and I reached Cottonwood at noon. We arrived at my parents' place just in time for lunch. We unpacked my things and put them in the shed and took the car out. Everything arrived in one piece except some of my designer couch cushions were a little damaged. The car was fine and drivable.

Chapter 24

I was home: Cottonwood, population 1,000, but I couldn't stop thinking about all the events from the past several months, the coincidences I noticed. I tried to connect the dots but I couldn't. *Was it a coincidence that Connor married someone while I was on vacation or was it a setup? One never knows with the FBI. Was it a coincidence that Sonya was at my apartment when I found out or was that a setup, too? Were Sonya and Conrad really FBI informants? Why did Professor Luigi single me out—a nobody? Was it a coincidence that Roy brought along the book 'Armageddon,' the book Sonya had talked to me about? And, was it a coincidence that Maureen and I had an accident on the same day?*

* * *

Paranoia naturally surrounds the work of intelligence agencies so I didn't know if I was thinking like an intelligence analyst or if I was sick. I know now that my extreme paranoia was mostly the manifested symptoms of the schizoaffective disorder I would later be diagnosed with, but during those years in California I had no clue I was sick.

* * *

Mom and Dad were Northwest conservatives who I felt could not possibly be mixed up in the espionage events I had just encountered. So, at last, I could breathe again. I had enough adventure for awhile. It felt good to be in the small farming community of Cottonwood with its one gas station, one drug store, a couple bars, large Catholic Church, small Christian Church and two grocery stores.

My parents lived in a six-bedroom, three-story, white house with a two-car garage at 1701 Lewiston Street. They had purchased the house and property in 1947 for $3600 and since made renovations. Because they lived in a small town, professionals didn't landscape the place.

Mom and Dad were amateurs who fit a tree and flower in where they could. The house had a large poplar tree on the side by the long driveway, flowerbeds surrounding it on all sides and two cement flowerbeds in front with bridle wreath bushes behind. Evergreens sat in the middle of the lawn on either side of the front sidewalk.

Mom grew flowers everywhere. There were irises in the side flower bed between us and the neighbors, petunias, pansies and tulips in the cement flower beds by the front sidewalk, a bleeding heart in front of the house as well as peony bushes, daffodils and geraniums. Two lilac bushes were located behind the house. Plum trees and an apple tree separated the property with the next door neighbor.

The remaining property included a half-acre vegetable garden with a fruit orchard. They grew corn, asparagus, beans, peas, carrots, cucumbers, potatoes, cabbage, and strawberries. Raspberry bushes were planted near the adjacent Sawmill property and the orchard behind the garden blossomed with apple and plum trees.

It felt good to be home. My baby sister, fourteen-year-old Maureen, was ok but she was suffering from a concussion and the accident left a scar on her face. I helped take care of her.

But I felt worthless, rejected, duped and paranoid. I looked to my parents for support, love and comfort but they couldn't understand me or the events in California. They acted as if nothing had happened to me. They were more concerned about Maureen. I was totally alone with the turmoil eating away inside me. And I felt certain someone was out to get me and my family. I was glad I was home to protect them, especially Maureen.

Her concussion, a brain injury, caused all sorts of bizarre behavior. She reverted to a two-year-old state, wanting constantly to be held by Mom. Little did I know, it would foreshadow my own future bizarre behavior due to a brain disorder. But, I knew nothing about that yet.

* * *

Coming home, I wasn't exactly welcomed with open arms. Mom was in the kitchen canning peaches. There was a large canner on the stove and she was wiping the jars with a white towel and putting them on the cabinet. Throughout the summer she canned apricots, pears, dill pickles, sauerkraut, made strawberry jam, applesauce and blackberry jelly and put huckleberries in the freezer. Now she was canning tomatoes and peaches. She checked other jars to make sure the lids were sealed and took off rings that unscrewed easily, getting ready to put the jars in the cellar in the basement. There was an air of sweetness in the kitchen from the syrup and a never-ending sense of urgency to get all the work done.

"How was the fair this year?" I said, making idle conversation.

"About the same as usual. The animals always steal the show."

"I assume you're talking about the 4-H Livestock Auction. It must be pretty hard to give up your animal after taking care of it for a whole year."

"One little boy was so pitiful. He just bawled his head off. I felt so sorry for him."

"Did you win any awards this year?"

"I got a blue ribbon on one of my quilts and a purple on the other one."

"Hmmn, slow year, huh?"

Her smile turned into a frown. Mom didn't appreciate my sense of humor. She looked like I had just aggravated her.

"Just kidding. Just kidding. Did you enter a loaf of bread this year?"

"I did but I only got a white ribbon on that. I just don't have luck with my bread anymore. I think that's the last time I'll enter bread in the fair."

"So, who are we having for dinner?" Mom was from Illinois so to her lunch was dinner and dinner was supper.

"Frances Coughlin and Dennis Sullivan."

"Aren't they Dad's friends?"

"Yes. He's the one Dad bought all those chainsaw dogs from for all the grandsons that one Christmas."

I always wondered why an old bald-headed guy like my Dad would befriend a guy with a ponytail. "What are we having for dinner?"

"Chicken and noodles."

We normally only ate chicken and homemade noodles on a holiday or a special occasion since they were a lot of work for Mom. "What's the occasion?"

"Well, I haven't had them over in awhile and now people can sleep in that big Beagle in Dog Bark Park. They've got beds in there now. That's something to celebrate."

"How much are they charging a night?"

"I don't know."

"Oh, Mom. You should make dog quilts for the beds. That would be so cute. You should do it, Mom."

She never liked my ideas. If it had been Marilyn or Connie who said that, she would have heartily agreed. "I have some other ones to make right now that I'm working on. You got some mail there."

"I did?"

"Yeah, it's on the writing desk. Did you put our address as your forwarding address?"

"Yeah, I did. I didn't know where I would end up."

"So, what do you plan to do now?"

"I don't know. I thought . . ."

"Well, I hope you don't think you're moving back in here. I told you before that you're not welcome to live here ever again."

"I never said I was, did I?" My voice rose with anger. She struck a nerve with me. *Why was it always so difficult with her? Why couldn't we ever get along? Why couldn't I have been born to another mother?*

"Don't you smart mouth me you ol' big mouth!" She raised her hand as if to hit me. "Now hurry up and get the table set. Dad and Dennis will be coming home any minute."

* * *

My mother reminded me of Grandma Hoene, a widow who strong-armed her children to keep the family farm. Mom's Dad died when she was one year old. They lived in Effingham, Illinois where Mom grew up. As a child, I thought Grandma was the meanest and nastiest old lady I ever met. But she was left with seven kids and a dairy farm to manage after her husband died so you could say she had a reason to be crabby. She used to come out to Cottonwood, to visit us. I dreaded her month-long visits. And that half-man/half-woman was Mom's role model. In my eyes Mom became bossy like her.

My mother learned to work hard at an early age. Getting the work done was always uppermost in her mind. I did appreciate Mom's hard work in canning. Mom never told me she loved me but she would smile and give me a jar of dill pickles or sauerkraut. She knew it would please me. Although it was certainly a funny way of showing it, that was her way of demonstrating her love.

Living at home again, I found my relationship with my mother had not changed since high school. I had been rebellious as a teenager. She and I didn't see eye-to-eye during that time or for that matter, forever after that. It was easy to see why she didn't want me living with them again.

* * *

I sought refuge in Dad. I remember driving down to Lewiston one Sunday in my high school years with just me and my Dad in the car. Tears started streaming down my face and I began crying with pent up anger. Finally, I let it all out.

"Dad, I hate her. I just can't stand it anymore. Nothing I ever do pleases her. And, she's so bossy. I hate her."

He looked at me with a surprised look on his face. "Well, I'm not going to divorce her."

His remark startled me. I wasn't asking him to choose between us. I just wanted a little sympathy.

He looked at me with loving eyes that told me he understood. "Well, I knew after I married her there might be problems. You see, she tried to imitate Grandma Hoene. And we both know what she is like. Lord knows it's probably because your mother only has an eighth grade education. I tried to get her to learn more but she just refused. I just always felt it was my cross to carry."

I wondered why devout Catholics like to suffer instead of doing something about it, solving the problem, alleviating the suffering. "Dad, you should have done something. She has affected us all."

Nothing ever became of that conversation. Dad never did anything about it, never sought psychiatric help. We lived below the poverty level and in those days living in a small town, psychiatric help was not an option. But I felt my Dad understood me better now and was on my side. It seemed like a million years had gone by since our discussion. Dad and I were still close but it was definitely Mom who ruled the roost and I got nowhere with her.

The next day, a Thursday, after I helped Mom carry the jars of fruit to the basement cellar, I left Cottonwood and drove one hour to Lewiston. I stayed overnight in Lewiston with Theresa and Roy.

* * *

They were in the Lewiston Civic Theatre production of "Gypsy". The show started at 8:00 p.m. They had to be there early so they gave me directions on how to get there.

I arrived by myself in my yellow VW Bug and watched a little of the play but had to go because I felt I was going to burst out crying. I felt like my wretched life was like that of Gypsy Rose Lee. After fifteen minutes, I went back to Roy and Theresa's house.

I could not stop crying. I cried all the way back to their house and I sobbed alone in the guest room for the whole night. I was lonely, starting over again, and didn't know anybody; I didn't know what was happening to me. Mom telling me I was not welcome in her house had me feeling unwanted and unloved.

I heard Theresa and Roy and the kids come home later but my light was out. Tears were streaming down my face but I was silent. I didn't want them to hear me. I didn't want to be a problem to anyone. I thought I could handle my problems alone.

When I saw them at breakfast, Theresa had a puzzled look on her face but I just told her I wasn't feeling well. No one else said another word to me about the fact that I might have looked like I had been crying. They were excited and wanted to tell me about the play. After breakfast I went on my way.

Chapter 25

Being turned down by my mother for a temporary place to live, I headed to Spokane, Washington where my older sister lived. Population 200,000, Spokane is located near the Idaho border on the eastern side of the state. A married-with-children kind of town. Californians come to Spokane because they can get more house and land for their money which brings up the price of real estate. Local residents are not amused. And, Spokane attracts outdoor enthusiasts who love good, clean water and fresh country air. There is excellent hunting, fishing, camping, hiking, biking, boating, skiing, horseback riding and mountain climbing. Beautiful Lake Coeur d' Alene in Idaho is only an hour drive away.

I didn't like living in Spokane. I didn't participate in any of the above outdoor activities. I was only there because my relatives lived there. In Spokane, singles, like me, wither and die a slow death and pray for divorces. Even department stores have a tough time making it in Spokane because many people wear the same clothes for three years or more and Spokane shoppers pounce like vultures on anything to do with a sale including a garage sale. People living in Spokane learn to be frugal out of necessity. Most salaries aren't high. My sister, Marilyn, dressed her whole house and household with sale items, including garage sales. She figured she could double her buying power by being thrifty.

Marilyn, a receptionist for a group of Sacred Heart Hospital doctors and a board member of St. Augustine's Catholic Church, as well as her husband, Dan, an Assistant Director of the Morning Star Boys Ranch, invited me to live with them in their two-story, Craftsman-style four-bedroom home on 20th Avenue in Spokane's prestigious South Hill.

They harbored more than one of my siblings previously. My sister, Connie, was trained to be a Special Ed teacher and she stayed with Marilyn for five months before Marilyn was married while Connie did her student teaching. My brother, Don, stayed with them for seven months after he graduated from college because he had no money and lots of debt and couldn't afford an apartment. And, my youngest brother,

Larry, also stayed with Dan and Marilyn for five months after he graduated from college before he got his own apartment. We call their house The Kuhlmann Hotel. So, it was natural for them to offer me a place to stay before I could afford my own place.

Marilyn and I weren't that close. She offered to let me live with her family for a couple of months but it was conditional.

"You can stay with us, but . . ."

"Yes? But, what?"

"Well, Verla told me that someone she knew had a girl living with them and the girl started having an affair with her husband." She looked at me as if she was an interrogator in The Inquisition.

"Who is Verla?"

"My friend, Verla. She used to be a Duman."

"Oh, her. Just because it happened to someone you don't really know, then you think it would happen to you and me. Marilyn, don't be ridiculous. I'm your sister, for Chrissakes."

"It could happen . . ."

"Do you really think I'd be interested in Dan after all I've been through? I don't trust men, period. Ok?"

"Well, I'm just trying to be careful."

I could see Marilyn was apprehensive about letting me stay. I was welcome . . . up to a point. I had no interest in Dan. I was too depressed. And, besides, I was paranoid and thought he was a communist.

So, I moved in with Marilyn, Dan, and their two young boys, Justin and Jeremy, and I ended up staying for six months. I was severely depressed and couldn't quit thinking about California and Connor and all the events that happened there so I was not always pleasant to be around. Depressed people certainly don't bring joy into your life.

I didn't always make people sad, though. Sometimes Marilyn and Dan would go out for the evening and I would babysit three-year-old Justin and two-year-old Jeremy for them. What I usually did was take them to the basement where we would do exercises to wear out their energy. We'd do jumping jacks, push-ups, touch our toes and run in place. Little Jeremy made me laugh. He became frustrated because he tried hard but he could not touch his toes.

Although I appeared to be functioning somewhat normally on the outside, I was dying on the inside. I coped with my losses as best I could. I lost a boyfriend. I lost the love we shared. I lost a social life. I lost an income and, thus, lost my independence and freedom. I lost my identity as a straight A student in college. And I lost the comfort of having my own home in familiar surroundings. It is no wonder I was depressed.

Dan came home from work one day and he seemed to notice that I had been crying. Even though I tried hard to hide it, my eyes were puffy and red and I wasn't very communicative. I went down to the basement where my bedroom was and Dan told Marilyn to go down and talk to me. He should have told her to go *listen* to me.

I was very negative about everything but based on what I had been through this was probably normal. Dan had us join hands at the dinner table and thank God for something. I couldn't bring myself to thank God for anything. I hated life so why should I be thankful? I know Dan was trying to get me to be more positive but my problem was a chemical imbalance in the brain that couldn't be treated by anything less than drugs and therapy. But I wasn't ready for help yet.

Marilyn, a "devout Catholic" like my Mom was not educated past high school, never took a psychology course, never read any books except romance novels and, worse yet, she didn't know how to listen. When I would complain about how Mom treated me, instead of reflecting back my feelings, she appeared to think she had to defend Mom. She never listened to my side of the story, how I felt, what I had gone through. She just added to my troubles. She made things much worse. I had no one who offered me support. Now, besides my Mom, I also had a sister I couldn't get along with. It made me feel even more alone and misunderstood. I was also having a religious crisis in addition to my own personal mental health crisis.

"Mom doesn't love me," I complained. Children know when they are loved. I never knew Mom's love. I never felt she really cared about me. Mom put a crack in my emotional pot a long time ago and it never really healed so every time I had new hurts, negative emotions would spill out of the pot. And I always looked for another Mom, a Mom substitute, a surrogate mother like my sister, Connie, to fill up that pot with positive emotions.

"Joanie, she does too. She cleans the house for you. She gives you jars of homemade canned fruit, pickles and sauerkraut. What more do you want?"

"She's never hugged or kissed me. She doesn't tell me she loves me so how would I know? I'm not one of her favorites."

"She doesn't have any favorites."

"Yes, she does. When Connie was in the first grade, Mom brought cupcakes and Kool-Aid to her class to surprise her. She never did that for me even though she promised she would. If that isn't having favorites, I don't know what is."

"I can't believe you're still mad at her for that. You're just being stupid."

"I am not. It hurt and it still does." I started crying.

"Get over it. Mom loves you as much as she does any of her kids."

"Oh, sure! She loves me all right! How come when I was in high school and I used up all my babysitting money to paint and wallpaper my room, put new curtains up, bought a pretty new bedspread and sanded my dressers . . . when she came home early from vacation in Illinois, all she did was complain about the mess? She never did thank me for beautifying a part of *her* house. I was only going to live there for another year and a half."

"Well, she didn't like the color."

"She never said anything when I showed her my plans for it. I worked hard on that. I sanded all the baseboards and put putty in every hole. Grandpa and Dad used scrap wood upstairs when they built those rooms and besides, no one redid that room and hallway for twenty years. Mom never had the money. I used my babysitting money but she never appreciated it."

"It's over with now. Just forget it. She loves you just like any of her ten children."

"Oh, yeah! She sure has a funny way of showing it. Besides, that's easy for you to say. You never had to stay with Aunt Johanna."

"What has that got to do with anything?"

"Remember Uncle Ben died of a heart attack before Mom and Dad were supposed to go back to Illinois to visit relatives. Aunt Johanna was afraid to stay alone so Mom made me stay with her. Connie was home, too, but she didn't make *her* stay with Johanna."

"Mom did what she thought was best."

"For who? Not me! I was a junior in high school and Johanna was grieving, crying all the time, every time we prayed the rosary, every time she thought of Ben, every time she'd notice something in the house that reminded her of him, every time she went to bed—and I didn't know what to do or say to comfort her. I was too young for that kind of responsibility."

"If that was the worst thing that happened to you, you have nothing to complain about."

"Oh, yeah! You didn't have to sleep with her. She was not only afraid to stay alone, she was also afraid to sleep alone. She told me I had to sleep with her so I did. During the night she would roll over and reach for Ben and since I was his stand-in, she grabbed me. I was a high school kid, for Chrissakes!"

"You've had such a horrible life," she said sarcastically.

"Yeah, and when I started my period in the 6th grade, Mom never told me anything about it. She just said, 'Go see Connie.' Connie became my mother, not Mom."

"Well, she had a lot of children to raise. She probably didn't have time to tell you anything at that time. She had a lot of other work to do."

"Yeah, work was more important than telling her own daughter about sex."

I was going to tell her about The Applesauce Story when I stood up for my little sister, Karen, when Mom chastised her for burning the applesauce and Dad ended up belting me, leaving a scar, but Marilyn would probably only say I deserved the belting so I didn't bring it up. We shouted at each other and I just wanted her to go away.

Chapter 26

A week or two passed before I finally sought help. I turned to a young priest at St. Augustine's parish on the South Hill. I went to the rectory and was greeted by this priest who had reddish blond hair, wore black glasses and looked like he was in his 40's. There was another priest there, an older priest, who did not offer to counsel me.

I considered myself lucky. The younger priest would know more than me and would be able to pinpoint my problem, although I was not sure I even had a problem. I felt I was only misunderstood. My depression manifested itself in that the tiniest task seemed to take on gigantic proportions. It was an effort to shower every day and blow-dry my hair. I much preferred to sleep in my clothes and get up the next day foregoing a shower, even though I knew this was unacceptable in public. My room was a mess. I also let junk mail pile up before I had the energy to toss it out.

Friends and relatives seemed to cut me off when I tried to talk to them. I felt I just needed someone who would listen to my whole story from beginning to end and help me sort it all out.

I had two sessions with the priest. By the third week I was really looking forward to our counseling session, as I was having problems at school, but the young priest was unavailable. I had enrolled at Gonzaga University. During the first semester I tried talking with two Jesuits about my life in California.

"An FBI agent I was dating for six months married someone else while I was on vacation and then this Professor of Economics embarrassed me a couple of times in front of class and then I had a car accident which wasn't my fault." I didn't really make a whole lot of sense because I wasn't giving many details. But it was a first effort at trying to get someone to understand the trauma of the recent events in California.

One of the Jesuits looked at me and said, "You should read the part about Job in the Bible."

I felt like screaming, "Go read Job yourself." I just wanted someone to listen to me.

I struck up a conversation with an acquaintance, Brenda, one day. She asked me, "Why did you decide to go to Gonzaga?"

I hated Gonzaga. I hated being an older student at a predominantly younger campus. I wondered why I came myself. I stuck out like a sore thumb because all the students were younger than me. I was also poor and it seemed like a lot of the students were from wealthy families. I couldn't even afford to get my hair high-lighted any more. Brenda's question wasn't making it any easier. The look on her face made me feel even more out of place. But I had to give her some answer. I didn't feel I could spend an hour telling her that a Professor at City College had embarrassed me in front of class several times and I had a car accident which wasn't my fault and I had an FBI agent boyfriend who jilted me so I jumped schools to try to alleviate some of the stress. I still hadn't sorted out my life in San Francisco. Besides, it was a casual question. It wasn't as if she was a personal friend. So I just said, "Gonzaga has a reputation for being a good school."

"What do you plan to do after college?"

Was she inferring that even with a college degree I wouldn't be able to get a job? Did she think my life wasn't planned? Would I stick out in the marketplace like I stuck out at Gonzaga? Would I continually be punished for not attending college with my peers when I should have?

I might have answered her question with, "I'm going to be a stockbroker" which sounded promising and like I was going to make my fortune in life. But, feeling very depressed and beaten down, I said, "I don't know."

After my last class, I went to see the priest at St. Augustine's. I wanted to be comforted, to be told that life would get better and not to worry. I needed one person, one human being to be on my side. I met him at the door to the rectory.

"Hi, Father."

"Hi, Joan. Listen, I won't be able to see you today. I've got a penance service I have to prepare for and I don't have enough time."

He must've seen the disappointment in my eyes.

"Are you ok, Joan?"

"Yeah," I answered. I decided never to come back to him for counseling. I didn't really know what was wrong with me or how bad it was but the priest bailing on me was the last straw.

I was suicidal. I had no gun. Knives seemed too messy and besides if I didn't succeed, I might end up in an insane asylum, which seemed worse than death. I was desperate. I had bottomed out. There was no hope left.

That first call I had to make to get help was the hardest. I had a relative, a great Aunt who spent forty years in what we called the insane asylum in Orofino, Idaho, not far from my hometown. She also had the "Hoene curse" as it was called on my mother's side of the family. (I later unsuccessfully tried to get medical records on her; however, they were on unreadable microfilm. Nevertheless, the death certificate revealed she died from a stroke and secondly, a contributing cause from schizophrenic reactive chronic "undifferentiated type" which meant she was not paranoid. With modern drugs, she never would have been in sanitariums. More importantly, however, the diagnosis was probably bad because doctors didn't understand as much about depression and schizophrenia as they do today.) At the time, I didn't know how we were related or what her diagnosis was or how long she had lived there. I just knew she existed. If I contacted someone there, would they commit me also?

On my Dad's side of the family, Aunt Claire had written about the heated arguments the Kopczynskis would have saying, "It might appear as if the Kop Klan would come to blows, but the consensus at that time was that airing opinions in a verbal debate was better than people carrying inward grudges and eventually ending up on a psychiatrist's couch." I took that as a negative view of psychiatrists. It made me afraid of them. But there was definitely something wrong with me and I knew I needed to get help. If I didn't get someone to listen to me soon, I felt like I was going to explode.

I had previously been a housekeeper/nanny for Mary Higgins and her husband, Dr. Curran Higgins. Mary was the Director of the Mental Health Clinic in Spokane. Mary reminded me of the actress, Elizabeth Taylor—a classy, dark-haired beauty, a strong woman, with a good sense of humor. She was good natured, kind, intelligent and an eloquent speaker.

I lived with the Higginses while I attended Kinman Business University. Kinman had a program designed for students who needed financial aid where students received room and board in exchange for babysitting and light housekeeping duties. I had been in that program before I left for Washington, DC where I worked for the CIA.

The Higginses had two small children and a teenage son who stayed in his room a lot. I was responsible for babysitting the two younger ones, doing the laundry, straightening up the house, getting the groceries and cooking the meals on weekdays. It was heaven compared to what I was used to.

Cooking was easy. The first night I made a box of Hamburger Helper for the family. I only added hamburger to the ready-made mix. Dr. Higgins and Mary thanked me profusely and told me how good it tasted and that I was a great cook. It was as if I had made them a gourmet meal. I turned red in embarrassment. I was suffering from low self-esteem. I wasn't used to being praised, especially for something so simple. My mother never praised me for anything. Mary praised me for whatever I did for them. I couldn't believe how nice she was. It was a joy to work for her. Mary must've liked working with me, too, because she had offered me a job as a secretary in the Mental Health Clinic if I decided not to join the CIA.

In need of help now, I called her.

"Mrs. Higgins?"

"Yes."

"This is Joan Kopczynski. I used to be your housekeeper/nanny."

"I know who you are. How are you doing?"

"Not good."

"What can I do for you?"

"Well . . ." I was so choked with emotion I could barely talk. "I need somebody to talk to."

"Is it painful for you, Joanie?"

On the verge of tears, I said, "Yes." She seemed to intuitively understand. I instantly knew I could trust her. I knew she would help me.

"Why don't you come see my friend, Marilyn Wilson at the clinic? She's a good friend, a great therapist and I know she can help you. Ok?"

"Ok. Thanks."

"One of my staff will call you back to set up an appointment and I'll tell her you'll be coming. What's your number?"

I gave it to her and then said, "Thanks, Mrs. Higgins. Bye."

"Bye."

Chapter 27

I liked Marilyn Wilson right away. She was pretty, blond, and older than me but what mattered most was I finally found someone to listen to me. It sounds strange now but at the time I didn't know that's basically what therapists do. She spent a large part of her time focused on me, just listening. It was a dream come true. Oh, she'd throw in some comments there, too, once in awhile but mostly it was the listening that kept me coming back. And I wanted to talk to her for hours, get my whole story out but like all good therapists and psychiatrists, she always told me when my hour was up and I had to wait until the next time I saw her to continue with my story. I learned that most therapists or psychiatrists won't tell you what you should do. They help you figure it out for yourself.

And, since I didn't have any money, I was glad to know I could pay on a sliding scale. Once when I was in the waiting room with other patients, I noticed many seemed agitated. One was doing strange things with her hands. I later asked Marilyn if I was as mentally sick as that lady. As yet, I had no diagnosis. She told me, "No."

I talked to Marilyn a lot about my Mom and she listened and gave me feedback.

"Do you think your Mom is a good person?"

"She's good to others. She did a lot of charity work even while raising us. She'd clean house for Cousin Johnnie Hoene who was considered the town drunk. She visited all the widows in need of company. To repay the debt she felt she owed to the town of Cottonwood, Mom gave away baked goods or quilts to practically everyone in town for special occasions or just when they were sick or down on their luck. There was hardly a family in town who hasn't been a recipient of Mom's cooking. Besides cooking for Prairie Middle School, she also cooked for weddings and funerals. She'd bake rolls and cookies for the needy family down the street and did volunteer work for the hospital at one time. Her hobby was quilting and she kept records of how many quilts she gave away."

"How many?"

"She gave away over 800 quilts."

"That's a lot. What kind were they?"

"There were a variety including Wedding Ring, Star-Embroidery, Log Cabin, Necktie, Dogwood, Friendship, Star and 9-Patch. She quilted mostly for other people and made a lot of baby quilts as well as tied quilts."

"Why did she feel indebted to Cottonwood?"

"In November 1958 Mom came down with rheumatic fever and went to the hospital via ambulance leaving eight kids and a husband behind. Theresa, the oldest, was in the 7th grade and Karen, the baby, was only six months old. Dad hired Mrs. Nelson to help us but everyone in town brought food and made doll clothes and shopped for Christmas gifts. Dad helped out but he didn't do much laundry or cooking. Mom came home a week before Christmas and never forgot the generosity and kindness of the people of Cottonwood and vowed that she would one day repay their kindness."

"So, that's why she felt she was in their debt?"

"Yeah and in the fall of 1965 Mom and Dad faced a medical and financial crisis. My older sister, Carole, who had her right eye removed when she was eleven years old, sought help at Mayo Clinic in Rochester, Minnesota to determine what they could do for her that the doctors in the Northwest couldn't do. She was fifteen years old when she went to the Mayo Clinic."

"What did they find out?"

"They found she had a disease she was born with called von Recklingshausen. She had surgery there at the Clinic and was recuperating at the Blocks Downtown Apt. House in Rochester when the doctors told Mom and Dad Carole would need another surgery. Mom said that was about the hardest thing she ever thought she would have to do. When Carole was still weak from the other surgery they had to take her in for another. Mom wrote in her diary that she felt like she and Dad were leading an innocent lamb to the slaughter. She said knowing that their friends were praying helped so much. But they felt alone and it seemed like the world was folding in on them. They were getting so tired of it all. So many, many hours they just sat waiting and wondering. Sitting around waiting, doing nothing was extremely hard for my mother who always liked to be busy doing some kind of work."

"Hmmmn, Mayo Clinic. It must have cost a bundle. How could your folks afford that?"

"Considering how poor we were, medical expenses of this magnitude would have financially bankrupted our family. But Cottonwood was a small town and word spread like red dye in a glass of water. Before too long, donations of money were coming in from friends and relatives. The Cottonwood Jaycees held a benefit dance in town and one day Boots Mader, representing them, knocked on our door and gave Mom an envelope with a lot of money in it. The Kopczynski and Hoene relatives also gave a lot of money and support during this time. My Mom and our family never forgot everyone's kindness so she vowed that one day she would repay their generosity."

"So, you think she's good to others but not to you. Is that it?"

"Yes. She has been an excellent mother to my sister, Carole, and to the people of Cottonwood. But, you know, she's hardly ever nice to me. She can't ever find anything good to say about me. She always criticizes me. She thinks I'm fat. She hates my hair. She thinks it should be short like hers. We have completely opposite tastes in clothes. She swears she is going to bury me in that ugly dress in the upstairs closet. She finds fault with who I go out with. When I was in high school, she told me Mike Tews was a womanizer and to stay away from him. She thought that because he had dated practically every girl on the Camas Prairie. I felt special though because he chose me as the girl he wanted to date long term. But Mom wanted me to quit seeing him. He's a really nice guy and if she had just given him a chance, she'd have thought so, too.

"She is so different from some of the other women I know. Mom doesn't ever treat me like an adult. She just thinks I'm somebody she can push around. She likes to order me to do the work around the house and it's never-ending."

"How do the other women you know treat you?"

"With respect. I call them my surrogate mothers."

"Who are they?"

"Well, Connie is one. My favorite sister and the one closest to my age. She's a year older than me. She and I were so close it was almost as if we were twins. I often fought with her as a kid. We fought about the usual things—who got the hand-me-downs, who got the most or best Christmas or birthday presents and who had to do certain chores. I would often complain that she only had to sweep the floor while I had to wash or dry dishes. I always accused her of being Mom's favorite child. Mom would usually tell me to shut up. I was a typical middle child and I believed in fairness. But for the most part, Connie and I got along."

"Do you two look alike?"

"A little. She's tall like me and has chestnut brown hair and for as long as I can remember she was always a size 10. But, it isn't really how she looks that is special; it is how you feel when you are with her.

"She is the one who touches your soul. She is the peacemaker and the best listener in the family. She is the one who cares whether you know you are loved, who tries to mend hurts between family members and is the most sympathetic when you are ill or ill-fortuned. You could say she is a combination of St. Francis and Mother Teresa. I look up to her; she always gives me advice and she helps me solve my problems and make my decisions. I sometimes share my dreams, goals and aspirations with her and whenever I have problems, she is the first one I turn to. Even though she was Mom's favorite child, there was no enmity between us because of that."

"So, who are your other surrogate mothers?"

"There were three other women who were very influential in my teenage years—Marianne Wren, Maggie Driscoll and Mary Higgins."

"I know Mary Higgins so tell me about the other two."

"Marianne is a bubbly blonde who loves people, loves to laugh and loves to talk. Constantly battling her family's meager finances, she always had money-making schemes which never really made much but never deterred her from enthusiastically promoting them."

"How did she come to be one of your surrogate mothers?"

"I babysat for her. Wrens had ten children, all under the age of eleven, four in diapers. They had a child every year, skipped one year and then had twins one year.

"Marianne was the first woman I could relate to outside of the family. Unlike my mother, people were a higher priority to Marianne than work. Her house might not be clean or her dishes done but she always had time to sit and chat with friends and me. She was the mother who listened to my problems, my dreams and my opinions. My own mother never had time to do that or never made time. She was only concerned with getting the work done. That caused a lot of friction between us."

"I can imagine that must have been a great deal of responsibility."

"Yes, it was. The Wren kids were pretty easy to supervise so I spent most of my time cleaning their house and doing laundry. I babysat once or twice a week for seven years. From the fall of 1965 until the summer of 1972. For babysitting ten kids, cleaning their house, doing their mending and laundry I got paid 50 cents an hour and I never got a raise in seven years. Even though it wasn't very much money, it was, nevertheless, more money than I'd ever had. Growing up below the poverty level made me grateful for any money I received. Besides, Marianne was always very appreciative and I liked her so much, I thought it was worthwhile. I noticed she didn't belittle her kids or destroy their self-esteem when she chewed them out. She treated her kids with the same respect that she treated me."

"You seem very mature but that was a lot of work, caring for ten kids."

"Yes, it was. Babysitting them was a lot of hard work. I babysat so much my grades suffered. I got B's and C's in high school. I found out later I had a genius-level IQ. At that time, I suffered from low self-esteem. I always thought I was stupid. I should have done better. My guess is that I didn't have enough time to study. It wasn't only the babysitting though. I had other cleaning jobs, which competed for my time. I helped Mom clean the grade school and I was custodian of the Community Hall. I also cleaned house for a couple of people. At that time, I usually put in ten or twelve-hour days and I always worked weekends. I had jobs ever since the third grade when I carried newspapers for five years. I loved the feeling of independence and freedom money gave me and I thought that hard work was the best way to get ahead."

"So, did you want to have ten kids when you grew up?"

"No. I knew then that I wanted to do something with my life besides raise children or at least not raise ten. Marriage and being saddled with ten children never was a goal of mine. Instead, I sought independence and freedom."

"Do you still feel this way?"

"Yes. On top of all this, when the Wrens took a vacation to California one summer, I completely redecorated their only bathroom in the house. I paid for everything. I had a nice surprise for them when they came back home. They were very grateful."

"That's a nice story, Joan. And who was the other lady you mentioned?"

"Maggie Driscoll. She is Mary Higgins' sister-in-law. I was a nanny to Maggie and John Driscoll's kids at their Liberty Lake home for two summers in high school."

"That must have been fun."

"It was. Red-haired, freckled, Maggie was always so full of life. I never met anyone more cheerful. Prettier than a springtime flower, she was so good-natured. Talking to her was like a warm fuzzy. She was like a comfortable old shoe, fun to be around with a good sense of humor. Her smile lit up the room, melted even the most disagreeable person and brought sunshine into the life of others. She was so unlike my own mother, at least at the time I thought so."

"Why?"

"Maggie lived to become a college graduate and a modern woman. My mother had an 8th grade education and was old fashioned. Maggie chose to be well read and well informed. My mother thought reading was a waste of time.

"Maggie treated me with respect and like an adult even though I was only a freshman in high school. My mother destroyed my younger sister's and my self esteem."

"Maybe she felt threatened by you, by your good looks."

"If that was so, it was stupid because Mom was pretty good looking in her day."

"So, you lived with the Driscoll's?"

"Yeah. Although I did a lot of babysitting for other families before, it was the first time I actually lived with another family when I stayed at the lake. I saw how Maggie interacted with her husband and the kids. Mom nagged my Dad to death."

"So, Maggie was important to you?"

"She was an intelligent role model. She gave me hope that there was something better out there and that I wouldn't be subjected to people like Mom my whole life. Mom complained that I always thought I knew better. I knew that what I saw *was* better.

"That's it. The last one was Mary Higgins and you know her. She treated me like an adult, too."

"Well, Joan, it is normal for a woman your age who hasn't married and hasn't had children to blame her mother for the person she became and to start choosing her own identity. Normally a woman goes through this when she gets married and has children. She chooses what she likes about her mother and wants to continue doing and discards what she doesn't like."

"Oh. Maybe you're right."

"The other problem you seem to have is a lack of self esteem. This could have been caused by your Mom's critical remarks about you, or it could be caused by someone else. Have you ever read the book, 'Born to Win'?"

"No,"

"Well, you can find it in any bookstore. It's real popular now. I want you to read it and tell me what you think. Our time is up."

Chapter 28

At Christmas, I drove down to Cottonwood via Lewiston and Clarkston and stayed overnight with Roy and Theresa. Lewiston, Idaho and Clarkston, Washington are located across the Snake River from each other in a valley. I loved driving down the Lewiston grade at night seeing the lights of the two cities in the valley below. I remembered riding in an American Express bus tour driving down such a grade in Austria years before with many of the passengers oohing and ahhing at the night-lights. I remember feeling smug because we had the same thing at home although no one ever took notice.

Roy and Theresa lived in a ranch-style four-bedroom home on a hill in a new subdivision in Clarkston Heights. When I arrived, Theresa was busy stringing popcorn and cranberries to put on the Christmas tree. I made myself at home, and then sat down at the round oak table to write.

"What are you working on?"

"I'm writing a play. I thought it would help boost my self-esteem. My therapist told me that's what I suffered from most."

"Good for you. What's it about?"

"It's a spoof on our family. Act One is about Mom and Dad. Let me read it to you."

"Ok."

"Mom's on the center stage, ragging about something and ready to nag Dad like always. Dad comes in from the side, takes his hat off, looks at Mom, puts his cap back on, shakes his head and turns around and tries to leave.

'Where are you going?' she says.

'To Church,' he says.

'I thought you just came from there.'

'I did,' he says as he leaves, smiling."

I laughed. Theresa laughed, too. "That's a good one," she said.

"See, even though it never happened, it's just a typical scene about Mom and Dad. It says a lot about them, their relationship and about what was most important to Dad, how he coped with Mom's nagging. You see, every act in my play is going to be like that about a different member of the family."

"That's really good, Joanie. What did you write about me?"

"I don't have that one yet. I think I'll make you the harried housewife and Roy the Disco King."

We both laughed. I felt loved, and stronger, like I was coming out of my shell, like I was human again. She made me feel excited about the play. It was good to be around Theresa. Unlike Marilyn and Mom, Theresa listened to what I had to say. I was important to her.

I left the next day for Cottonwood. When I arrived home two of my siblings were in the living room. I couldn't wait to tell them about my play and I tried to enlist them in being actors in it. They, however, didn't share my enthusiasm. After I read Act One to them, they let me have it.

"You're going to hurt Mom and Dad's feelings with that stupid play!"

"It's just a spoof on our family life," I said.

"You're making fun of them. We're not doing it." I had never seen them so mad.

"It's only a play," I said.

"Well, it's stupid and we're not doing it and neither are you!"

I ran upstairs crying. I felt like the two of them were ganging up on me. I wasn't strong enough to withstand their criticism. My eyes felt like they were on fire and my shoulders shook with each gut-wrenching sob. I tore the play up and threw it in the trash.

Theresa came in the front door and they told her what happened.

"I can't believe you guys. Joanie worked so hard on that play. She was trying to build up her self-esteem. Where is she?"

"Upstairs."

I heard her call my name and heard her coming up the steps so I got out of bed and met her halfway down the hall.

"Joanie, I'm so sorry." She took me in her arms and hugged me tight for what seemed an eternity. It was a hug that both of us would later remember for a long time. My eyes were red and I could barely talk but I felt the way I did when I was a little kid and I scraped my knee and I ran to Mom for comfort. This time it wasn't Mom but my oldest sister who had a comforting, calming effect on me.

"No matter what I do, it always turns out bad," I blubbered in the midst of tears.

"No it doesn't," she said. "It was a good play. You worked so hard on it. They are just insensitive."

Theresa that day acted as judge, peacemaker, mother and friend. In my fragile state of mind, I was grateful for her comfort.

Chapter 29

A month later I returned to see Marilyn Wilson. I wanted to talk to her about the book, "Born to Win."

"I read the book you recommended."

"And how did you like it?"

"I was astonished. It asked questions like, 'Who was the person in your family to tell you that you weren't funny?'"

"And who was it?"

"I thought it was my Mom but it wasn't. It was one of my siblings, who at a very young age got a pair of cowboy boots for Christmas one year and he used to kick me constantly when I didn't do what he said. Although he was younger than I was, he always seemed to want to be the boss of me. And I hated it."

"Don't you see? He's still got a hold on you. Now you kick yourself if you think he wouldn't approve."

From that day on, I quit taking crap from my little brother. Therapy was priceless.

* * *

I continued with my classes at Gonzaga but I was still so depressed and out of it my grades slipped. I had attention and memory deficits. I couldn't concentrate in my classes because of all the unresolved conflicts that were ruminating inside my head. To keep from going insane I fed my passion for writing. In addition to my studies, I wrote ten poems, a short story about whitewater rafting, a barnyard children's story and reported for the school newspaper. For my work-study job I created a newsletter called "Career Strategy" for the Career and Placement Center and another newsletter for the few older students on campus.

During this time, I also had problems with insomnia and my judgment process was impaired. One of the Jesuits remarked to me that perhaps I should quit for a while and come back later when things were better. I was not a quitter. I had gotten straight A's at City College in San Francisco but at Gonzaga I got B's and C's. I tried hard not to let it bother me.

At the time, I hadn't been diagnosed yet and I had no idea what my limitations were because of the brain disorder. I blamed my problems on others and myself instead of my illness. I reasoned that no one asks about your grades in life. They mostly care about work experience. I was doing the best I could, considering the circumstances.

A girl came up to me in the Crosby Library where I usually hung out.

"Say, you're in my Statistics Class, aren't you?"

I looked at her briefly, then glanced away. "I guess," I said in a low, depressed voice.

She started to sit down at my table. "Did you understand that problem we had in class today?" I felt panicky. She acted like she wanted to be my best friend but I didn't want any friends. I just wanted to be left alone.

"Leave me ALONE!" I said as loud as I could get away with it in a library. It was obvious that I was even more depressed and irritable than I ever imagined.

She stood up to leave, rebuffed. She looked at me with a scowl on her face. "Hey, I was only trying to help you."

She left and I couldn't believe I had just bitten her head off for trying to help me. *What was wrong with me? Would I ever feel normal again?*

* * *

My paranoia manifested itself in telling my sister, Connie, shortly after I came back to the Northwest that I thought my brother-in-law, Dan, was a communist and that I thought Connie's husband, Garry, was a communist, too, and I didn't like the fact that Garry owned guns. I thought there were people out there—maybe the FBI, maybe Barry and his friends—who didn't want me talking about what I knew, who might fake my suicide death to shut me up.

Even though I liked their two little boys and used to babysit them off and on, I found it difficult to continue living with Marilyn and Dan. I needed my own space and I suffered from insomnia and made poor decisions, besides the paranoia. I was not on any medication and obviously had no prescription for sleeping pills. So, one day in Spokane, I called up the Republican Party in town. I was so paranoid I made the call from a phone booth on the street so the call couldn't be traced. A man answered.

"Hello."

"Yes, could you please give me the name of a Republican realtor? I need to find an apartment and I want to be sure it's in a good neighborhood if you know what I mean."

"Mrs. 'Smith' has been active in the Republican party. I think she could help you."

"Thanks."

I dialed her number.

"Hello."

"Yes, Mrs. Smith?"

"Yes."

"You were referred to me by the Republican party as a good realtor. I am a student at Gonzaga and I need an apartment nearby and, of course, I don't have a lot of money to spend. Do you think you could help me?"

"I think I have just the thing. Meet me on the corner of Bridgeport and Nevada. There is one on Bridgeport not far from there. What time could you be there?"

"I'll be there in ten minutes."

We walked up the stairs in the back to a nice little apartment on top of a house. It had a bedroom, living room, kitchen and bathroom. No dining room but I didn't have a table and chairs anyway. I felt like I would be living in Anne Frank's hideout in Amsterdam.

I was finally peaceful, at home. I was more comfortable in my own surroundings. However, I isolated myself from school and family. I had no friends. I didn't trust anyone—not men or women—the loss of trust would continue to haunt me for many years.

I didn't have a job lined up for the summer so I signed up for door-to-door sales with the Southwestern Company in Nashville,

Tennessee. I sold the Volume Library, a mini-encyclopedia and two sets of children's books. I relocated for two summers to Texas, walked thirteen or more hours each day selling books, associated with positive people and came back with a healthy check at the end of the summer. My depression went away each summer but came back when I returned to Spokane in September, where I didn't get as much sunlight; had no friends and I didn't get the exercise I'd get in warmer climates. There were no inside running tracks, at least none that I could afford. I didn't own a treadmill. My Spokane circumstances frustrated me.

After one summer I came back to some startling news. My Republican realtor, Mrs. Smith, had been killed. Her nephew came and talked to me one day about it.

"You sub-let the apartment to someone this summer, didn't you?"

"Yes."

"Well, you signed an agreement that said you would let my aunt know if you did that."

"I completely forgot. I'm sorry."

"Yeah, and now my aunt is dead."

"Do you know who killed her?"

"Some guys. We don't know if there was a connection."

"But, the girl I sub-let to goes to Gonzaga. She is from a good home in Sandpoint, Idaho. She only rented it for the summer."

"Yeah, but she kept having run-ins with my aunt. She was always complaining because the lawn wasn't mowed to her satisfaction."

Had I inadvertently caused the realtor's death? Was I just being paranoid to wonder if I did?

Chapter 30

One day after I had come back from a Southwestern summer, I turned up the heat in my bedroom as the weather had already started to get chilly. Because the apartment was in the upstairs and not insulated well, it got hot in the summer and cold in the winter months. To save money I heated only the bedroom.

I finished reading my Economics textbook and put down my assignment, then I stopped to take a break and called my Mom. I hadn't been sleeping well and I was depressed. My brain wouldn't let go of all the unresolved conflicts in my life. I still couldn't sort out all the stuff that happened to me in California. I'd wake up in the middle of the night thinking about it and couldn't get back to sleep. The insomnia started in San Francisco after Connor jilted me and it continued for four years now. I didn't have any sleeping pills and never thought about going to see a doctor to get some. The past couple nights I barely slept at all. I complained to Mom about the depression and insomnia but she discounted it as unnecessary worry.

"Oh well, we all have trouble sleeping. It's just old age. Joanie, what's that noise I hear in the background?"

"Oh, it's my stereo."

"Why do you have it turned up so loud? I can barely hear you."

"So they can't listen in on our conversation."

"What? Who's they?"

I didn't know. I had heard before that you were supposed to turn the stereo on so voices couldn't be picked up clearly by a bug, but I didn't tell her that. I changed the subject. This odd behavior though probably made my Mom frightened of me. I was different from her other kids. She didn't know how to deal with my peculiar behavior.

"You know those woodcarvings I have of German people . . ."

"What about them?"

"I want you to give them to the Monastery at St. Gertrude's' in Cottonwood. I don't want them anymore."

"No, Joanie. You keep them. I thought they were special to you."

"They are but I don't want them now. Will you do that for me?"

"All right. Are you ok, Joanie?"

"Yeah, I'm just a little depressed. I hate it here. I hate school. I hate my life."

"You need to get out and take a walk. You've been cooped up inside too much."

I learned later that giving away prized possessions was one of the signs of suicide.

Later that week I combed the walls looking for pinholes. I remembered being at a briefing once in the CIA that showed an Ambassador's office was bugged through a pinhole in the Great Seal. I never learned more about how bugging worked. I was just afraid of bugging and skeptical of pinholes. I thought someone was listening in to my conversations or could read my thoughts even when I hadn't talked to anyone. I had the feeling that someone knew about things in my life and I never told them. Having few conversations, I could remember exactly what I told people. I decided my phone was bugged because of paint marks underneath it. It sounds so ridiculous now but it was very real to me at the time. I brought the phone to the house of a boy who I had tried to recruit for the Southwestern sales program. I knew from his application that his father had been in the police. I knocked on his door. A man opened the door.

"Hi, I'm Joan. I know you used to work for the police and I think my phone is bugged. Look here underneath it where the paint marks are." I brought my phone to show him.

The man must've certainly been surprised and puzzled but he didn't laugh. "Take it down to the police station which is behind the courthouse and tell them."

"Ok," I said, hurrying on my way.

I parked nearby on Broadway and took the phone to Spokane's main police station at 1100 West Mallon. I brought it to the front desk in a paper bag.

"I think my phone is bugged. See the paint."

The officer behind the desk looked at me but didn't laugh at me either. "Give me your name and address. Here, write it down on this piece of paper."

When I did, the officer said, "We'll investigate." And so I left.

The next week, I wrote a poem to Allen Clements, a Vice President of the Southwestern Company who I admired very much. It was really a cry for help. It was something about death. I took the letter and flew out of my house, got in my yellow Volkswagen bug and tooled down the road. A policeman stopped me.

"Ma'am, may I see your driver's license and registration?"

I gave them to him.

"Oh," he said, like now he understood because he knew I was the one who had brought the phone to the police station.

"Do you know what you just did?"

"No." I was spacey as hell and agitated.

"You turned left on a one-way street going the opposite direction. Where are you going?"

"To the Post Office," I said.

He never gave me a ticket. He told me how to get to the Post Office. The Postman would have picked up mail at the house but I guess I was too paranoid to let that happen.

The next week I told my therapist, Marilyn, about this. She made me see a psychiatrist at the clinic. Even though I protested, she told me I could no longer see her unless I did.

I saw a psychiatrist at the Clinic and he did not give me a diagnosis, only a prescription for Mellarill. I didn't have to take it on a regular basis, only a couple at one time as needed. I remember attending classes at Gonzaga during that time. The Mellarill made things dark, like all the lights were turned down low. The paranoia went away and I was fine again. I saw Marilyn for the next six to eight months and never had a recurrence of paranoia during that period.

I finally graduated from Gonzaga August 18, 1984 "summa cum mediocre." I didn't care. My life would not be valued by the grades I got at Gonzaga. I also had a different approach to studying. I wanted to study the things I didn't know about, the courses that were difficult for me—economics, political science, finance and business—rather than the things I was good at—English—even though it stressed me out more. I wanted to understand my world better.

The poor Jesuits. They never knew what to do with me. I was an older student and definitely didn't fit in. I think they also suspected my mental illness. My accounting professor, who was trying to get tenure, tried to find out what my problem was and tried to fix it. I gave him a glorious end-of-the-year critique. He went beyond what was necessary to try to help me. Most of all, however, I just wanted to be left alone. I thought I could fix my problem myself.

Except for Marilyn, I kept my personal life to myself at Gonzaga. It had been a wrong choice to attend Gonzaga because I never fit in and I was only trying to escape from my problems in California but I had made the best of it. When I graduated, my family gave me some money, which I used it to buy business suits and shoes for my new career as a stockbroker. I put in storage my designer rattan sofa bed and chair and plush white rug and my other things, thinking I would be able to move them later as I made more money in the Washington, DC area. Money was tight so I opted not to buy the insurance on my storage unit.

Chapter 31

In August of 1984, I moved back to the Washington, DC area. I was thirty years old. I planned to stay with my friend, Eleanor, and her husband, Pete, in Northern Virginia until I could afford a place of my own. This was the second time I had moved to Virginia from Washington State or as Pete said, "I drifted in and out occasionally."

There are many Virginia cities in the suburbs of Washington, DC but none quite so memorable as Tyson's Corner. Back then, Tyson's Corner was the location of one of the largest and greatest shopping malls (10,000 parking spaces) on the East Coast.

Nearby McLean was where lobbyists and the really wealthy lived. The type of people who lived in these big brick homes were Senators, Representatives, Pentagon officials, FBI, CIA, Justice, Supreme Court, government officials in HUD, HEW, IRS, FAA, Dept. of Education, BLM, GAO, DOE, oil company executives, Association executives and lobbyists.

All those people get paid by American taxpayers, but if you take a look at where and how they live, it's clear that most of them feel no public obligation. They live in the nicest homes on the nicest streets with the nicest landscaping and the average American pays for it one way or another. Somehow this didn't strike me as being fair to the folks back home in Spokane, yet as a budding stockbroker I wanted to capitalize on it. I chose DC over New York City because I had lived in the DC area before so it was familiar to me.

Driving the DC area is not like driving in Spokane. Beltway driving (also known as 495 or the Capital Beltway which circles the DC area) is like no other. If you miss your exit, you just keep driving around the Beltway for an hour or so until you come upon it again. Less than a car length in front of you is appropriate; otherwise, someone will cut you off. Police never stop cars for following too closely. It would slow down traffic and they'd have to stop everyone. And many of the Beltway drivers have driven on the German autobahn where there is no speed limit and if you're behind a car going too slow, you flash your lights at them to get out of your way. Some of these super highways are only two lanes with traffic lights like Route 50 but others, like 66, are eight lanes, no stopping. And construction crews keep widening the roads to lighten the congestion.

Luscious, green, leafy trees—oak, maple, ash, scrub cedar, black walnut, locust, birch, sumac, white pine, hickory, spruce—cascade the roadways and have a calming effect on drivers. It seems the Federal Government spends more on roads and landscaping than it does on IRS agents. No one drives junkers on these roads either. There are no potholes, no ruts in the roads like back in Spokane.

The weather is generally good in the DC metro area. They have a short winter (from December to early March) although you do have to put up with high humidity in the summer in 100 degree heat which makes your clothes feel clammy and the air smell musty. August is a good time to take a vacation out of the city.

The Northern Virginia suburbs have everything in abundance as opposed to Spokane—more money, people, traffic, kinds of trees and even items in stores. I fell in love with Northern Virginia and knew it would be more lucrative to be a stockbroker there rather than in Spokane. After doing some initial interviewing, I found that I needed phone sales experience besides the door-to-door selling experience, so I immediately got a job in telemarketing with DialAmerica Marketing in Tyson's Corner and kept that job until May 1985. Off and on I also worked as a temp for Kelly Services.

The telemarketing room was small and smoke-filled at that time, but I read a little script, sold magazine subscriptions and children's books over the phone and with the help of the two managers, I was successful. But I remained broke. Telemarketing didn't pay much more than minimum wage but I was getting the experience I needed to put on my resume.

I didn't own a car. I never got the body of my VW Bug fixed after my accident and now it was toast. I left it in Spokane. Eleanor and Pete let me borrow their Volkswagen Bug. I ended up staying with them for six months and couldn't afford to pay them back till much later. I finally bought a car—a Ford Tempo which turned out to be a lemon.

I continued to interview for stockbrokerage jobs without any luck. Then I answered an ad in *The Washington Post* for a part-time, evening position as a Parabroker at Paine Webber for two financial consultants setting appointments for them. Again, the pay was not spectacular, but the experience, for me, was to-die-for.

One morning I got a phone call from my sister, Marilyn. "The storage company found water in your storage unit so do you want me to get rid of your stuff?"

I was shocked and couldn't believe my luck. "Did Larry's unit get water in it, too?" My brother, Larry, had a unit next to mine.

"No, his was fine. I don't know all the details. I just know that yours has water in it. What do you want me to do?"

"Well, maybe it wasn't much water. Maybe my rattan sofa-bed and chair will be ok."

"They're wood, Joanie. There was two to three inches of water. They'll warp."

"Oh, God! My designer furniture. So, what would you do?"

"Well, you can't leave it in there. You'll have to keep paying for the storage unit. I'd suggest trying to sell what we can in a garage sale and get rid of the storage unit."

"Ok. I guess so." My voice was low. I was again depressed. "Thanks for calling me, Marilyn."

* * *

Sunday, she called me back saying she sold the sofa-bed, chair and coffee table for less than half of what I had paid for it. However, those were the only things that sold. I was bummed but grateful for her handling my stuff when I couldn't be there. Then she proceeded to tell me what she did with the rest of my stuff. My sister and my family helped themselves.

"Mom wanted your white carpet. She's going to put it in Carole's room upstairs in her house. Karen took the desk and she wanted your skis and ski suit. Mom and Dad took the TV. Maureen took the typewriter. Connie took your bike. You said I could take your tape deck since you owed me money. Allan and Lisa took the Bose speakers. We had trouble finding the ski suit. We had trouble finding your green floral spray cushions for your couch, too. We looked in all your boxes."

I had visions of them rooting through all my carefully organized boxes. "What else didn't sell?"

"Your dresser and nightstand and bed didn't sell. I thought I would take them. We can use the nightstand for our telephone table and we can put the queen-size bed in Jeremy's room in the basement. Oh, and your Lane cedar chest didn't sell either. We can take that, too. And Dan wanted your tent. He wants to go camping with the boys."

I felt like Jesus Christ when the Roman Centurions cast lots for his clothes. My devout Catholic relatives. None of them paid me a dime. They thought they were all doing a good deed by getting rid of my things so I wouldn't have to pay the $30/mo. for a storage unit. I agreed that they were doing what was necessary but it left me with nothing.

I envisioned my sisters and mother picking over my possessions as if I had died, or had held a garage sale where the items were all free for the taking. I grieved for my possessions. I was starting over . . . again.

Chapter 32

I worked as a Parabroker for six months when the broker sitting next to me commented, "You're really good. Why aren't you a broker?"

"I don't know," I said shyly. I was good at reeling in the big fish. One older man in the firm offered me a job as his Assistant. It looked like I would inherit his book but he also had a son who worked there.

"Listen, I know someone at Laidlaw, Adams & Peck. I think I could get you an interview if you want it."

Although I had never heard of that firm, I was hungry. "I'd love it," I said.

I was too much in a hurry and thought I was good enough to become a stockbroker myself so I declined the man at PaineWebber who offered me a job as his assistant and instead interviewed at Laidlaw, Adams & Peck, located in the middle red brick/black windows Centennial Plaza II office building on Old Courthouse Road in Tyson's Corner. The office was very nice. Very professional looking. Lots of free parking. Laidlaw sounded like a law firm but it was actually the second oldest stockbrokerage firm on the New York Stock Exchange.

I got the job. I was thirty-one-years old. While I was helping some friends move that following weekend, depression hit again. I felt stressed out and sorry for myself. I was single, no prospects, no possessions, no house and no kid. In the '80's, this seemed like a major crisis for a woman my age. But so what? I tried to tell myself that this was no big deal. I had been through worse. So, why am I so weepy? I didn't know what it was but I didn't feel normal and I knew I needed to seek help, again.

I looked in the yellow pages and found an ad for depression and schizophrenia at the Northern Virginia Institute of Psychiatry (NVIP) in Springfield. I had worked for a small, private mental health clinic in Virginia as a Kelly temporary and they had some brochures on schizophrenia and manic depression which I took and saved. Now I thought I was one or both but I didn't know which one. I dialed NVIP's number.

"I need to see someone."

"Have you been in our office before?"

"No."

"Have you seen a psychiatrist before?"

"Yes."

"Where?"

"In Spokane, Washington."

"All right. I'm going to set you up with Dr. Paul Peckar and a therapist."

I hated to see a psychiatrist. I felt they were the last resort but I had no cards left in my deck. "And what is the charge?"

"The charge is $80 for a psychiatrist, $55 for a therapist and you need to pay before you see them."

I also had to pay $200 for blood tests and over $40 for medication. My insurance didn't cover any of it, except part of the medication.

The Northern Virginia Institute of Psychiatry was located in a dark brown secluded colonial office building on Hemstead Way. I liked the privacy. I walked to it on a sidewalk in the middle of an atrium of overhanging trees with dark brown benches. Secluded. Comfortingly private. The inside, however, with its white walls and dumpy office furniture didn't match the elegance of the outside.

I was shown to an office where Dr. Peckar questioned me about my prior illness.

"Who did you see at the Mental Health Clinic in Spokane?"

"A therapist named Marilyn Wilson and I don't know the name of the psychiatrist I saw. I only saw him once."

"What drug did he give you? Do you remember?"

"Yeah, I remember. It was called Mellarill. I didn't like it."

"Why not?"

"It had yucky side effects. It made it so all the lights seemed like they were turned down low. Even sunlight."

All the while I spoke to him I couldn't stop crying. For every word, it seemed there was an accompanying tear or tears. I was embarrassed but I couldn't control it.

Dr. Peckar didn't comment on the crying. He just gave me a box of tissue. "Were you having problems with paranoia?"

"Yes, I thought my phone was bugged. I brought it to the police station."

"Did the medicine help clear up your paranoia?"

"Yeah, I never had another experience."

"And what's going on in your life now?"

"My friends just moved into a new house and I'm afraid I'm just feeling sorry for myself."

After an hour or more of quizzing me, he looked satisfied and then wrote two prescriptions. One was for lithium and the other was for Trilafon, an anti-psychotic drug sometimes used in combination with lithium for manic depression.

"What is my diagnosis?"

"Bipolar, schizoaffective."

I guessed it was a good thing I saw that ad because I was both. Wow! Double whammy, I thought. I was dumbfounded. Bipolar and schizophrenic were strange words to me that were not yet in my vocabulary. I knew what bipolar meant. But, I asked him to clarify schizoaffective. He said I was definitely not schizophrenic, however, "schizo" comes from the word schizophrenic and "affective" just means it is a mood disorder. So, perhaps I had some, but not all, of the traits of a schizophrenic.

Dr. Peckar seemed to think my depression was biological; however, it seemed to me my depression was mostly situational considering the magnitude of my life crisis. But, I let it go. I didn't say anything because I was in shock. I needed to go home and have time to digest what he just told me.

I drove home and called my sister, Connie, and told her about the doctor visit and the diagnosis. Connie was shocked. She could hardly believe it and was concerned for me.

"I'm not bipolar or schizoaffective, am I? That Dr. was weird. All psychiatrists are weird. I'm not taking any of that stupid medicine. I've quit crying now. I'm fine."

"Joanie, you've had problems. Maybe you should just try taking one pill and see what you feel like. Did you get the prescriptions filled?"

"Yes, but I'm ok now. I don't need the medicine."

"Maybe you do. How will you know unless you take the pills? Just take some and call me back."

"But . . ."

"Just take them."

"Alright. I'll call you back."

I took them and in a couple of hours I called Connie back.

"You won't believe this."

"What?"

"I feel normal. One of the pills—either lithium or Trilafon or maybe both—made me feel like I've just woken up from a dream. It's as if I was in a fog and now I can feel things more clearly. For the first time in my life I feel normal."

"You took the pills?"

"Yes. And I can't believe how good I feel." I giggled as if I had been holding in the laughter for weeks.

"See. I guess that doctor wasn't so dumb after all. I'm glad for you, Joanie. You deserve to feel good. Now don't forget to take them every day."

"I won't. Remember when we were kids and Dad made us sit at the table till we took our vitamins?"

"Yeah, Dad made us take vitamins every day to ensure our health."

"Didn't we eat pretty good back then? Why did we need to take vitamins? Mom was such a good cook. She made miracle meals out of the $25 Dad gave her for groceries each week for twelve people. We didn't have much money but we had a big vegetable garden. I remember hating to hoe or weed that garden but they made us."

"I remember eating Macaroni and cheese and slush a lot—something that went far with our big family. Meat was a treat. No pop. No potato chips. They were luxuries we couldn't afford. Don't you remember? Dad read *Prevention Magazine* long before it became popular. He didn't want us to get sick. Who knows how much he spent on vitamins but they weren't expensive like they are today."

"Even the little kids had to take pills and because we didn't know what they were or what they were for, we named them. Do you remember some of the names we had for them?"

"There were roly pills. They were vitamins E and A."

"And teeth pills which were bone meal and mustard pills which were vitamin B."

"Oh, don't forget pepper pills. Who knows what they were!"

"And my personal favorite—sour pills which were vitamin C. We not only had to clean our plates, but we had to sit at the table in the morning until we took our pills. Sometimes it took us over an hour to wash down those pills."

"Oh, we hated taking those pills. Do you remember how we devised ways to get out of it? We'd pretend to have to go to the bathroom and when Mom and Dad weren't looking, we'd stuff the pills in our pocket and dump them down the toilet."

We both laughed.

"Another favorite place to hide the pills was behind a hole in the bedroom wall which was next to the kitchen."

"I almost forgot about that."

"When Dad tore down this wall later on to enlarge the living room, to his amazement, he found our stash of pills. Of course, we were grown by then."

"Well, you shouldn't have any problems remembering to take your pills now."

"I guess not."

Chapter 33

At work on Monday, I resolved to tell my Manager about my diagnosis. I was afraid a mentally ill person couldn't work in a brokerage firm and that I would have to give up the wealthy life I had planned for myself. My imagination was doing overtime. So, with tears in my eyes I told Steve my illness. I was amazed at his reaction. Steve's wife was a nurse so he probably knew about mental illness from her and although he had a surprised look on his face, he comforted me.

"You don't care?" I asked, shocked.

"No, I don't care. You can work here. That's fine."

Although puzzled, I had the biggest I-just-won-one grin on my face and returned to the bullpen to work. I was the only female broker in the office and none of the guys seemed to want to train me or maybe they just didn't have the time, so I perused the bookstore and found a book for $5 called, "Successful Telephone Selling in the '80s" by Shafiroff and Shook which was very informative. I put together my own little script and then I used the street directories for Maryland and Northern Virginia and with a little coaching from Steve, I sold some Alaska Housing bonds my first week. That was the only week I was on guaranteed salary.

We got paid monthly and I gave almost that whole paycheck to my friends, Eleanor and Pete for allowing me to stay with them. It amounted to about $1,000. I didn't think it was enough to repay their kindness but that's all I could afford at the time. After that I would be on straight commission—or straight poverty.

Meanwhile, Steve advised me to prospect in Vienna, Virginia because he said, "Everyone calls McLean, Virginia and Potomac and Bethesda, Maryland." He was the manager so I assumed he knew best. Day after day and night after night I called the streets of Vienna without any luck. I would offer prospects a stock, usually Nordstrom's, which they hadn't heard of, or Nuveen, a product which was like a mutual fund of municipal bonds.

Then one afternoon, I hit pay dirt. The guy on the other end of the line, Jack Hashian, told me a short, suspenseful story. He was unmistakably the author of a book I had read.

I immediately said, "You wrote Shubumi!"

"Yes." He laughed this deep, baritone laugh.

"I couldn't put that book down. I thought a woman wrote it. So, you are Trevanian?"

He laughed that baritone laugh again, deep down in his belly. "It's my middle name."

He told me he didn't have any money to invest—that most of it was tied up with his financial advisor in Boston. So I made some notes on a 3x5 card, thinking that I would call him back another time in the future when I had something "hot."

I called him back several weeks later when I was prospecting with the stock for a company called Wickes. There had been articles about it on the front page of *The Washington Post.* I sent Jack the articles and he bought some shares from me. He also invited me out to lunch a couple of times and gave me a book written under his true name, called *Mamigon.* He even autographed it for me. Inside, it said: "To Joan, my quiet friend." I felt insulted but I never said anything. I was an introvert and he was obviously an extrovert and if he hadn't been flapping his jaws so much, maybe I would've gotten a word in.

Unfortunately, the price of Wickes soon dropped and I had to face telling him that I had lost money for him. The lady who bought the Alaska Housing bonds from me also ended up losing money and she chewed me out on the phone when I told her. I HATED this aspect of being a stockbroker. I just wasn't built for it. I didn't know how to apologize and still manage to keep the client.

In the office there was a single parent who sometimes offered me some fatherly advice. He told me the real deal. "It's churn and burn, baby," he said.

I looked at him in astonishment.

"You heard what I said. You go from one brokerage firm and after you churn and burn all your clients, you go to another firm and start all over doing the same thing there."

I must've had naïve written all over my face. "Whatever happened to caring about the client?"

"We care about them but we also care a great deal about eating."

* * *

Jack first asked me to lunch in December 1985, shortly before Christmas. We had lunch at a restaurant in Tyson's Corner. The food and the place were not so memorable but what he said was. I devoured every word. He told me about his past.

"My mother died in a car accident when I was three years old."

"You poor thing. Well, if it makes you feel any better, I never liked my mother. I always liked my father better."

"My father died from pneumonia two years later."

"So, you grew up without parents. Who took care of you?"

"Well, I got tossed around in foster homes after that. I lived with my Aunt in Montreal for a while but nobody seemed to want me. That's where I learned French, by the way. Then I lived with Mamigon, my male guardian for several years. Boy he was a brute—macho like me and he wouldn't entertain any foolishness. I was under strict orders to read all the classics and get straight A's in all my studies. This experience was actually very good for me. It taught me a lot but unfortunately I had this archaic idea of women. That was the one problem I had in my writing."

"Did you ever marry?"

"Yes. I married a girl from my youth after I returned from the Navy. I remember I went over to her house and asked her Dad if I could take her out. He was totally impressed."

"Where is she now? Are you still married?"

"She later had an affair with the next door neighbor, an insurance salesman. I found out about it from my city editor on the Boston newspaper where I was an editor. I was so hurt I went to see a psychiatrist. That was a horrible period in my life. I don't even like to think about it.

"Why do you think she did that?"

"Well, I used to spend from 9:00 p.m. until midnight every night writing books on the Civil War. She must've felt like a widow all those years and I guess it's no wonder she turned to someone else for affection."

"That's sad."

"Yes. Well, anyway I left Boston and divorced her and moved to Washington, DC. First I moved to Cleveland, Ohio but that is another story. Anyway, I had to leave behind all my children in Boston. It was hard."

"How many children do you have?"

"Four and they're all grown. They're all older than you."

"Tell me about them. What do they do for a living?"

"I have three boys and a girl. My oldest son is a successful business executive who makes more than $100,000 a year and is married to a woman who makes the same kind of money."

I couldn't help but be impressed but I wondered what Jack saw in me. *Did he think I was wealthy, too, just because I was a stockbroker?*

"My next son is the drummer in a popular music group and is married to a Playboy bunny. They have two kids—my only grandchildren."

"What type of music does he play?"

"I think it's hard rock. I'm not really sure. I've only heard them a couple of times. One time they played in the Capital Center in Washington, DC. They put me on stage with earplugs in." He laughed.

"Why did you have earplugs in?"

"Well, I just wanted to watch the crowd and their music was too loud."

"And what about your daughter? What does she do?"

"Kathy is a studying junkie. She has about ten master's degrees. I'm exaggerating a little bit but she does have several and she is a teacher. She was formerly married to a professional hockey player. She is a petite little thing—probably a size 2."

I hated her already. I was 5'9" and a size 14. "And who are we forgetting? Who is your third son?"

"Michael. I call him Michelevich. He and I are close. I love all my kids the same but Michael and I share an interest in sex that I don't share with the other two boys."

"What does he do for a living?"

"He works at the Post Office. He's a Vietnam Vet who was very affected by the war. He still has nightmares and he has some very interesting stories to tell about his time over there."

"Do all your boys have your beautiful, sexy, deep, baritone voice?

"I never noticed. I don't know but thank you for the compliment, Ma'am."

"It must hurt to be away from your kids. I can imagine it is hard for you."

"It is."

"You've been through a lot. But, you know what Goethe said."

"What?"

"That which does not kill you makes you stronger."

He laughed.

"Speaking of that, you lost money in Wickes."

"Well, it happens. It's not the first time. My money manager will rake me over the coals for this. He handles my money in Boston. It seems like every time I try to do it myself, I end up losing money."

"I'm sorry," was all I could muster. "I feel terrible." I wondered if I'd ever see him again.

"Don't worry. I won't hold it against you." After dinner, he politely escorted me to my car, said goodnight and left. He was a perfect gentleman.

Jack was kind about me losing his money but he never gave me any more to invest and I never asked him for any. We remained close friends, however. I was always honest with him and, of course, intrigued by him.

Chapter 34

"Ok, all you dancing girls can go home now." Jack would laugh and then I would nervously laugh with him. He'd be on the phone talking to me and then pretend to holler to someone else but, of course, no one was there.

I'd call him to see how his day went and though my heart raced with fear that another woman might be in his life, that maybe I might get jilted again, Jack always calmed my fears. It had been seven years since I had trusted a man; seven years without sex, seven years since I let my heart wander out without heavily guarding it. Jack must have sensed that I did not trust men and he made me laugh about it.

I told him about my sister, Carole. "She had one eye removed when she was eleven."

"Where does Carole live?"

"In Moscow, Idaho."

"What does she do for a living?"

"She's a cook at a little restaurant. She doesn't make much money but she has managed to put away a nice nest egg. She's really a great cook, too, and she has the best figure in the family. She was blessed with boobs, small hips and a tiny waist."

"Is she married?"

"No, but she would like to be. She's so hopeful even though she's never even dated."

"She is exactly what I am looking for—no debt, good cook, nice body and she'll probably treat me better than you do. Tell her I'm available. Why am I wasting time with you? Call her now. Tell her I'm available."

We both laughed.

Jack was always a gentleman. He was never the type of man to push sex or lure a woman in without full knowledge of what was about to transpire. But I couldn't believe the filthy language coming out of his mouth. It didn't fit a man of such importance, of such high stature. Here he was a best-selling author, a successful speechwriter, a millionaire and a high government spy and he was talking dirty to me.

And I couldn't believe the power it had over me. He could make me come with only words. Embarrassed and a little offended, I wanted to believe his words weren't that powerful but my body said otherwise. I can't even remember what he said. I just remember I had to cross my legs. My panties were moist, almost wet. To him, I think it was foreplay.

One evening we were laying on the pink couch in his study and he was slowly undressing me. He seemed to notice I was turned off.

"But, what?" he said.

"But, you have a bald head."

"So . . ."

"So, my Dad has a bald head. And, since you shaved your beard off, you look like my Dad or one of his brothers. This feels like incest. I can't do it. Let's get dressed."

Jack laughed his deep, baritone laugh from down in his gut. "Oh, come on. I'm not your father," he said smiling.

"Well, ok." Then I got a sudden idea. "I know. I'll close my eyes. Ok, I'm ready. Let's get it over with."

This time we both laughed.

Then he kissed me and I kissed him back and after about five minutes the bells and whistles were going off when he suddenly started fiddling with himself, fiddling with his balls. My mind raced. I did not know what to think of it. I was surprised and taken aback. I wondered if he was gay or something. I wondered if I should say something.

"What are you doing?" I said.

"This damn thing. I'll have to get it fixed. I'm sorry Miss Humperdink but we'll have to do this another time."

"Get what fixed? What are you talking about?"

"Oh, I never told you?"

"Told me what?"

He looked frustrated that he had to explain. "I was married to the heir of a well known soap fortune."

"But, I thought you said . . ."

"She was my second wife."

I looked at him in amazement.

"Well, she was a nasty drunk and evidently suffered from depression and drank to medicate herself."

"How long were you married to her?"

"Three days, I think. My memory is fuzzy. And, to make matters worse, I deeded her several properties in Virginia as a wedding gift. I was showing off to her dad."

"So, I don't see the connection . . ."

"Let me finish. One night while I was sleeping, the nasty drunk came in with a board and maimed me for life. She ruined my penis. I had to have a penal implant put in and now I guess the darned thing isn't working. The mechanism to make it hard must be broken."

"Don't worry, I won't hold it against you."

He laughed. "Yeah, because it's limp, that's why."

* * *

Jack showered me with gifts—a luxurious bathrobe, some trendy perfume, and a microwave oven. The bathrobe was pink and a size Small.

"Try it on," he said.

"No. I already know it won't fit. I wear a size Large." I gave it back to him.

He wasn't letting me off easy. He gave it back. "Just put it on. Put it on for Chrissakes!"

"Ok." I tried it on. The sleeves came up to my elbows and I couldn't get the front closed. "Satisfied?"

"Ok, I'll give it to my daughter, Kathy, and get you another one."

He bought me a beautiful, soft, royal blue bathrobe, size X-Large. He liked shopping in department stores and loved having the salesladies wait on him hand and foot. I absolutely loved the gifts and him.

In a letter to his kids that he shared with me, he wrote, "I have been seeing a woman of magnificent proportions . . . she's five-ten . . . whom I got to know when she was my stockbroker. As usual, I'm too old for her and certainly can't support a woman in my straited circumstances . . .Her name is Joan." I thought that was a rather nice way of telling them I was tall and fat.

* * *

Jack's birthday was February 2. He was born in 1926 and was 60 years old. I was 32. He wanted to celebrate his birthday by going to dinner and a movie. I was nervous because what in the hell do you get a millionaire for his birthday? And, since he showered me with so many expensive gifts, I couldn't think of anything comparable that I could afford. It had to be thoughtful, classy, pricey but not too expensive. I wracked my brain. Nothing came to mind. I finally settled on a gold Cross pen and I had his name engraved on it. I figured he could use it signing those bestseller books of his.

Before he opened the present at dinner, he said, "My kids tell me I'm not very good at receiving gifts. I hope you won't be disappointed."

I couldn't imagine that he wasn't good at it because he was so good at giving gifts but his kids were right. There was no surprise in his face, no giddy, child-like wonder, nothing. He was unbelievably matter-of-fact and dull about it. But, at least he thanked me a couple of times.

In the movie theater he kept trying to hold my hand and I kept subtly pushing him away. I'm sure he was puzzled but for Christsakes, he was twice as old as I was and a zillion times as rich. *What am I doing with him? Does he see me as a plaything? His daughter-in-law is a Playboy bunny. Am I Jack's Playboy bunny?*

* * *

By March work was rolling along at the office. One top producer with a corner office was a Jewish guy who I nick-named Hercules. Fresh from drug rehab, he was an extremely strong closer and he would go around trying to steal clients from unsuspecting brokers. He had his own clients or prospects snowed into believing he knew exactly what the economy would do in the future even though at the time most government experts did not know.

A broker he successfully stole clients from was a man who Ellen, the cashier, called "the chicken man." She called him that because he was always talking about going to Roy Rogers for chicken. Phil was a tall guy with black hair and glasses and had a large belly on him. He snacked all day and made smacking sounds with his lips and tongue. He tended to repeat things over and over, and he liked to reminisce—he'd tell you details about various Senators or DC gossip or who used to be down on 14th Street at the old DC office. He repeated this sometimes several times a day. Will Moncure, a trader, mimicked him flapping his arms and squawking like a chicken.

One morning a client of Phil's arrived while he was back at his desk getting a prospectus. Hercules wandered in, monopolized the client and persuaded her to become *his* client. It was obvious Phil was hurt by this but he never raised a fuss. He just let him take her. I wanted to tell Hercules off for Phil but as my mother would say, it wasn't any of my business so I kept my mouth shut.

I set up an appointment on Saturday morning with a couple who had $100,000 in their children's trust fund. Hercules showed up, although he never worked on Saturdays. Because the bullpen was so open and my voice carried, he must've heard me make the appointment the day before. He sauntered into the conference room where we were sitting to make a pot of coffee and made some casual remarks to my prospects. I had never seen him make a pot of coffee before and I suspected he was trying to monopolize my clients. I didn't let him. I effectively punted him.

He was about to say something when I said, "Are you through there?"

He looked at me, scowling and then left the room.

I had to walk to the storage room next door to get a prospectus of the fund I was trying to sell and there was Hercules.

"Don't you ever talk to me like that again!" he shouted.

"Look, I know what you are trying to do and it just ain't going to happen! Stay away from my clients!"

"Or else what?"

"Just stay away! They're mine. You didn't bring them in!" My voice rose.

"You're just going to lose them."

"If I lose them, then it's my own business. I brought them in so it's my right to try and sell them."

"You stink!"

"You stink worse!"

I left. Burning in anger, I had to return to sit with my prospects and pretend like nothing ever happened. They never gave me their account. I wrote up what happened that day and the manager sent it up to our Vice President in New York. Hercules left the office shortly after that to go with a firm in Reston. I never saw him again.

If I hadn't had so much therapy, I would never have had the courage to stand up to him like I did. I functioned very well in the office. It was as if I was normal and fighting battles as a normally assertive person would. At that time, I did not tell Dr. Peckar of the clash. I assumed personal relations were not his business. I also did not discuss it with Jack. I dealt with conflict myself as best I could.

Chapter 35

"If you want to be a writer," Jack told me, "sit on your butt and don't move and write." I consider that the best piece of advice I ever got. Although I wanted his help with my writing, when I was dating him, we never discussed it.

We did, however, discuss his books. I read all his books. Whenever I finished one, I called him to discuss it. No matter what he was doing or who he had visiting, he always stopped and gave me a few moments to discuss it.

He wrote four bestsellers (*The Eiger Sanction, The Loo Sanction, The Main and Shibumi*) and received $250,000 for each one.

"What was your favorite book that you wrote?"

"I don't know," he said, pausing to think. "Probably *The Main* I guess. That has a lot of me in it."

"I thought the ending was awesome. Do you actually play pinochle?"

"Yes. Why?"

"My folks play it. Are you sure you're not my father or one of my uncles?"

He laughed.

I was in awe of Jack for being such an accomplished writer. Of course, he had written thirteen novels about the Civil War prior to ever publishing his first bestseller and none of those were ever published. With pressure from his kids, after his fourth bestseller he sold the rights to his pen name to his Agent, and then wrote several books under his true name; however, these were never as successful.

"Say, Jack, what church did you tell me you go to?"

"I belong to the Orthodox church. Why?"

"Could I go to church with you sometime? I want to hear your beautiful baritone voice singing." Our relationship had grown closer over the last couple of months. I even held his hand in public. The age difference no longer bothered me. I was beginning to think of him as a possible candidate for marriage but I wanted to test the waters. In my hometown of Cottonwood, if you were serious about someone, you brought them to church, especially around the holidays. If Jack was serious about me, I was sure he would take me to church.

"No, that's not a good idea."

"Why not?" This sent up a red flag to me. I was feeling him out. I thought Jack was only interested in me sexually. I was his plaything, his Playboy bunny, but I wasn't good enough for him to take me to church.

"I could sing for you now." He bellowed out a couple of tunes. I wondered why he kept skirting the issue.

"But I'd like to see your church. Is it because of some of your older lady friends at church who ogle after the best-selling author?"

"Don't be ridiculous." He squirmed like he wanted to change the subject. I wasn't about to let him go this easy. I knew I had uncovered the real reason.

"I thought older women didn't do it."

He looked surprised but he seemed to realize I was serious. "Some do."

"But, aren't they all dried up?"

"They use lubricating cream."

I was always amazed at the little tidbits of knowledge I learned from him.

* * *

In April my roommate, Leslie, left so I placed another ad in *The Washington Post*. It took about a month to find someone. A girl named Sandra who was younger but more persuasive than me answered my ad and came to look at the place but since we were both in the same boat, trying to get a roommate; she wanted me to move to her place instead. Sandy said she lived on Commons Dr. in colonial brick apartments in Annandale near the Heritage Village Shopping Center. Since I could no longer afford to pay full rent at my place, she convinced me to give up my place and move in with her.

Meanwhile, Laidlaw had given me an old typewriter and this humongous desk which I moved to my new place. I thought for sure it was a sign that I had done the right thing.

I was so broke yet I had to see Dr. Peckar once a month in order to get refills on my prescriptions. He was not sympathetic to my financial problems.

"I don't have any money to pay you this month. Can I defer the payment until I make enough money to cover it?" I always paid him at the beginning of each session so if I couldn't pay, we didn't have a session.

He flatly refused. "No, if you don't have any money, you can go to a clinic in Alexandria where you can pay on a sliding scale."

I didn't think he heard me. "I said I don't have ANY money."

"I'm not a charity organization, Joan, and you can either borrow the money to pay me or you can go to the clinic."

I wasn't living a life of luxury. I lived in an apartment with a roommate. I didn't go out to eat. I never went to a movie. I never bought any clothes. I scrimped on groceries. Yet I continued to believe the dream was always just around the corner. I worked hard on the phone selling for eight to twelve hours each day and partial days on Saturdays, and thought it would soon pay off. I just needed time.

I thought it unfair of Dr. Peckar to refuse to see me unless I could pay and that obviously he was only in the business of psychiatry for the money. To go to another psychiatrist meant I would have to start all over again with my meds and my life history. Just thinking about it exasperated me. I felt tied to him because he had been able to correctly diagnose my problem and the medicine worked so well, I appeared normal. No one could tell I had a mental illness. And, besides, I felt I would probably get someone inferior because if they worked at a clinic, they weren't good enough to have their own practice. I swallowed my pride, braced myself for more stress from Mom and borrowed the money from Dad.

I wanted to think that luck was in the next phone call like I had always believed, but I was having difficulty selling at the brokerage firm. I wasn't good at closing and, worse yet, face-to-face and conversational selling bothered me because of my memory deficits. Selling over the phone was fine because I could use cheat sheets about the products but when clients came in the office to set up an account or discuss further investments I had to make eye contact with them. Seeing their facial reactions distracted me. I'd lose my train of thought. I had to look away to focus and then I couldn't remember what I was trying to say. I worked very hard, putting in long hours to compensate for my shortcomings and I blamed myself for not being up to par with other brokers in the business but I later learned it was part of my illness.

By July, I was having difficulty paying rent so Sandy kicked me out. I didn't think I could ask my friends to help me move again. I was embarrassed. So, I moved my stuff in storage myself and left my desk and bed with Sandy.

I wasn't making enough money at the brokerage firm so I did some temporary work through Kelly Services to supplement my meager brokerage income. I felt like a failure but I had no other choice. I had no money and now I had no home. I spent four nights sleeping in my car and one night sleeping in Dunn Loring Park, only to find a policeman, shining his flashlight in my face, ask me what I was doing there. I thought it was obvious. I was homeless and too embarrassed to ask anyone for help, including Jack.

Mom was screaming about all the money I was borrowing and I didn't know myself when or if I would be able to pay it back. Although I couldn't afford it, I needed my own place. Tired of roommates, especially ones who kicked me out because I couldn't pay; I applied to get an apartment at the Hamlets in Alexandria. The apartment I wanted wouldn't be vacant for two months. It overlooked beautiful trees in the back. I waited for that apartment.

For the next two months, I slept on a couch in the basement of my sister's old boyfriend's condo.

I was afraid to tell Jack about my financial woes. I thought he might never want to see me again.

I didn't talk to my psychiatrist, Dr. Peckar, about it as he wasn't very sympathetic about my financial problems. If I could cut out his monthly visits, I'd have more money, but then I wouldn't be able to get the drugs I needed. It was a vicious cycle.

I made $18,000 each year. The median income in the Washington, DC area was $30,000. I came up short each month. And I couldn't keep borrowing from Dad. Every time I called home Mom made a snide remark about all the money they were giving me. I knew my folks weren't rich and I agonized over the stress it caused.

* * *

My two brothers and their wives came to visit in October, shortly after moving into my new apartment. They visited the Smithsonian during the day and we ate out but they were a little surprised at what they found for accommodations at my place. I had no furniture whatsoever. I had my electric typewriter on a cardboard box on the floor. The only other thing I had was an inflatable air mattress. I let Allan and Lisa sleep on that with my comforter. We moved the "bed" to the living room. Don and Melissa and I slept on the hardwood floor under Melissa's blanket. Melissa had made a patchwork quilt as a wedding present but she felt so sorry for me she gave it to me.

I'm sure they went back home with stories about how their sister, the stockbroker, was living. I continued to be grateful for the $1,500 Dad sent to me earlier that year but I did not live in luxury.

I lived in that apartment without any furniture for over a year until one day my dear friend, Eleanor, came to my door. She and her friend, Simone, delivered a black Colonial couch which had a missing cushion so she gave me a green striped one to replace it. It was fine although the three of us had difficulty getting it in the door. I covered the odd cushion with a red and black plaid car blanket and it almost looked like it was supposed to be that way. Having a couch to sit on was like being back in civilization after a long trip through the bush. Their generosity touched my heart. I never cried in front of them. I don't like people to see me cry. But tears streamed down my face after they left.

One day Jack and I were in Alexandria in the vicinity of my apartment and he wanted to stop and see my place. I panicked. I had this queasy feeling that I would lose his friendship if he saw how I lived but I decided to go through with it anyway.

It was not the life that he had imagined that I lived as his stockbroker—everyone "knows" stockbrokers are wealthy. My one-bedroom apartment in the Hamlets was located on Dunster Ct. with beautiful trees surrounding the back and a façade of dark brick in the front. Upon entering, he gasped and said, "Maybe I should've bought you some furniture."

Inside there were bare floors and the black couch that Eleanor and her friend, Simone, had given me with the red plaid car blanket covering one cushion. No coffee table. No end tables. No other chairs. The connecting dining area had a cheap, white plastic table and chairs, more suitable for an outside patio. On it stood my electric typewriter. There was no bed or dresser in the bedroom. I slept on the floor on the double air mattress.

We never made it to the bedroom, however. I wanted to take his mind off my pitiful place so I started fooling around with him in the living room. We ended up making love on that old couch. He never ever said a word about my place again.

Chapter 36

We were in bed when I asked, "How many ex-wives do you have in that closet of yours?"

"Only three."

"Why didn't you tell me that before? I thought you were married twice."

"I was too embarrassed to say that I had been married three times."

"I told you my secrets, and that I'm bipolar schizoaffective. You said it didn't matter to you."

"It doesn't."

"Well, then why did you think three wives would matter to me?"

"Good point. I'm sorry."

"Who is the third one? What does she do?"

"She's a psychologist."

"Why did you divorce her?"

"We got along very well, actually. She even called the kids "our kids." There were no problems until one day I wanted it and she no longer did."

"Sex?"

"Yes."

I had never met any of his ex-wives and only one son, Michael, who had a deep baritone voice like his Dad. His kids were all older than I was, extremely successful and I was penniless, hadn't done anything of importance with my life and felt they would treat me with contempt. I imagined that they thought the only reason I was in love with Jack was for the money. Because Jack was very wealthy, he always had people around him asking for a handout or a loan. I didn't want Jack's money. I wanted to make my own way in this world. Of course, I wanted him to tell me how to become a bestselling author but I should've realized that he had had many women in the past who wanted the exact same thing. While we dated, he never offered any advice and I never pressed him for any.

I realized I loved Jack the day a little bird fell injured in his backyard. Jack went out of his way to nurture that little bird back to health. He tried hard in everything he did. He drove a couple of miles to the grocery store with the sole purpose of buying blueberries for the little bird. They were out of season and expensive but he bought them. And he was so tickled at the little bird's progress in recovering. He gave me blow-by-blow reports each day by phone.

That is what I felt he did to all God's creatures whether it is someone down on their luck, or stuck in a lowly occupation, or someone who was struggling to get ahead without the help of privilege. He often befriended lower class people who he thought were intelligent or had other redeeming qualities. He took me under his wing, accepted me for me. Unconditional love—that's what it was. That's why I loved him. I never forgot it.

Funny thing was I started accepting him for him, too. He always wore this god-awful navy blue knit cap. I hated it. I thought he should have worn something to show more his status as a successful author and millionaire—maybe an English tweed or a gray fedora. But he wore that damned old cap all the time. To me he looked like a garbage man or a hood in that cap. He even wore it in the author's photo on one of his espionage books. I never told him how much I hated it. Then one day when I realized the unconditional love he offered me, I decided it didn't matter what hat he wore as long as *he* liked it and felt comfortable in it.

I loved almost everything about him—except when he corrected what I thought was my excellent English, or told me how to drive and it was never good enough for him and, of course, wore the ugly old navy blue cap.

* * *

In January 1987, I saw an ad in *The Washington Post* for a part-time telemarketer position that paid an hourly wage. It was for a company called Colorado Prime that sold a shop-at-home food service. Colorado Prime was located in a two-story gray office building at 7115 Leesburg Pike near Haycock Rd. in Falls Church, Virginia not far from Tyson's Corner.

I called to inquire about it and they told me to call back. That was a test they used to see how I sounded on the phone and whether I could sell myself. I would be setting appointments for a Food Sales Representative to come into a customer's home and sell freezers and frozen foods. I liked sales, anything that wasn't straight commission, so I hired on. I worked twenty hours a week, evenings and Saturdays and got paid approximately $8,000 per year for it. I liked it so well I kept the job for four years.

The best telemarketer in the room was an older lady named Marty Crocker, sort of a grandma-type, good at building rapport with the customers and just as good at cutting them off at the pass so they didn't divulge their whole life history before she could set an appointment. Then there was Polly Flores, a roly-poly telemarketing manager with a big heart, and Murray Yeoman, the Puerto Rican sales manager who I teased because I thought he was stuck on himself. A lot of others came and went. There was a high turnover.

I loved this telemarketing room. I found it relatively easy to set appointments and it was fun to compete like the old days in selling books door-to-door. I always came in second to Marty in the room. I found a richness in the people who worked there. Each was unique. Each one had his or her own story, which could fill a book. They made me laugh at life. And we were all in the same boat—struggling to make our own dream of prosperity come true.

* * *

During the two-year time period from May 1985 to August 1987 while I was a stockbroker, I had borrowed a total of $3,500 from my parents plus they had given me some money for trips. Dad sent me $450 for Connie's wedding and $400 to take a trip up to New York City in 1987 to visit the Shrine of Our Lady of the Roses and pray to the Blessed Virgin Mary in Flushing, New York, which was my Dad's idea so that I would not continue to live in poverty the rest of my life. He really thought I would receive a miracle.

I hadn't even been going to church regularly but I went to see the appearance of the Blessed Virgin Mary and prayed the rosary and paid my respects to the "beautiful" statue. Yet I thought the whole thing was rather hokey and contrived. And it didn't create any miracles. I remained near the poverty level. The trip was Dad's way of saying he and Mom were tired of all the money I was borrowing from them. Dad never complained about it to me. He was always cheerful in giving to a family member in need. But Mom was a whole different story.

"You can't keep borrowing money from us, Joanie. What do you think we are—millionaires?"

"I know, Mom. I don't plan to."

"I mean it. That's enough."

"Ok. I just don't have enough to pay rent and I have to pay for all my stupid medicine and my doctor visits, too."

"Then why don't you get a real job? We're not a bank."

"No one said you were. Things will turn around at work. You'll see."

"Awk. You'll be draining us of all our savings before that happens. What about those secretarial jobs? Why don't you go back to them? You used to have enough money to live on."

"Yeah, yeah. That's why I got a college degree—to go back to secretarial work."

"Well, at least it paid the bills."

"All right. I won't borrow any more money from you. Happy now?"

* * *

On July 17, 1987 four of us rookies in the office were let go due to lack of production. Jock Hazeltine who was manager at the time said, "If anyone should have succeeded, it should have been Joan because she worked so hard."

Being fired might have devastated me or sent me into a deep depression if I had not been on lithium. I always took my medication faithfully so being fired only made me feel a sense of relief that my struggle was over. I had lost and now I could go on with my life. I had chances to go to other firms but they were all straight commission and at this time I felt pressure from Mom and Dad about all the money they were giving me and I was tired of poverty so I got out of the business altogether.

A headhunter had called me a month ago and told me that if I didn't find a mentor in the business pretty soon, I would go out of the business. She was dead right. The only mentor I found, the only person I have ever wanted to be like in my whole life was Jack Hashian. I finally admitted that my true vocation in life wasn't being a stockbroker.

For the next three months I worked for Kelly Services as a temp. Then in October I got a day job as a secretary for the Institute for Defense Analysis (IDA) located near my apartment on Beauregard Street in Alexandria. My Mom said, "Hallelujah!" It was so close I could walk to work. Basically a military think-tank, my little department worked on the Critical Technologies Project—preventing U.S. technology secrets from escaping into the wrong hands, e.g., the Soviet Union, China, etc.

Chapter 37

In the Spring of 1988 I offered to give Jack a ride to the hospital for his surgery. I was working for IDA at the time. He was having surgery to fix his penal implant. There wasn't much you could give him that he didn't already have or that he couldn't buy himself. But helping him when he needed it was a form of love, which I could give him.

He had to be at the hospital at 6:30 a.m. for tests. The hospital was in Maryland. I wanted to drive my Ford Tempo because I was familiar with it but Jack wouldn't hear of it. He wanted me to test drive his light blue Mazda 626 while he was in the hospital and at home recuperating. He encouraged me to buy the Mazda, saying it was far superior to the Tempo. I didn't know anything about cars so I agreed.

We were running a little late and I didn't have time to adjust the mirrors. That was my second mistake. My first mistake was offering to drive the old bag of wind. It was a drive from hell.

We got out on the Beltway with Jack yelling at me about my driving. Then I couldn't see in the driver's side mirror when a car came up alongside me and I cut him off. The guy blasted his horn and I thought Jack was going to go through the roof. When he got to the hospital, his blood pressure was so high he had to wait till it subsided until he took the tests.

When he was ready to come home I sheepishly called him and he didn't have any other offers and was anxious to get home so he agreed to let me come and get him. I brought along a box of Russell Stover chocolates—his favorites. This time I had adjusted the mirrors and tuned the radio in to the station I liked. He later got mad at me for doing both. The ride went without a hitch.

After I brought Jack home from the hospital, I tried to take over. He had stitches on his balls and I could imagine how sore they must've felt. Unfortunately, I added to his pain. "I'm in charge now," I said.

I thought of what my mother would do if her child was sick or hurt. Attention and love were scarce commodities around our house.

There wasn't enough mother to go around to ten children. But when I was sick, I got all sorts of attention. It was the one and only time I felt loved by her. Mom would feed me chicken noodle soup and pour cold orange juice or hot lemon juice or fenugreek tea down me. She'd put Vick's Vaporub on my chest with a diaper she had warmed in the oven. She'd check in on me frequently during the day, making sure my pillows were fluffed and that I had enough covers. Normally she'd never touch me except for a spanking but when I was sick she'd feel my forehead for fever, plump my pillows and rub my back. Being sick to me meant you were pampered and loved.

I wanted to do the same thing for Jack. Here was my chance to make points with him. But, he snarled. This was obviously the wrong thing to say. He stomped his feet and gave me a stubborn look of pure hatred. It was as if a foreign agent had just double-crossed him and he was going in for the kill.

"Oh, for Christ's sake. You're not in charge. Why do women always have to think they're in charge? I'm the man. I'm in charge."

He said it so vehemently and so loud it frightened me. He didn't take kindly to this affront to his manhood. He wanted to make sure I knew my place and that I was not in charge of him. He was raised mostly by a guardian who was a tough son-of-a-bitch and taught him to be macho and "take it like a man." But I wasn't giving up.

"You are not!! You're sick and I'm in charge now. I want to change those sheets on your bed. They probably haven't been changed in awhile and I don't want you sleeping with dirty sheets. I brought this clean pair to put on. They're the dark brown ones. The ones you like." I had bought them overseas at the PX. I thought they looked lovely with his intricately carved, mahogany, queen-size, four-poster bed with canopy. "I'm giving them to you. Now go sit down while I finish changing your bed."

"Oh my God! You're not changing my sheets." He was yelling at me. Jack's blood pressure went through the roof again.

"I am too." I yelled back.

"Lady, I don't know where you get off but you're not changing my sheets. My sheets are fine." He said this as if it were the last word. He didn't know me very well. Persistence is my middle name.

I started removing the white sheets from his bed. He soon saw that I wasn't about to take no for an answer so he began helping me, although begrudgingly. He mumbled something inaudible and kept snarling words at me in another language, probably Turkish, maybe Armenian.

Now I was seething inside. My good deed turned out to be a disaster. My mother, who had dominated my father, had obviously left something out in her example of how to handle men.

We both walked away with wounded egos and hurt feelings. Jack treated me like a stranger and fed me some of my own silent treatment medicine. This unnerved me. He was the gregarious extrovert in the relationship while I was normally the quiet one.

Then he went to the store to get a prescription filled and he brought me back a piece of gourmet fish as a sort of peace offering. I refused it, saying "I don't want it. I want to go home. Could you please move your car? It's in back of mine." I was not going to be appeased by a stupid piece of fish. Jack looked baffled. "Ok, then. I'll give the fish to my friend, Steve."

"Go ahead. I don't care." I felt bad being this much trouble, asking him to move his car, when I knew he must be in pain but there was no way I would stay there unwanted and unloved. If I saw him again anytime soon it would be both our misfortune.

We made up after that and Jack never held it against me. He didn't hold grudges. But he later remarked he was amazed that he had spoken to me as if I were his wife.

* * *

I finally found another job—through my sister, Connie. She had a friend, Susan Kuwana, who was a manager at a company called BTG (the letters don't stand for anything). I got a job there through her in August 1988. Basically, a software engineering firm, I was hired as a Configuration Management Specialist. Our department worked on contract documents for the Federal Aviation Administration (FAA). Every time even a minor change was made to the FAA contract, we had to document that change.

BTG was housed in the block long, white, ten-story high Department of Transportation building near L'Enfant Plaza on Virginia and D Streets in southwest Washington, DC. When printed out, contract attachments were voluminous and we carted several boxes of them, on a regular basis, over to the FAA five or six blocks away, pushing a dolly over old, crumbling sidewalks in our suits and heels. Rarely did I find a gentleman willing to help.

Chapter 38

One day I drove over to Jack's red brick house with black shutters on the long pipe-stemmed driveway. He opened the front door and stood on the step and motioned for me to come to him. We were about the same height but when he stood on the step he was taller than me. He liked this. He smiled.

"Do you want to go for a drink with me in Vienna?"

"Sure. The Vienna Inn?"

"No, I thought we could go somewhere else. Sort of a last fling in case something happens."

"What are you talking about? What's going to happen?"

"Oh, nothing. That's probably a bad idea. You'd better go. I don't want you to be here when they pick me up."

"Who is picking you up? What are you talking about?" I suddenly got it. It was the spy stuff he was involved in. "You mean them, don't you?"

"Yes, and I don't want you to be here."

"Ok, I won't." That ended going out to dinner. "How are they picking you up? By car?"

"No, by helicopter."

"Where? I don't understand."

"Behind the house. Now, will you please go?"

"Ok, I won't ask any more questions. I'll just leave."

"Are you afraid for me?"

"No, why? Should I be?"

He assumed I knew more than I did. I didn't know anything but I remembered someone at the CIA talking fondly of Trevanian as if he worked for the Company but I never associated the two until now.

I thought he must be a high level spy if they came to pick him up in a helicopter. Once when I was at his house he showed me a check he had gotten for doing something. The envelope did not say it was from the CIA. So, who did he work for? He wouldn't tell me what he did but I thought the money was probably too little.

"I always get afraid before I go. It turns my stomach into knots. You'd better leave now, Miss Humperdink. They'll be here any minute."

I kissed him on the forehead. "Go with God, Hash. I suppose you'll come back with a sun tan." Last winter he came back from somewhere with a golden tan. He never said a word about any of his trips, what he did or who he saw. It was all a secret.

We kissed and I left before the helicopter arrived.

* * *

In August 1988 Jack was ready to retire and I went to Charlottesville, Virginia house hunting with him. I thought I was helping *him* find a house but Jack saw it differently. We didn't really see anything we liked, and on the long ride home, he commented to me about us being together. He smiled.

I wrinkled up my nose and said, "You should be with your kids." I didn't ever want to come between him and his kids. I thought he had a right to know his grandkids in his old age.

He grew quiet which was unusual. He didn't say anything the rest of the way home. After that trip he turned on me. He was always a little antagonistic toward me and he flatly said that he was going to give his furniture to the neighbors and then laughed sadistically even though he knew I needed decent furniture desperately. I felt like I had lost him and I didn't know what I had done to deserve such punishment.

He never said goodbye. I called his house once and the phone was disconnected.

Chapter 39

One Saturday I fetched *The Washington Post* from my front door and casually tossed it on my bed. I went to the kitchen, made a pot of coffee and took a cup back to my room so that I could have my coffee and read the newspaper. I hurriedly glanced at the front page and then took a second look.

To my astonishment, there on the front page was Dr. Peckar, my psychiatrist. Someone had sent him a pipe bomb in the mail and it blew up in his face. This happened on June 1, 1990. Three-fourths of his body was burned and his office and windows were blown away.

The bombing not only devastated Dr. Peckar's life; it would soon devastate my life as well. Not long after the bombing, I received a call from a psychiatrist who was helping re-direct Dr. Peckar's patients to other psychiatrists in the area. I had a choice between a woman, Dr. Cynthia Denver, who believed heavily in psychotherapy and a young, male psychiatrist, Dr. Geoffrey Adler, who had done a lot of research at NIMH and who basically believed in medication to treat patients. I chose Dr. Adler because I felt my problem was basically a chemical imbalance in the brain and with medication, I was normal. I didn't think I needed therapy.

I saw Dr. Adler, who was a year younger than me, from June 1990 until the end of June 1991. He and Dr. Denver both initially examined me and they both thought I was over-medicated. I had been taking about five Trilafon pills, 4 mg., and they felt I exhibited a flat affect. They felt my arms and said I was rigid. They also commented on my monotone voice. So they both agreed I should be weaned off that drug.

I hated and feared changing psychiatrists. I had to start all over with my meds and life history. As is normal, they decreased the dosage each month until I was completely weaned off the drug by December. I was ecstatic that I didn't have to take so much medicine and I actually felt better. My voice wasn't so monotone anymore and I didn't feel so drugged.

In December I started experiencing chronic insomnia, although at the time I never discussed it with Dr. Adler because I didn't see that it related to my illness. One of the greatest aspects of experiencing mania is this euphoric, maybe a little wild, state of mind. Some people quit taking their meds because of that.

My creativity skyrocketed around Christmas; I put a doggie stocking on the door of some of my cohorts with their name on it in gold letters. The stocking was red and green, small, and said, "Doggie Doggie Doggie Doggie Doggie Doggie" across the top of it. It also had a white cloth bone with a red ribbon hanging from the top of the stocking. So, on Friday, my last day with the FAA's AAP, after they had gone home, I passed out envelopes on everyone's desk with a dog biscuit in it and a note which read:

> *Frank Bassett has a little Doggie stocking hanging on his door. This is a little something to go with it. Take it to him when he comes in and bark like your favorite dog or wish him a Merry Christmas. Thank you for your cooperation.*

I lucked out. No one had ever played a joke on him before. I also played the joke on Murray at Colorado Prime. It was a tremendous hit at both the FAA and Colorado Prime. At a regional sales meeting in Delaware shortly before Christmas, Polly, our telemarketing manager, told the group what I had done to Murray. They said the Regional Sales Manager, Tom Scovolla, thought it was so good he couldn't stop laughing. Murray was a good sport about the whole thing. He was an attractive guy but sometimes he had an over inflated sense of his self worth and I let him know it.

I also wrapped up two Christmas boxes with nothing in them and enclosed the following note:

> *You seemed to enjoy the Christmas present that I gave you last year so much that this year I wrapped it. Merry Christmas!*

I gave these to two different people and told them to pass it on if they smiled when they read the note.

I also ran around taking pictures of people in the office—single shots and later gave them each their own picture after I had them developed. One of the sales reps at Colorado Prime put a red stocking cap on and in the background was a picture on the wall of Saddam Hussein that you could clearly see. I drew a bull's eye on this photo and wrote "Merry Christmas from Saddam Hussein." It was priceless. I also had Murray pose with his hands on his desk in front of him. He didn't know what it was for. I surprised him by cutting out a doghouse to put around him. He looked like a bulldog. The joke was on him.

Chapter 40

In January the Gulf War was heating up. Seeing men in green army fatigues on TV reminded me of my old boyfriend, Michael. I remembered peeling away those clothes off him in Berlin.

I had not forgotten him. The Gulf War triggered old memories but I had lost touch with him. We had not spoken since my midnight phone call to him years ago, after Connor dumped me, when he told me he did not love me.

There was an African-American guy who worked for Colorado Prime in the evenings who was in the army and had access to the Pentagon's finder index who told me he could get Michael's phone number if I gave him his full name, even though I didn't know his rank. He came back with the news that Army Major Michael Glenn O'Neill was living in Ft. Bragg, North Carolina and gave me his phone number.

I was ecstatic. I immediately called but got a message the phone had been disconnected. I went back to the guy who gave me the phone number and told him I thought it was a wrong number. He assured me that it was the right number and to keep trying. I called the next weekend and got through.

The delight in Michael's voice to hear from me, to hear that I had gone through the trouble of looking him up was my reward.

"How did we lose touch?"

"Oh, I guess because of the war. It doesn't matter. The important thing is we found each other again. I'm glad you called."

"You won't believe what I went through to find you."

"I'm blushing."

"You should blush. You owe me one. I called last week and I got a recording that said the number was disconnected. I almost gave up."

"I was away in the Gulf war."

"Are you still a company commander like you were in Berlin?"

"No, they told me I'd never have another job like that again. It was my favorite job. Now I'm just an Army Major in charge of airborne troops. I have some folks under me but it's not like Berlin."

I wondered what he had done to piss somebody off since he had only made it to the rank of Major. I expected him to be a Colonel by now.

"I'm getting out of this business pretty soon. I'm taking early retirement. I told you many years ago that I'm just a peacetime soldier."

"What will you do then?"

"Oh, I hope to work for some Defense Contractor if they'll have me. You said you live up in Washington, DC, didn't you?"

"Yes."

"Well, I'm going to interview with a company up there pretty soon. My sister, BJ, lives in Maryland. I'll probably stay with her but I'd love to see you again."

"I'd love to see you, too."

"Hey, do you know anything about resumes?"

"Yeah, I just put together a resume book for the men at IDA. What do you want to know?"

"I'd like your opinion on mine. Do you mind if I send it to you?"

"No, not at all."

"I have to go back to the war soon but I'll let you know when I can come up. Let me give you my military address. I've always liked the letters you wrote me."

* * *

Since the war and my manic side seemed to be at its height, on February 14, 1991, I wrote a letter to Michael's troops in the Gulf War.

Dear Troops:

Everyone in Washington is talking about the war. We hear it every day all the time at work. In the morning, at breaks, at noon. Everyone wants to know if there are any new developments. They are sad to hear of casualties, glad to hear about the success of bombings in Iraq. None of us even know anyone who is over there. We still care. That's why I'm writing you this letter.

I do know someone who knows you all though. To me he is just Michael or Sweet Pea, but you probably know him better as Major O'Neill. None other than the soldier who serves only in times of peace. But he swears he is patriotic.

Now I don't know what sort of advice he gave you to win the war (probably none, he said you all were smarter than he was) but I'd like to take this opportunity to send you some of my advice. Here are three things which you should do:

Whatever you do, don't give up. Persistence will pay off in the end. I know what it's like to be in battle. I have been in pursuit of a devil the likes of Saddam Hussein for 15 years now—Major O'Neill. I have had several skirmishes with the enemy (OTHER WOMEN) and have experienced some casualties. It seems as soon as I get close and whisper that forbidden word (marriage) in his ear, he breaks camp, ducks and hides for years at a stretch. But nothing good ever comes easy. Fortunately he is within reach now. I'm determined to get the sucker within the next year or two. I'm going to shoot one of those love darts right between his two Irish eyes. He will never know what hit him.

Be courageous. Try hard, then try harder. No one becomes a Hero unless whatever they did was extremely hard or difficult. I'm trying hard to muster the courage to ask my Sweet Pea for his hand in marriage this year, possibly next year. The hardest part for a woman under these conditions is deciding just what to wear. I think I will wear nothing but an American flag. He's so patriotic. I just know Sweet Pea will love it. Trouble is most men these days seem to prefer the YOUNG, DUMB, AND BUILT type. I am NONE OF THE ABOVE. One guy I dated described me as "of magnificent proportions"—a nice way of saying I'm tall and fat. Actually, my weight is perfect for my height . . . which varies. I'm enclosing a picture. You decide which one is me. I hope he won't notice that I've put on a few pounds since I've seen him last. I know I'm lucky. He says he likes the shy ones that don't say no and have a full refrigerator. Homeboy, my fridge is always bursting.

If danger looks imminent or you seem to be losing hope, do what I do—give it to God. Tell Him it's in His hands and let Him take care of it. I had planned to send you some St. Benedict's medals, the patron Saint for

Hopeless Cases, but there weren't enough to go around. My Dad gave me one years ago. I gave it to Michael who was more deserving.

By the way, please don't tell my Sweet Pea, er Major O'Neill, any of these secrets that I have leaked out to you in this letter. At times I have been known to have been an undercover agent for Major O'Neill but only in the winter. So, if I hear that any of you squealed, I am going to personally fly over to Saudi, get a great big scissors, and snip your tiny little pecker off!

Michael did say he loves you all. I knew he was Gay. No wonder I haven't been getting anywhere with him.

Your loving ally,

Joan K.

(my last name is Kopczynski but soon it will be O'Neill)

P.S. Don't forget to laugh. It's only a war.

P.P.S. Some of these lies are true!

I planned to include a picture of two women I knew at Colorado Prime who each had sixty-inch waists—one African-American and one Caucasian.

I loved the letter so much I wanted to share it with my old friend Jack. I called information in Boston and found his number and read it to him over the phone. He howled with laughter.

"Boy, his troops will really get a kick out of that. What was that guy's name?"

"Michael."

"How do you know him? I never heard you talk about him before."

"He is an old boyfriend. I haven't seen him in a couple of years."

"Hmmm. Well, I'm glad you found me. You went to a lot of trouble to find me."

"Not really. I just called information. But I am glad I found you again."

"Well, I'm glad, too. Say, listen. I miss you. Why don't you come up to Boston to see me?"

"No, I can't"

"Sure, you can. Don't you miss me?"

"Yes, but I love Michael." Really, I just wanted to get married and I thought Michael was a better prospect. I thought I was just a plaything to Jack. If he had been serious about me, he would have taken me with him to church or to Boston.

* * *

I continued to faithfully take my 1200 mg. of lithium each day yet each month after I was weaned off Trilafon, I exhibited many signs of mania, behavior I had never experienced before and stubbornly and fiercely refused to believe that it existed in me. I was flying high. I was impulsive. I had grandiose thoughts. I signed all my letters as "the world's greatest writer" even though the only thing I had been writing was a sucky piece, the beginning chapters to a book that depicted the FAA in Disney characters. How absurd!

And, although I never consciously thought of it, I acted like I thought I was a millionaire or I was going to be a millionaire after I published this pathetic piece. I didn't know that it takes forever to get an agent and it may take years to publish a book once you land an agent. I wouldn't have listened to anyone who told me that at the time. I just thought it was magical. Jack had written for many years before he hit pay dirt. He wrote thirteen novels about the Civil War before he published a bestseller, an espionage thriller, but I was going to be an overnight success. No one had told me that it takes fifteen years of hard work to become an overnight success.

Some force inside me was pushing me on, it seemed. Everyone experiences a little voice inside them sometimes suggesting they buy a certain thing (it just jumped out at me); however, the voice is a fog horn in a person who is manic. And I listened to no one during this time—not my doctor, not my best friend, Eleanor, and not my favorite sister, Connie. I was headstrong in believing I was doing the right thing. My judgment was so way off, a symptom of the illness. I was in la la land.

I shopped at Tyson's Corner a lot. I'd enter by Hecht's department store on the upper level and usually hit Tyson's Hallmark and Monte's, a novelty store, (both were near the mall entrance) and stroll down toward the Fashion Court, hitting Brooks Brothers on the way. Hallmark was one of my favorite stores at the time, I think because it boosted my imagination (as if I needed a boost).

I was buying gifts for everyone. I was also buying bunnies and bears for a children's museum I planned to build in Spokane, Washington. I saw a big, 6 ft. stuffed bear outside one of the mall entrances but didn't know who to ask about getting it back to Spokane. Thank God. A lot of the stuff I bought was the musical wind-up types or collector's items. I wonder how I thought a museum curator would have enough time to go around winding up these toys for museum patrons. The idea was odd, too, because I was single, never had children and never would have children. Why was I planning something for children? It was that little voice inside me that was telling me to do it.

My credit cards became weapons of mass debt (WMD). Whereas before I had always been careful with my money, never buying anything I couldn't afford and faithfully paying off the balance at the end of the month, now I was reckless and stupid with my money, never counting up the total I had spent before I was using that little plastic card again. It was as if I had told the shopkeepers my spending limit and gave them free reign to run up my balance. And I never kept a running total on my checking account. It never stopped me from writing checks and plenty were bad.

I left the mall laden with so many shopping bags it was difficult to carry them and I was so out of shape my breathing was labored. Besides Tyson's, I'd also hit Landmark Shopping Center in Alexandria, a smaller mall but closer to my home, and occasionally Fair Oaks Shopping Center which had JC Penney as one of its anchors. Fair Oaks was off Route 50 and on my way to Middleburg and then Front Royal where my friend, Eleanor, lived. Once or twice I wondered if I was doing the right thing but that little voice inside me told me to keep spending.

I was buying gifts for people who had done something for me in my life, trying to reciprocate their kindness. I guess I tried to spread a lot of love around. Each person received almost $1,000 of stuff. Most of the gifts had a theme. I had never bought in themes before or since and I don't know why I did then. It was bizarre!

I sent Jack Hashian jungle toys for his grandkids. Imagine $1,000 worth of jungle toys. I wanted him to invite his grandkids over for a big party in Boston. My brother Larry who lived in Lewiston, Idaho, and who had given me two round-trip tickets to fly home in the past, got the fish theme for his house. My sister, Connie, and her husband, Garry, who lived on a wheat farm in Moscow, Idaho, received the farm theme. My brother, Allan and his wife, Lisa, who lived in southern California near Irvine, received toys for their two-year-old son, Brian. I sent Michael O'Neill five or six stuffed Garfields because he said he liked Garfield and shirts and ties worth $1,000 total because he had just retired from the Army and was going into civilian life. I also bought Michael an expensive ring which I suppose was meant to be an engagement ring which is a good example of how far my judgment was off. For myself, I bought a wardrobe full of Gulf War t-shirts.

I gave gifts to the people in our little department inside BTG. The work was extremely boring to me and there was no outlet for my creativity so in my manic state, I unleashed it on them.

I gave my friend and coworker, Brooke Lanham, Michael Jordan sweats. He was an African-American man I sat next to. Brooke was a big basketball nut and I loved him to death. Every time you asked him to do something, he always replied, "No problem." Those were the words he was known by in the office. Once we had a little ceremony in the office where I adopted him as my big brother. We pierced our fingers with a pin and smeared the blood together and I gave him Adoption Papers which I framed for him. I thought it was very creative, very clever. It said:

ADOPTION PAPERS

Because of his sterling qualities of loyalty, honesty, trustworthiness, counseling ability, dedication, tremendous wit, upbeat personality and ability to fool us all, I hereby request the State of Maryland to grant me the extreme pleasure of adopting as my Big Brother

Mr. Brooke No Problem Lanham, Jr.

On this Thursday, the 11th day of April in the year of our Lord, Nineteen Hundred and Ninety One.

Joan M. Kopczynski

____

Adopter

I hereby accept the adoption:
Brooke No Problem Lanham, Jr.

____

Adoptee
(signature required for those over 40)

Witnesses:____

I also had calling cards made up with a basketball hoop on them that said his name BROOKE NO PROBLEM LANHAM KOPCZYNSKI. It also said: “Warning—I am armed and dangerous. If I have a basketball, I will shoot.” Michael Jordan would have been proud.

At the time, I spoke almost solely to Brooke about the current love of my life—Michael—which was odd because I normally spoke to my best friend, Eleanor, about men. Brooke was married and I liked getting a male viewpoint on it. I often wondered what his wife thought about this strange white woman giving Brooke all this stuff. One younger girl in the office, an African-American Marine Sgt. Linda Savage, who had served in the Persian Gulf War (I think she had a tour of duty in London), came back to this welcome:

!!WELCOME BACK, LINDA!!

In grateful appreciation of the U.S. Marine Corp’s thoughtfulness in reserving a special place in history for our beloved reservist Sgt. Linda Savage, in the Persian Gulf War, whose name shall be indelibly etched in the minds and hearts of those she loves and those who love her for centuries to come, please take a few moments out of your busy schedule to honor her today. A salute would be fine, but Linda says money thrown at her would be better. No (British) pounds please!! Linda said she’s already carrying around a lot more of those than she wanted since she got back from her all-expense paid vacation in Europe, complimentary of the U.S. Taxpayers.

To Linda we say CONGRATULATIONS!! on making it back alive. We know all those quaint English stores, theatres and exotic foods were real obstacles to overcome. Her reservist training helped, but her reservist pay helped her stay away from them even more.

CONGRATULATIONS!!, too, Linda, on capturing that POW (Poor ol' Wimp) of your dreams upon your return. That is really what war is all about for women—put up a big military front, go shopping and come home to a man waiting to be held in your arms.

* * *

Linda got married and no one in the office seemed to step up to give her a party so, being the leader I thought I was, I organized a potluck for her along with a cowboy skit which was pretty lame but I guess it got a few laughs.

I also bought a coffee mug that said something about pissing someone off. The president of BTG had the last name of Bersoff. In my Disney FAA story, I had a character whose name was Bers and, of course, you never wanted to piss Bers off. At the time, I thought it was so clever. I sent the cup to the president who I didn't know and had never met. Of course, my story was never published and Mr. Bersoff was puzzled and offended by my gift. When I left the company, he probably clapped.

And I was collecting "dog stuff" for Murray and "cat stuff" for Polly at Colorado Prime. I had large boxes of the stuff—t-shirts, knick-knacks, stuffed animals. I don't know why I bought them gifts because they were not close friends.

Chapter 41

I wrote a letter to my Mom for Mother's Day, May 12, 1991.

Dear Mom:

As usual, I am sending you a gift for Mother's Day but really this letter is the special gift. I know I hurt you deeply years ago when I sent you that awful letter blaming you for the hurts in my life. I can't say that I'm sorry that I sent it. We both grew as a result of it. You finally started treating me as an adult. I no longer blamed you for the person I became. I started choosing my own identity.

I do have something to blame you for now. In my heart I know I am destined to become one of the world's greatest writers of all time. I owe a great deal of the credit to you. You were the one who made me sit down each week and write a letter to Grandma Hoene in Illinois. I remember complaining, "But, I don't know what to write!" and you would show me how. I later won a Letter Writing Award at Kinman Business University, thanks to you and all that practice.

You were also the one who made magic come alive during the holidays. You successfully pulled off a delightful Halloween when you had your friend, Alma Poxleitner, pose as a witch in our house for the whole day and you even kept her identity a secret for 15-20 years. And I'll never forget that year you asked Father Method, that Benedictine Monk from St. Gertrude's Academy, to pose as St. Nicholas. He came in wearing a full Bishop's outfit complete with golden ring and staff and was accompanied by an entourage of attendants. I was in the early grades of grammar school and when he asked me to recite the Hail Mary I almost peed my pants. I was so scared I couldn't remember all the words. I was afraid of being punished for slipping up and also of not getting a bag of candy he had ready for those who performed flawlessly. You told me years later that you did it because you really wanted us to believe. Those memories are so special to me. I like to do things like that now, to share that same excitement about holidays or special days. Thanks, Mom.

You were also the one to kindle my creativity. The best teacher is by example. You spent a great deal of time making quilts ever since I was a kid and that exposed me to a wide variety of patterns, shapes and colors. You also taught us how to sew, knit and make craft items. It's amazing you managed to find time for it with all the work you had raising 10 children, your jobs outside the home and all the charity work you did. Thanks, Mom.

Now, Mom, I am very close to getting published in a magazine and I can't but help remember who gave me my start, both in life and in writing. I know I gave you pain coming out of the womb and more growing pain when I was going through each successive school—grammar, high school and college. I'm afraid you may experience more pain in the coming years because of what I may write. I may not be the Catholic, goody two shoes daughter you had hoped for. If anyone ever gives you grief about it, just remember, you started me but I am finishing me. I hope that one day you can look back and admire the masterpiece you created. Thanks for all the pain you suffered through because of me, Mom. It will all be worth it. You'll see.

If you've cried half as much reading this letter as I have writing it, we're even, Mom. I hope you have a very special day. Thanks again. I love you.

Your loving daughter and world's greatest writer,
Joan K.

My mother never said anything to me about the letter and never kept it, which makes me think she never treasured it as I intended. She kept the letter I wrote to my Dad for Father's Day and gave it back to me along with the card I had given him but she never returned the letter I had written to her so I guess she never thought it was special. Considering the few letters I had written to her previously which were hurtful, I thought she should've considered this one priceless.

I don't remember which magazine I was trying to get published in but it was probably *Guideposts* because I had submitted to them a lot and never realized my dream. I thought of myself as "the world's greatest writer. You'd think I would have come down from that high but I was so headstrong, so gung ho, so incredibly naïve.

* * *

I wrote a letter to my Dad for Father's Day, June 16, 1991.

Dear Dad:

As usual, I am sending you a gift for Father's Day, something you can enjoy giving away to your children or grandchildren, but really this letter is the special gift.

I know I have hurt you deeply by not attending Catholic mass each Sunday. Church is probably the most important thing in your life. It always has been and always will be. I'd like to be able to say that for your Father's Day gift this year I will return to the Church. I can't though. That would be the wrong reason for going back. I wouldn't rule it out completely in the future but at this time I cannot give that gift to you. I'm sorry.

What I can give you though is something we always gave you as kids when we didn't have the money to buy a gift. I am enclosing my Spiritual Bouquet for you. I will begin the prayers and masses starting on Father's Day. I know you will treasure it more than any material gift I could give you. I want you also to know that it was by far more difficult for me to give. I relish sleeping in on Sunday mornings so it will be an extreme sacrifice.

This sacrifice, however, does not compare to the sacrifice you and Mom made for all of us kids. I know you had money headaches in the extreme, Dad, and yet you kept all those worries to yourself. We didn't even know we were poor. I have those worries myself now and I am learning that it might be better to suffer in silence. I don't know. That's difficult for me to do because I've always been a screamer whenever pain was inflicted upon me. Speaking of pain and sacrifices, Dad, I wonder how many times you went without so that we could have something we needed or wanted badly. You never said anything but I know you made sacrifices like that. Anyway, thanks, Dad for all the sacrifices you made for me.

You know I have something else to thank you for. Your faith in God is so powerful and so awesome; I was often astonished by it. What it did for me, I realized, is to give me a strong belief in something, too—myself. I often remember you standing up for what you believed in when all those around you said you were crazy. Well, you proved to us who the crazies were. Now I am faced with the same dilemma. Everyone has chastised me for being generous before I make any money as a writer. Dad, I know I will be one of the world's greatest writers and I know that I am about to publish soon. I believe in myself. God, or someone, has gathered all these people around me to help me and I want dearly to reciprocate before my story gets printed so that they'll know that I appreciate their efforts. See, it probably sounds crazy to you all. So did what you used to tell us. But you believed and so do I, thanks to your example. Thanks Dad!

Dad, there's something else I'd like to thank you for. When we were small you sat each of us by your side and you tried to teach us to learn to play the piano. I never quite made it. Sister Anna, O.S.B. didn't give me much hope for she hit my hands with a ruler whenever I didn't do what she wanted me to. It's hard to learn with negative reinforcement like that. Then in the 4th grade Sister Cecile, O.S.B. wouldn't let me play in the piano recital for she said I had missed too many lessons because I was sick with mononucleosis that year. I felt like I could've played the piece o.k. but she ended up calling Mom and even made her cry on the phone and to this day I don't know what she said to her. I quit taking lessons after that. Connie and Karen went gung ho though. It's funny cause it was Connie and Karen who told me I couldn't carry a tune. I love music and sing a lot but only when I am by myself so no one else will hear because "I'm convinced I can't carry a tune."

I never realized what power they had over me until last year when Polly, my telemarketing manager, was riding in the car with me and asked why I didn't sing along with the songs like she did. When I finally did, she told me she thought I had a great voice and sang real good. I remember one time I was in Church and Mom made a similar comment. She said she heard this lovely voice and looked around to see where it was coming from and was surprised that it was me.

Music will always be a part of my life, Dad, thanks to you. I'm going to learn how to play the piano, maybe take singing lessons and for certain I will write lyrics for songs. Your efforts have not been in vain, Dad. Thanks for bringing music into my life. I cannot go a day without it.

Dad, there's just one more thing I'd like to thank you for. I know you like to pray and I know you have been going to Church twice on Sundays to make up for some of your kids who don't go. I remember the all night vigils you made during the Vietnam War. I remember the litanies you would recite by heart each night after our daily family rosary. I remember you getting up early during the week so that you could attend daily mass before going to work. I remember the Angelus you would recite by heart before we were allowed to touch our food. Your whole life has been centered around prayer. It's a good thing because we would never have made it without you or your devotion to God. I still need the prayers. I seem to need them more each day. Dad, thanks for all the praying you've done for me or about me. I hope that one day you'll be able to say that all your efforts were worth it.

Now, Dad, I know I am very close to getting published in a magazine and I can't help but remember who it was that instilled that faith in me, who showed me how to rise above those that say I am crazy. It was your example, Dad. It is difficult but I know I can do it because I'll always remember what you did.

I may not be the Catholic, goody two shoes daughter you had hoped for. Like I told Mom, if anyone ever gives you grief about it, just remember, you started me but I am finishing me. I sincerely hope that one day you can look back and admire the masterpiece you created. Thanks for all the sacrifices you made for me, Dad. It will all be worth it. You'll see. I hope you have a very special day. Thanks again. I love you.

Your loving daughter and world's greatest writer,
Joan K.

Here is the Spiritual Bouquet I gave my Dad which I had framed:

SPIRITUAL BOUQUET

Catholic Masses	15
Catholic Rosaries	15
Our Fathers	50
Hail Marys	50
Glory Be's	100
Acts of Kindness	100
Acts of Generosity	100
Genuflections (Knee-Bends)	50
Standing Up For What I Believe In	10
Public Confessions	1
Working Miracles (getting published)	1
Good Intentions	10,000

Start: Father's Day, June 16, 1991
End: December 31, 1991

The other gift I gave my Dad, which accompanied this letter, was a gold family tree that I had engraved with names of his parents and grandparents and all his brothers and sisters. Dad's astrological sign was Cancer and he was big on family. It cost $500 at the time. I never thought to give Mom a family tree with the names of her family engraved. She was probably hurt by this and I regret that deeply. But, I did later give her a priceless porcelain mouse collection and some Irish crystal wine glasses.

Chapter 42

I gave Dr. Adler a $100 gift certificate for Brooks Brothers, a prestigious men's clothing store, and he refused it, giving it back to me, but didn't make a big deal about it and probably didn't think anything of it. Then my sister, Connie, called and said, "Larry doesn't want fish for every room of his house." I had sent him $1,000 worth of fish stuff which included a wall hanging of Caribbean fish that he really liked. He hung it in his dining room. Then I sent him fish plates for the kitchen, a fish shower curtain and fish toothbrush holder for the bathroom and a down comforter and fish duvet cover for the bedroom. It never dawned on me that he wouldn't want it. I thought it was rude of him to turn down my gifts.

Connie asked if she could call Dr. Adler and talk to him. I said, "Sure." I gave her his number. She was the main one in the family concerned about me. Like I said, she was always my surrogate mother. I never sent any gifts to Mom and Dad or my best friend, Eleanor. I knew they wouldn't understand and certainly wouldn't approve which is odd because other people didn't understand or approve either.

When Connie called and talked to Dr. Adler, she told him about the shopping (and she didn't know about all of it) and the fact that the family was concerned because they knew I couldn't afford it.

Dr. Adler never suspected mania in me until that phone call. I had never mentioned in my sessions with him that I was doing a lot of shopping. The next time I visited him, he confronted me about being manic.

"I had a phone call from your sister, Connie."

"So?"

"So, I think you're manic. I want you to start taking Trilafon again."

"I am not manic. What did she tell you?" There was anger in my voice.

Dr. Adler was losing his voice but tried to speak above a whisper. "She said you were doing a lot of shopping. That's a sign of mania."

"I have never been manic in my whole life and I'm not manic now. I don't care what you think. I am not taking Trilafon again. I'm a lot better since I've been off of it."

"You are manic," he screamed at me.

"I am not," I shouted back.

"You are, too." Dr. Adler sighed. He wrote out two prescriptions, one for Trilafon. "Here. Take this. I want you to start taking these."

"I refuse. You can't make me. You were the one who weaned me off of them. And furthermore, you are not to talk to Connie again. I forbid it." At the time, family members were prohibited from talking to the patient's psychiatrist without the patient's consent. So, his hands were tied. I was a horrible patient.

In June someone called and said Dr. Peckar wanted to see his patients as part of his healing process. I went to see him. He looked awful. His arms and hands were in bandages and the expression on his face looked droopy. His eyes looked sad. I told him I was moving to Florida to be with Michael. He said he thought that was a good idea. We talked about my medications and he told me he thought I should start taking Trilafon again. I didn't say anything but I wasn't planning on going back on that drug.

* * *

One day I had to take off from work to go see the U.S. Postal Inspectors at L'Enfant Plaza who were investigating the Peckar bombing. They had jurisdiction instead of the FBI because the bomb was sent through the mail. Thankfully and coincidentally it was within walking distance of the Transportation building where I worked. L'Enfant Plaza is a relatively small mall, full of shops and restaurants and on the west side is the Postal Building. I took the elevator and went up to one of the office suites.

After the initial warm-up of questions as to who I was, one of the gentlemen in a nice navy pin-striped suit asked me if there was anything unusual about any of my sessions with Dr. Peckar.

"Dr. Peckar once took his shoes off in one of our sessions."

I saw surprise in their faces. "Did that bother you? Were you afraid he might do something?"

"Dr. Peckar was an old soft shoe. He said his feet hurt. I don't think he would harm anyone and if you're asking me was I afraid he'd rape me? No. He was rather unprofessional but I wasn't afraid of him. He was just weird."

They were finished with the questions and then asked me if I had anything further to say.

"Well, the suspect *had* to be one of Dr. Peckar's patients."

"Why do you think that?"

"Because no one else would have known he opened up his own mail. He didn't have a secretary."

"Did you see him open up his mail?"

"Yes, my appointments were usually around lunch when the mailman delivered the mail."

"Do you think he deserved this?"

"No. No way."

Chapter 43

I normally saw Dr. Adler once a month but he wanted to see me almost every week before I left for Florida. I thought it was for the money and since I was throwing money away I didn't mind. I also needed the prescription for lithium so I thought I had to be nice to him. I continued to take my lithium pills faithfully except I wouldn't go back on the Trilafon. I had chronic insomnia and no prescription for sleeping pills. After I saw Dr. Peckar again, I went to see Dr. Adler. He still wasn't through arguing with me.

"Now, I think you should stay here in Washington and not go to Florida with Michael. What did Dr. Peckar say about that?"

"He said he thought I should go to Florida."

"What did Dr. Peckar say about you taking the Trilafon?"

"He said he thought I should take it."

"So, now we had a difference of opinion about Florida but we both think you should take the Trilafon. What are you going to do?'

"I'm really fine without it. I don't think I need it."

"But Dr. Peckar thinks you need it and I think you need it."

"Well, Dr. Peckar hasn't really seen me without it except that one time.

* * *

During my manic state, I believed I was invincible. Always timid in groups before, suddenly I was a leader, unafraid to speak my mind. My judgment was way off.

I told my close friend, Sue, that it was wrong for her to have an abortion. *Never faced with that choice myself because I never had children or would have children, why did I feel it was important to lay that guilt on my friend? I don't know.* It wasn't any of my business and I was way out of line but I was convinced I was right and I felt compelled to tell her. My views on abortion had come from Fr. Hebert, a Catholic priest, who I delivered newspapers to from the third grade on in grammar school. He wrote many an editorial in *The Lewiston Morning Tribune* against abortion. Although I was too young to fully understand the issue at the time, I admired him for standing up for what he believed in. In that way, he reminded me of my Dad.

I told my friend, Eleanor, what I had done and she chewed my butt. She told me to go back to Sue and apologize. My judgment was so way off I wouldn't listen to anyone, not even my best friend. I refused to apologize and I lost Sue's friendship. Sue dropped contact after that. I don't blame her. She never realized it was because of my illness and by the time I got better and realized the magnitude of what I had done, I didn't feel she would understand or forgive me. Losing friends or relationships has been one of the negative side effects of the illness I've had to deal with.

* * *

I exhibited signs of full-blown mania for approximately six months in Washington, DC from January to the end of June 1991 without detection by my psychiatrist, Dr. Adler, until my sister, Connie, talked to him. If it hadn't been for her, I wonder how long it would have taken him to realize it or if he would have ever known. I don't remember what I talked to him about but I think it was mostly about my medications, certainly not about all the shopping I was doing. (I later tried to get my medical records from Dr. Adler but he was unable to locate them.)

I managed to wreak havoc on my bank account, writing checks that bounced and going over credit card limits. ITT Financial Services sent me a signature loan in the mail and I signed it and got $5,000. I also leased a 1991 Mazda 626 from GE Capital. I thought it would be fun to order a car by phone so I called up the Mazda dealership and told them what I wanted and had them deliver it to my office. They did. I also cashed in what I could of my 401(k) plans. I had called Jack once and in the conversation asked him, "If I make a million dollars from my writing, then I won't need my 401(k) plans, will I?" He said, "No." I had one with Colorado Prime, one with Institute for Defense

Analysis (IDA) and one with BTG. I wrote letters and asked them to send me the proceeds, not even considering the tax consequences.

I bought a big, expensive TV set which I knew I couldn't take with me to Florida, and a top-of-the-line stereo system, then thought my Major Michael could buy me newer and better, so I sold them to a neighbor for a dirt cheap price.

My one-eyed sister, Carole, sent me a check in the mail for $1,000 and told me to pay my creditors off. She said she couldn't sleep just thinking about it. She didn't understand my illness. It drove her crazy to hear about all the bills I was racking up. Receiving her check broke my heart because Carole was a cook at a Fraternity and barely made more than minimum wage. I had so many bills, I had difficulty deciding who I should pay and who I shouldn't, and the $1,000 didn't put a dent in my damage.

Chapter 44

I loaded up my car with what was left of my belongings. I knew I could replace my dishes, pots and pans and silverware and the South American family who cleaned my apartment were poor and struggling to make it so I gave the contents of my kitchen to them. I also gave them my carpets. I used to play the song, "Don't Cry For Me, Argentina" over and over again and I guess I thought I was Eva Peron.

Once the mother of the cleaning crew came in and looked lovingly at my sewing machine, the sewing machine that Dad had given me long ago, which I rarely used but had lately been piecing together a quilt on it. I'd started it in San Francisco. It was to be a gift to my friend, Tina. She had picked out the colors and fabric with me. I had about six more blocks to go before I turned it over to my mother to quilt. I wanted to give that lady the sewing machine but I also needed to finish the quilt so I made her a deal. I said if you can make me six blocks like the ones I have finished, the machine is yours. The lady did not speak or understand English but her daughter translated it for her. She protested at first but she really wanted the sewing machine so she agreed. She proudly came back to me with the six blocks and I let her take the sewing machine.

After my mother quilted the peach and brown quilt, she wanted me to promise that I would not give it to my friend, Tina. I refused. It was typical of Mom trying to tell me what to do and me rebelling. I tried to find Tina in San Francisco but she had moved. I still have the quilt. They were Tina's colors and tastes and she was a very good friend and if I ever find her, I will give her the quilt.

I took the microwave Jack had given me and gave it to a store in Annandale which had a sign inside representing an organization where you could drop off items for the homeless. They must've been surprised at my almost new microwave. I also took my royal blue velour bathrobe that Jack had given me and gave it to the homeless. That sacrifice hurt the most but I was determined not to keep anything around that would remind me of the love I shared with another man. Michael had never given me a thing and I didn't want to confuse my love for him or his love for me by material things which another man had given me. I told Jack what I had done and he was not only puzzled but heartbroken.

* * *

My sister-in-law, Lisa, came to visit me in June 1991. I planned to meet her plane at the airport gate; however, due to miscommunication we got our wires crossed. After waiting for awhile, I gave up and was going to leave. Then I realized I didn't have any money to pay for parking so I decided to stay and had her paged. Luckily, I found her.

Lisa came home with me and one of the first things she wanted to do was go grocery shopping. Connie had sent her money to help pay for groceries. We went to the local Giant supermarket in my apartment complex. Lisa pushed the cart and I pointed out things I ate. I got the feeling that she didn't trust me to buy groceries and thought I would've spent the money on gifts. She was probably right. I hadn't been eating or sleeping very well. Some nights I only got an hour or two of sleep. My psychiatrist hadn't prescribed any sleeping medication for my chronic insomnia—I probably never told him about it.

Lisa tried unsuccessfully to get me to change my mind about Florida, about giving away gifts and things but I was so cocksure at the time, I wouldn't listen.

"When are you going to Florida?"

"At the end of this month."

"Don't you think it would be better to go back to Spokane to be closer to your family?"

"No. My family doesn't love me. Michael loves me."

"Have you seen your doctor lately?"

"Yeah, I just saw him last week. Why?"

"What does he say about you going to Florida?"

"He thinks I should stay in Washington, DC."

"So . . ."

"So, he also thinks I should start taking Trilafon again. He's the one who took me off it."

"I think you should do what your doctor says."

"No."

"Why not?"

"He's weird. All psychiatrists are weird. They all have something wrong with them. That's why they went into the business."

"That's not true."

"It is. Dr. Peckar once cut a lithium pill in half and shared it with me."

"Why did he do that?"

"So we could taste it."

"Well, most doctors don't do that. What are you doing with those Christmas decorations you have here?"

"I'm going to give them to the homeless."

"But you got them in Germany. They have a lot of memories." Lisa looked frustrated. She was getting nowhere with me.

"I don't care. The homeless need some, too."

"I think you should keep them. You might regret it later on."

"No."

"Why?"

"I can buy new stuff. I'm going to be rich."

"How are you going to be rich? You're giving up your job."

"I just will. You'll see."

"Joan, you're not making any sense."

Exasperated, I replied, "I'm writing a book. So there!"

"What's it about?"

"It's very creative. I don't know if I should tell you."

"Tell me. I won't tell anybody."

"Ok, it's about the FAA."

"And you think this is going to be a bestseller?"

"I know it is."

"You know, Joan, Allan and I don't want any more gifts sent to us. We have enough. We don't want to spoil Brian."

"Ok. I won't send any more to you. Did you like them though? Wasn't that train terrific? It was just made for a two-year-old."

"It was very special. Brian can work it himself. But please don't send any more. You need the money for Florida."

"Ok. Do you want to see what I bought Michael? You can't tell anyone though. This is our little secret."

"What is it?"

I showed her the $500 ring I had bought from JB Robinson's Jewelers.

* * *

On my way to Florida, while driving through Old Towne Alexandria, I stopped at a doll shop and on impulse bought a white lace canopy doll's bed and porcelain doll for $500. This was going in my museum. I had no specific plan for what my museum would be, I just collected stuff on impulse. That day it was a rather expensive impulse.

I drove down Highway I-95, passing by Richmond, Virginia; Raleigh, North Carolina; Florence, South Carolina; Savannah, Georgia and Jacksonville, Florida in my silver bullet, my silver Mazda 626 leased car. I was on a mission and no one was going to stop me.

Dr. Adler asked me if I had told Michael I was coming to Florida to be with him. I couldn't get through to him on the phone but I wasn't worried. Even though my judgment was way off, I was so stubborn no one could persuade me not to go. Dr. Adler then suggested I send Michael a telegram or two. I thought that was a good idea. The telegrams were cryptic, kind of like a cable the CIA would send. I've since destroyed them so I don't remember what they said exactly but I do remember saying something about the silver bullet going to Florida. Michael never answered any of the telegrams, never told me not to come. So I knew in my heart I was doing the right thing.

Dr. Adler finally persuaded me to stay in my current job at BTG. So, one day I went in and told Anthony, the Ops Manager, that I had changed my mind. He said, "I'm sorry, but I already planned for you to leave." They no longer had a place for me. I didn't fight it. It seemed clear to me then that had I stayed I might have been fired. This gave me confidence that I was doing the right thing by leaving.

I never once looked back on the job I left, the possessions I gave away, the credit I ruined, the relationships I destroyed, or how many people told me not to go. I was riding high on a wave of euphoria and was so sure things would fall into place in Florida.

I woke up early, drove down Highway I-95 south, arrived in Melbourne fifteen hours later on July 2 and checked into the Mariott Courtyard Hotel on West New Haven Avenue. I wrote a poem for Melbourne:

MELBOURNE

Breezes from the ocean
Cooling off 80,000 people
From 90 degree heat.
Small strips of sandy beach
Line the ocean
For snowbirds who
Come in the winter,
Old folks mostly,
Though the average age
Of Melbourne's finest
Is 38.

All summer long
Until October,
The city is visited
Each afternoon by
Lightning and thunderstorms
Which wreak havoc
On Shuttle watchers.
Then come Fall and next
Spring you see bugs,
Lots of them,
Everywhere.

Little ants, big ants,
Sweet ants and termite-like
Ants—
Wall-to-wall in
New houses and old,
Dripping from ceiling fans,
Waking you up in the middle of
The night for a bite to eat.
And they eat your t-shirts,
10 holes in each one,
While they are hanging up
Clean on a hangar.

Another skeleton in the closet
Is their water.
Neighbor Palm Bay found a
Cancer cluster which was blamed
On the water.
Don't ever get thirsty or
You may die.

Chapter 45

My heart swelled with anticipation at the prospect of seeing Michael again. We had been exchanging letters and phone calls for months. Finally, I would be united with my sweetheart. I felt relaxed, light-headed, giddy, on top of the world, able to conquer my biggest fears. Nothing mattered except the excitement of seeing Michael again. I never once thought about all the shopping I had done and tooling down to Florida to be with a man who had once told me he didn't love me. Thoughts of Michael and the expectation of love consumed me.

When I arrived in Florida, this young, weird guy that Michael knew came and visited me at the hotel. I put more makeup on than usual and didn't exactly look my best but I figured he was only this strange guy, not Michael. I was overweight and didn't feel good about myself—how I looked, what I wore. I suspected Michael had sent this person over to check me out. I wondered why he didn't come himself. But I thought I knew. Michael spent years being a body builder and he never cared how much brains the woman had but he cared a great deal how she looked. Looks were everything, I later remembered. I couldn't see that I was doomed.

His friend came in. We sat on the bed. I must've told him I was going to be one of the greatest writers of all time. He wanted to hear some of the stories I had written so I read him my children's espionage Christmas story called "Santa's Secret Keeper" and another one about farm animals. Finally, he left. He said Michael would call me tomorrow, the 4th of July.

The next morning I went to a nearby convenience store and bought two beers. Normally I drink only one beer in a year's time, if that, but I bought these two beers and guzzled them down at 9:45 in the morning. I didn't know it but I was medicating myself. I was trying to come down from this magnificent maniacal high I had been on.

I noticed I had chewed my index fingernail down to the quick. I went in to the bathroom to get a tissue to wipe the blood off my finger.

I came back out and my stomach felt queasy. I didn't think I had the flu so why did I feel like I was about to throw up? I picked up the phone to see if the line was dead. There was a tone on the other end so I put the receiver back down. I could not sit still. I straightened the covers on my bed. I straightened them again. I looked at my watch. It was close to 10. I wondered when Michael would call. Would he be happy to hear from me? Surely, after all this time, after all I had gone through to get to Florida to finally be with him, surely he would forgive me for being overweight.

Then right at 10 o'clock Michael called. I don't remember what he said because all he did was shout at me. He was furious that I had followed him to Florida. He did not want to see me. If I was trying to come down from my high, this negative jolt did the trick. My judgment suddenly seemed clear as I picked myself off the floor. Michael did not love me. It was as if I had woken up from a bad dream. I started taking Trilafon again. I think I took four tablets, 4 mg. each.

* * *

I hung around Melbourne trying to decide what to do. *Should I stay in Florida? Should I move back home to the Northwest? Should I go back to Washington, DC? Did I hope Michael would change his mind?* I moved into the Sun Breeze Apartments on Woodwind Trail. They were in close proximity to a packaging place on North Wickham Road called P.k.g.'s. I had shipped my set of Britannica's down from Virginia and picked them up at this store and noticed the nearby apartments.

I didn't have any furniture so I made my usual bed from sheets and a pillow on the floor. One day I was napping in the afternoon and I felt something biting me. I woke up to find I was covered with ants, termite-like ants devouring my clothes. I screamed and went to my closet to get a new t-shirt and found ants on my clean clothes hanging on a hanger. They had chewed holes in each t-shirt, looking for sweat, I guess, or maybe laundry detergent. So much for my Gulf War wardrobe. Then I called the rental office manager. She said they would take care of it but they never sprayed until the time came around for more rent money.

I sent out resumes. I sent a resume to NASA for configuration management but the guy told me they didn't have an opening at the time and it might take awhile. I sent a resume to Boeing Aerospace and even Disney World at Lake Buena Vista. By now it was the end of July. I didn't stay around long enough to hear back from them.

Meanwhile, I kept busy by taking odd telemarketing jobs. I hired on at Colorado Prime again but was soon dismissed because of what Murray Yeoman told one of the managers. Murray had fired me during my manic state in Virginia for mouthing off. I got a job selling gift checkbooks, a booklet like Entertainment Books which had 2-for-1 coupons for restaurants and other things. I did well there but an attorney shut them down. I also worked for Metro Mechanical on Penn Street but I don't remember what we sold. And I worked selling water softeners for about a day.

I went to Melbourne Psychiatry on Silver Palm Ave. and saw Dr. Peabody. I needed my medications right away and couldn't get in to see Dr. Peabody for a month so I called Dr. Adler in Virginia and he called my prescriptions into the Florida pharmacy. I only saw Dr. Peabody once and my impression of him was not very favorable. I must've seemed odd to him also with my letter telling of all the shopping I had done. I refused to let Dr. Adler write about my mania so he wrote that I had been doing a lot of shopping.

I continued to think of Michael, and the magnitude of what had transpired in my life the past six months set in. I had ruined my life. I was not a millionaire. Everything went bust. All the good deeds I thought I was doing soured. They all turned out bad. Jack Hashian didn't even thank me for the stuff I sent him. He just complained that it was too much. Larry couldn't stomach the fish I sent him for every room of his house. Connie and Allan asked me to quit sending stuff. Connie was taking back the things I gave her to stores and getting the money, which she later gave back to me. I didn't become a success. I hadn't sold a book yet. *What do I do now about all the money I owe? What happened to the wealthy life I had planned? Where will I go now? What will I do? I can't stay here. I hate it here.*

I went to the pharmacy and asked the pharmacist for the drug inserts that the pharmacy gets on my medications. I told him I wanted to read about the adverse side effects of my drugs. He said, "Lady, everything in here causes adverse side effects. There isn't a drug on the market that doesn't cause something else." After being so kindly reassured, I took them home and read the tiny little print myself. The one for Trilafon said that in some people the absence of this drug can cause full blown mania if they are weaned off it. There I had my answer. I had become manic, did all the crazy shopping and destroyed my life because I had a doctor or doctors who weaned me off this drug. Not only Dr. Peckar's life was destroyed by the bombing.

I called Jack. "Michael refused to see me. All he did was yell at me. I don't know what he said." Jack listened with kind ears. He didn't interrupt. "Jack, I've ruined my life. You don't know, but I sent gifts to a lot of other people, including my brothers and sisters and even Michael. $1,000 each. I felt like I was paying them back for the good they had done for me. All the good I tried to do turned out bad. What should I do now? I don't know where to go."

"You should go home where you are surrounded by people who love and care about you. That way if you get in trouble again, you'll be with family. Go home, Joan."

By this time, I knew that in my manic state the biggest problem I had was that my judgment was way off. I also knew Jack was a lot smarter than me and I realized that he still genuinely cared about me. "Thank you. I think I'll do that."

"By the way, I have a new book out."

"Really, what's the name of it?"

"*Shanidar*. It's under my true name."

"I'll go to the bookstore tomorrow. How do you spell it?"

"S-h-a-n-i-d-a-r."

"I can't wait to read it. By the way, you're right about me needing to go home. Thanks again."

Chapter 46

One afternoon I was lying on my makeshift bed in my apartment resting when the phone rang. I said hello but didn't recognize the voice on the other end.

"Is this Joan Kopczynski?"

"Yes."

"I'm a friend of Michael O'Neill's. We're both jocks. We work out together every day."

"How did you get my number?"

"Information. Hey, look. I'm calling you because I have a sister who is bipolar so I sort of understand your situation. But, you sound pretty normal." There was surprise in his voice.

"I'm not manic anymore. I've come down." My voice was low.

"You were lucky. We never caught on to my sister until she had three grand pianos delivered to the house."

"Woo. She must've been pretty sick."

"She was. Say, Michael just opened all the boxes you sent him. What should he do with all of it?"

I had forgotten about the boxes. Insult added to injury. "He can have it. I don't want any of it back." I wondered what in the world I would do with twenty-five or more men's button down shirts, size 17-34 totaling $1,000. I'd have to find a dumpster. May as well let him have them although I wasn't feeling so kindly toward him at this point.

"What should he do with all the stuff he doesn't want?"

I had visions of the five stuffed Garfields. I thought it was rather rude of him to tell me he didn't want my gifts. I also thought it was rude that he didn't call himself instead of putting his friend up to it. Did he think I was poison or had AIDS or something? I figured he must've liked the shirts but his friend never said. "Throw it all away. I don't want it back."

"OK."

"Bye." I hung up. I thought about Michael, thinking he was my special friend, the friend I chased all the way to Florida, the man I thought I was destined to marry, the man I had bought the ring for. What kind of man, what kind of a friend did he turn out to be? He didn't even offer help when I was sick, when I was alone in a strange, foreign town and had nobody else to turn to. He wasn't much of a friend, much of a human being.

What about my friend, Jack Hashian? He still cared for me, he still loved me, and he helped me—even though I had rejected him for Michael. What a magnificent human being he was. He cared about more than what I looked like or what I could do for him in bed. He cared about my well-being. I was so wrong. Jack is the man I should have married. But I am not worthy to kiss his feet.

I devoured *Shanidar* practically in one day. Jack was the best writer I had ever read. I loved every one of his thriller books. On the cover of *Shanidar* was a picture of him playing spy in that old navy cap. It made me smile. His character Alison Arnold Davis in the last half of the book seemed oddly familiar to me. Even more familiar was the graphic sex scene he depicted with her. There was no doubt in my mind. It was unmistakably me. He taught me more in that one lesson in writing than all the self-help books I had been reading. Price I paid for sleeping with a writer. After I finished the book, I called him.

"Jack, you dog. Never ever sleep with a writer."

He knew exactly what I meant immediately. I heard his deep baritone laugh.

"I'm glad I got one. The store only had three left and I had to ask for it."

He laughed again. "They only put three in each store."

"I wasn't just after sexual attention, Jack, although I hadn't had any for seven years. I loved you but it was all so complicated with your kids."

"Do you remember when I took you house hunting in Charlottesville, Virginia?"

"Yes, what about it?"

"Well, we were driving home and I proposed to you."

"You did not."

"In my mind I did, too. I didn't say will you marry me? But I was trying to feel you out. I said something about us being together."

"What did I say?"

"You wrinkled up your nose and you said, 'you should be with your kids.'"

"Yeah, I remember. Is that why you got so mad at me and wouldn't speak to me and wouldn't even say goodbye? Is that why you moved back to Boston?"

"My kids have their own lives. We get together but not as often as I'd like. When I call them, they always have something else to do. And I can't even hold my grandson. When I pick him up, he always says, 'Put me down. Put me down.'"

"I'm sorry. I never realized that. I guess I was naïve. I didn't want to come between you and them."

I was hoping he'd say come to Boston but that would be asking too much. I was just grateful for his continued friendship.

The next day I made plans to drive across country to the Northwest. I got maps from AAA. I dropped off my boxes of encyclopedias at P.k.g.'s on North Wickham Road. The owner was suspicious of why I was sending them. Was I leaving? I never gave him a straight answer. He said Sun Breeze apartments had a lot of trouble with renters who only stayed a month or two and had signed a six-month lease. Most of them claimed bankruptcy so Sun Breeze couldn't go after them. I thought to myself, well, if they would tell you there are no jobs to be had here before you come and if they would take care of the ants, maybe they wouldn't have this problem.

I packed the rest of my things in my car, dropped the apartment key off in a box for the manager and never looked back. I took the middle route through Kansas and the only place I stopped was in Cunningham, Kansas to do some research on my father's family history, which I planned to write about. Cunningham was the highlight of my trip.

I arrived in Cottonwood around lunchtime and my folks seemed glad to see me.

"Well, if it isn't the prodigal child," Mom said.

I smiled. No hug or kiss hello. We just stared at one another. I wondered if they'd ask me about why I did all the shopping or why I followed Michael to Florida but they never said anything. I never got an opportunity to tell them. There never was a good time to ever bring it all out in the open and discuss it. But I tried.

"I can explain . . ."

"That's enough, Joanie. We've heard all about it. Put some silverware on the table now and let's eat. Carole is coming later and I want to have the dishes done before she comes so we can quilt."

I figured it was business as usual. I got the message that they assumed I was normal again and that all my foolishness had come to an end. They acted like nothing had ever happened. I stayed there a couple of days until my brother, Don, offered me a place to stay.

Chapter 47

When I arrived in Spokane for the second time in September 1991, I had to find a new doctor. I called a number in the phone book for a referral to a psychiatrist who was taking new patients. His name was Dr. David Bot. I had been through three psychiatrists in less than four months, none of whom I particularly cared for—Dr. Adler in Virginia, Dr. Peabody in Florida, Dr. I-can't-remember-his-last-name in Lewiston, Idaho—and now I appeared to be getting a Chinese doctor. I thought he might be Chinese because his last name was only three letters, common in Asian names. I wondered how we would relate but I had always thought my problem was chemical so it didn't matter. I didn't have much choice since I was poor.

I drove east on I-90 to the Division Street exit, turned right on south Division and found a very private looking, gray office building on the left-hand side of the street between 6th and 7th. The rain and dense fog made the roadway slick and made my first visit apprehensive. Glass lattice-like windows covered the right side of the front of the building. I walked though a wooden door with a round window in it.

I sat down in the waiting room on a royal blue chair and when it came time for my appointment, Dr. Bot opened the door to the back offices and called my name. I had trouble getting up from the chair. My first attempt failed. I looked at Dr. Bot who returned my glance. He was not Chinese. I scooted my butt further to the end of the seat. The cushion was obviously old and too soft. I wondered at the rate I was paying my psychiatrist, why did he have such old, dilapidated office furniture? I tried again and grunted. This time I made it. Then I followed Dr. Bot back to his office.

He surprised me. As tall as me, he had a slender build and looked very businesslike, wearing a blue shirt and tie. I thought he resembled in both looks and mannerisms the ABC News Anchor, Peter Jennings. I watched the Jennings' newscast daily on TV. I loved the tidbits of history he threw in with his reporting. So, every time I went to see Dr. Bot, I imagined myself sitting and discussing my problems with Peter Jennings.

I sat down in a winged back chair in front of his large, mahogany desk. We exchanged a few pleasantries and then we began.

"I'm bipolar schizoaffective. I need to get two prescriptions filled." My face showed no emotion and my voice was monotone.

"When were you first diagnosed?"

I briefly told him about my medical history—how it started in California when Connor jilted me and then in Spokane when I went to see Marilyn Wilson, the therapist and once to a psychiatrist at the Mental Health Clinic and then later in Virginia when Dr. Peckar gave me this diagnosis. I also told him about the bombing and having to get a new psychiatrist.

I gave him the letter from Dr. Adler. He frowned and looked puzzled. "You did a lot of shopping?"

"Yes. I wouldn't let Dr. Adler say I was manic so he wrote that I did a lot of shopping."

"And now do you think you were manic?"

"Yes, I guess so. But I've come down. I'm not on a high anymore."

"And you need prescriptions for lithium and Trilafon?"

"Yes. Will I need to see you every month like I saw Dr. Peckar?"

"No, only once every six months."

Wow! That was good news. "For an hour?"

"That's up to you. At the least I need to see you for a half session but if you feel you need more time, I can see you for a full session. Whatever you can afford. And I'll need to have you get a blood test each time before you come."

"How much is a half session?"

"$63." A half session was a half hour. At the time I thought he was expensive but since I only had to see him twice a year, I felt I could manage to fit it into my budget.

"Then I'll do a half session. I only had to have a blood test once a year in Virginia. Why do I need to get two blood tests?"

"Because that is what I require."

"But I hate getting blood tests."

"It gives me more of an accurate picture of how you are doing."

"But I always take my medications. My lithium level is always 1.0. You can check my records in Virginia."

"If you want to see me, that's what you'll have to do."

I could see Dr. Bot would not be a pushover. Definitely in control, I admired and respected him for that.

* * *

Soon after I started seeing Dr. Bot, I joined NAMI (National Association of Mentally Ill) in Spokane. I got their newsletters although I didn't like getting newsletters in the mail that said I was mentally ill. The stigma of being mentally ill still disturbed me. No one says a cancer patient is bodily ill so why do we say a person with a brain disorder is mentally ill? I did not want to be called mentally ill. I wished the newsletters came in a brown wrapper that didn't advertise the fact that it went to the mentally ill. I didn't want to be reminded or set apart. I was normal, after all, when I took my medication.

One day I called the office and learned they were having a meeting inside the First Presbyterian Church in Spokane on 3rd and south Cedar. The large, tan/gray stone, modified gothic building stood near the I-90 overpass. The meeting started at 7:00 p.m. I came early and went up the stairs to the meeting room where there were two NAMI leaders and some bipolar people as well as one guy I thought was schizophrenic.

We took turns introducing ourselves and each stated our diagnosis. I didn't like being around people with various brain disorders. It made me feel eerie, like it was a whole different world from the normal one I belonged to, like I was in a mental ward in the state hospital or something. Obviously there were degrees of severity. I didn't identify with these people. My problem was only a chemical imbalance. I felt like if I continued to socialize with them, I would become like them. They were weird. I never went back.

Chapter 48

I could not pay off my creditors, my brothers, sisters and parents did not offer to give me a loan and I could not absorb the debt so the only other alternative was to declare bankruptcy. My brother, Don, kindly offered me a place to stay for a while. He had matured to a wonderful, giving human being. I considered myself lucky.

Early one morning, the upstairs door opened and Melissa, Don's wife, hollered down the stairs. "Joan, you have a phone call."

Next, I heard the baby, two-year-old Kristen, start to cry. Barely awake, I looked at the clock which said 4:30 a.m. and ran upstairs. They didn't heat the basement so the cement floor was freezing cold and I didn't own a pair of slippers or a robe but that was the least of my worries. *Who in the world would be calling me at this hour?*

"Yes, this is Joan Kopczynski. Who's this?"

It was a woman with a man's gruff voice. "XYZ Collection Agency calling for ABC Credit Card Company. So, you think you can run up a lot of charges on your account and then skip town. Motherfucker. You blood sucking pig! Did you think we wouldn't come after you for not paying your bill? You good-for-nothing goddamn cunt."

"How did you get my number?"

"Your Mom gave it to us. We called her earlier."

Oh, boy. I had put my parents' address as my forwarding address because I didn't know where I would end up. "Do you realize what time it is here? You just woke up a baby." I felt guilty about waking up innocent people and I wanted her to feel guilty, too. This east coast vulture must not have known she was three hours ahead. Or did she know?

"We'll do a lot worse if you don't start paying back the money you owe ABC."

"You need to talk to my attorney."

I had recently contacted Attorney Greg Heline to represent me. I gave her his name, address and phone number and then hung up. I had similar calls like this on other days from other creditors but as soon as I gave them the attorney's information, they quit calling.

* * *

I filed for Chapter 7 bankruptcy on October 25, 1991, making it ten years before I could have any decent credit again. I went to the bankruptcy hearing by myself. I've always done everything alone and none of my siblings nor my Mom or Dad offered to come with me for moral support. I didn't know what to expect.

The Meeting of Creditors convened a month after I filed on November 26 at the Office of the U.S. Trustee, Wall Street, Hearing Room B, which was a small typical government office that held about ten to fifteen people. John M. Klobucher, Bankruptcy Judge for U.S. Bankruptcy Court Eastern District of Washington, presided, and Jack R. Reeves was Trustee.

The judge took roll call. When the judge came to my name, a tall gentleman from Gregory Heline's office stood up, turned and looked at me and said, "Hi, I'm your Attorney." I had never met him before. I think his name was John.

The judge said, "Assets or personal property?"

"$530," answered my attorney.

"Do you have the list of creditors?"

"Yes, here it is, your Honor." He handed him two legal-size sheets with all my creditors listed and the amounts I owed each one. I had previously given him the names and addresses of all fifteen creditors and he researched how much I owed each one.

"Let's see. Total debt is $22,077.81. Is that correct?"

"Yes, sir," my attorney said.

My debts were discharged January 31, 1992. That debt did not include Sun Breeze Apartments in Melbourne, Florida, which sent me a bill after the bankruptcy was discharged for $1,288.46. My attorney told me to send them a copy of my discharge so they quit hounding me and I never paid them. I later found out I owed my mother over $7,000.00, which I failed to put on my bankruptcy (big mistake). So the grand total of all my debts was actually $30,366.27.

Now the third time in my life that I had to live in poverty, I wondered if I would ever break free. Whatever happened to the life of wealth I had planned for myself?

My sister, Connie, gave me a card with a poem on it by Elisa Costanza which said: “Don’t ever give up your dreams . . . and never leave them behind. Find them; make them yours, and all through your life, cherish them, and never let them go.” Inside, Connie wrote: “You can do it!” It brought tears to my eyes. I keep it by my computer. I am also fond of Winston Churchill’s famous commencement address. “Never give up. Never give up. Never give up.” They are words I live by.

Chapter 49

I moved in with my brother, Don, and his family in a subdivision on the north side of Spokane called Arrowhead Point. The development had lots of young, rising executives, Don and his wife, Melissa, included. They opened up their four-bedroom, three-story, steel gray, cedar house to me in September 1991 while I recovered financially and mentally from my "foolishness" in Virginia.

Like my parents, Don never asked me about my "foolishness," never gave me a chance to explain. It was as if he denied the existence of my disorder and especially my bizarre behavior. Like my other siblings, he just treated me as if I was normal, as if nothing had ever happened. I sensed that my family blamed me though and I blamed myself for ruining my life.

I learned that my mental illness was actually very hard on my family, for they were often baffled or frustrated or angered by my behavior. They reacted to the only physical, tangible thing they saw—the behavior. They didn't recognize it as manifesting from an illness.

Don and his wife were godsends. Luckily, they refused to allow me to pay anything for rent, food or utilities while I lived with them. I don't know what I would have done without them.

While living with their family, I bonded with little two-year-old Kristen. She and I would play alligators. We'd get down on all fours and imagine we were in Florida. I'd paint a picture of the hot summer sun. Then we would pretend to bite each other and growl and hiss like alligators. Kristen loved it and always wanted to play whenever she saw me, but she had nightmares because of it and Melissa told me, "You're going to get up with her in the middle of the night when she screams." We stopped playing even though Kristen was too young to figure out why.

So that I wouldn't disrupt their family life, I headed downstairs after dinner each evening to my cold basement bedroom to write using my IBM Selectric typewriter. My icy fingers needed gloves but I was determined not to be a problem.

One night, not too long after I arrived at Don and Melissa's, Connie called.

"Hey, Joan, how are things?"

"Not bad. I found a job today through a want ad in the paper."

"Where?"

"It's for National Fundraising Associates out at the Incubator. They go by the name of Mama D's Pizza. I guess I'll get to eat as much pizza as I want."

"That's pretty cool. How much does it pay?"

"Not much. I figured I'll make $15,000 a year."

"Can you live on that?"

"If I continue staying with Don and Melissa I can. Otherwise, no. I made almost $40,000 a year back in Washington, DC. The only difference here is the cost of rent. All the other stuff—food, utilities, gas, phone—are the same here as they were there."

"Gee, it's no wonder you had to declare bankruptcy."

"I didn't have a choice. There is no way I could absorb that kind of debt on a $15,000 salary."

"So, what are you doing at Don's to keep out of trouble?"

"Well, I've almost finished that genealogical study of Dad's family. I've worked on it for twenty years now whenever I could or had the motivation. We, Don and I, have decided to call it The Kopczynski Family History Book. You should see what a great job he's been doing on the photos and layout. He has identified everyone in every photograph."

"So, you two have been getting along, huh? That's amazing."

"Hardly. Melissa is about ready to lock the door on us and give away the key. I'm exaggerating but we argue constantly about every stupid little detail. Do you know he's typing the whole thing himself and he's not a good typist? I wanted to do it but he won't let me. He actually refused to correct the typos. He said no one will notice them. That infuriated me."

"Well, Joan it was nice of him to give you a place to stay. Maybe you should bend a little bit on this."

"Connie, I went out and bought Don a $200 Don Quixote Lladro figurine and I got him a $300 gift certificate to Spokane Power Tool on Hamilton/Trent. He wants to buy something called a biscuit jointer. So, he is getting plenty of thanks from me. My name is going on the book. I should get some say in how it's done. I won't get any monetary reward, that's for sure."

"Why not? How much are you charging for it?"

"It's going to be a big, hardcover book which sells for $50 each. At that price, we'll just break even, not counting the phone calls I made."

"Well, Don is paying for all the photos and the layout, isn't he?"

"Yeah, but I am calling all of our hundreds of relatives to get their dates of birth, marriage and death information. It's costing me over $1,500. That doesn't include my time. Of course, each person has to get on the phone and gab, which runs up the bill. The phone company doesn't have any special rates right now on long distance calls."

"Wow, that's a gigantic job. When do you do it?"

"At night after dinner."

"Well, at least it keeps your mind off ruining your life and ending up in bankruptcy. So, how is your mental health these days? Have you run into any more communists?"

I laughed. "No. I am taking my medicine. Considering all of the losses again in my life this past year it's amazing I'm not depressed though. I take my drugs regularly and they work for me."

"That's a Yeah God!"

"Yes, it is."

Chapter 50

Six months passed; I still lived with Don and Melissa. They said I could stay with them for as long as I liked. I didn't bother them and they liked my company, even though Don and I argued about the Family History Book

Don, who was a manager at Avista, the local utilities company, came home one day and told me a guy from work had a daughter who needed a place to stay so they would be giving her my room in the basement and I could double up with one of the kids upstairs. The girl's father used to work for the FBI before his employment with Avista.

The house got a little crowded now, and I was faintly paranoid about Mary's connection to the FBI. My troubles began because I had once associated with an FBI Agent. I didn't like this arrangement and because I no longer had my own space, I moved to an apartment on the bottom of the South Hill, closer to where I worked and not far from where my sister, Marilyn, lived.

Since I had no furniture or possessions whatsoever, I asked Marilyn if I could have my bedroom furniture back. Five years was long enough for them to use them.

"Well, after all, I never gave them to you for keeps."

"Yes, you did. What would you have done with them if we hadn't taken them?"

"I gave you my tape deck to pay you back the money I owed. I didn't give you all my furniture. Look, I don't have any furniture."

"Well, you can have them back. I don't care. We can get another dresser."

I never said another word but when I went over to her house to retrieve the furniture, I felt every hair on my head turn gray. They had used the nightstand as a telephone table and her kids had carved things in the top and a screw was missing on the handle of one drawer. Then we went to the basement.

"One of the boys peed on your mattresses so they are toast. He had a little bedwetting problem for awhile." She laughed.

I hoped she'd say I'll give you $100 for them because I had already priced a set of discount mattresses and they cost $350 but Marilyn didn't offer. I wished she'd tell me that her son was going to take out a paper route to pay me back but that conversation didn't happen either. It was just my tough luck.

When I walked into the basement family room, I wanted to cry. They had taken the top of my Lane cedar chest off its hinges and treated it like a piece of cheap furniture. A heavy fish tank rested on the leather top which left an indelible impression that I felt I would never be able to get out completely. My old boyfriend, Bill Holbrook, had given me that cedar chest one romantic Christmas several years ago. The memories of love that it evoked were wiped out by their total lack of concern for my property.

"You can have that back, too."

Tears welled up in my eyes. "You ruined it by putting that fish tank on it."

"It's not ruined. It will be ok once we take it off there."

"You can't ever get that mark out of the leather."

"Oh, you can, too. Don't worry."

"I don't want it back."

"Ok, we'll keep it."

"No, I don't want to look at it at your house ever again. I want you to give it to Goodwill. I don't want to be reminded that you ruined it."

I tried not to care about my personal possessions. I learned then that it is not good to own things with sentimental value or at least not lend them to your relatives. Why, I wondered, are people tied to such inanimate objects? What in human nature makes us care about our possessions when we know we can't take them with us when we die?

Besides, Marilyn was just doing what I wanted her to. I let them have it because I had nowhere else to put it or store it. Looking back, I realize now what a burden my mental illness has put on my family. Not only did they have to try and get rid of my stuff, they had to suffer because of my ill feelings toward them.

I went back to my apartment and sat on my twenty-year-old yellow and green couch that Mom had given me. We had such different tastes.

I hated the color and told her I could sit on the floor until I could afford to buy one myself but she insisted I take it.

I hated being a charity case. I didn't like people's discards, especially Mom's, but since I had nothing I was expected to be grateful. I turned on the old TV set that Mom gave me. Like always, the channel occasionally blinked off so I had to get up off the couch and go switch it back. There wasn't anything good on TV so I turned it off and called Connie.

"Are you busy?"

"No, what's up?"

"I just came back from Marilyn's. She said I could have my bedroom furniture back but she ruined all of it . . ."

"All right. I don't want to hear about it. At least now you'll have some furniture."

"Yeah, I guess. I do have some other good news."

"What?"

"I got a raise at work."

"At the telemarketing company?"

"No, at Arby's. I thought I told you I was working there."

"I think you did. I just forgot. So, how much?"

"Well, I was no good as a cashier or on the fries so they gave me a job cleaning the floors and tables and making sure the condiments and ice machines were filled. Boy, you have to fill this big, heavy bucket with ice and stand on a chair and dump it over your head into the Machine."

"Ok, get to the point."

"One day the owner came into the store and he saw what a good job I was doing—it was exactly how he had wanted it done. I never met the man but soon after I received an unprecedented raise for my efforts—a nickel an hour."

Connie and I both howled.

"A nickel an hour? I thought. I can't do this so I saw an ad in The *Spokesman Review* for a telemarketer and I called the number. I had told Arby's management when I first hired on that I didn't like telemarketing but now I realize I can make more money telemarketing."

"So, did you interview for the job?"

"Yeah, a couple interviewed me—Jim and Helen Kraft. They hired me and then told me I would be working for their son, Patrick, a newly hired insurance agent for Farmer's Insurance."

"What's the pay?"

"$5 an hour. I'll be working 20 hours a week."

"Don't you think you're overdoing it? You'll be too tired to work a full time job and twenty more hours. That's sixty hours a week. You're not getting management wages for it. Is it really worth it?"

"I need the money. I'm still trying to pay off my student loans and I'm still making payments to Mom for that old Pontiac 6000 she sold me. I wonder why she thought it was worth $5,000. I've had nothing but repairs on that car."

"Well, your credit sucked so be grateful for the loan."

"I am but I was desperate and at her mercy when I bought it from her. And Mom says I'm lazy, sassy and spoiled. I'll show her. I just have to manage my time better."

"Won't the extra hours put a strain on your illness?"

"It won't affect my illness. I can still get enough sleep and I'll have less financial stress worries. I'll be fine."

Epilogue

Reflecting back on my life, my illness hasn't been the only obstacle but it has been the main one. Dr. Bot thinks I am definitely not schizophrenic but I am mostly schizoaffective, a vague set of symptoms that has traits of both mood disorder and schizophrenia but does not fit the strict criteria for either one. The way a person responds to medication largely determines the diagnosis. The Trilafon works wonders for me, relieving my symptoms of paranoia like an aspirin relieves a headache. Dr. Bot feels my depression has been more situational than biological. He has tried to wean me off lithium but I have taken it now for thirty years and I am afraid to give it up. I wonder if it would wreck my life like weaning me off Trilafon did. I have tried Prozac and Depakote but they did not work for me. In the twenty years that Dr. Bot has seen me, he has never seen symptoms of mania in me.

Because of the side effects of taking lithium and Trilafon so long, my lifestyle has radically changed. I have always loved to travel but now I dread it because I need to include plans to make sure a bathroom is close by at all times. Lithium killed my thyroid and put a strain on my kidneys. I take thyroid pills and I can't go for more than an hour and a half without having to pee, and may eventually need a kidney transplant. The Trilafon has wiped out any elasticity in my colon and I now have to drink MiraLAX every night for constipation.

My health insurance still doesn't cover my doctor visits. In thirty years, I have spent over $15,000 on doctor visits alone, another $3,800 on blood (lithium level) tests not covered by insurance and about $25,000 on medicine, including when my medicine wasn't covered by insurance. I have always been very independent and paid for all my care myself, not wishing to burden my family.

My mother had no qualms about burdening me, however. Through one of my sisters she repeatedly asked me to pay back the $7,000 Dad loaned me when I was poverty stricken even though I had undergone bankruptcy. Because I had no money, this was harder to swallow than finding out I was mentally ill. I ended up working two jobs for nine years and then worked six 80-hour weeks plus other weeks of more grueling hours of overtime at the telemarketing firm to pay back the debt before Dad died in August 2003.

In twenty-five years Mom never once asked me about my illness or gave me any sympathy. She gave my sister, Carole, a lot of sympathy and love because she had an illness she could see. I, however, had an illness she couldn't see so I felt I received no support and little love. Although I tried hard to educate her, she refused to learn. She died in November 2005.

In 2008, after coming out of the closet about my illness, I gave NAMI another try, consciously deciding not to care what my mailman and neighbors think about me having a mental illness. I feel it is very important to get NAMI's newsletters about new information concerning the illness and it helps make me feel less isolated and more connected.

To get out of poverty for the third time in my life, I got a job as an insurance agent at a telemarketing firm, selling insurance nationally over the phone. I also managed to write four (unpublished) espionage suspense novels which I hope will fund my retirement. And who knows, maybe if I make a lot of money, I can realize my dream of building a museum for "children and those wanting to be a child once more" in Spokane or Coeur d' Alene which I will call "Aunt Joan's House" although now without help from my mentor and friend, Jack Hashian. He died in April of 1999.

I have had many challenges in my life but I have persevered. I may not become the millionaire I dreamed of, but I will never be a burden to anyone. I will never give up.

Baby portrait. *Photo by Len's Studio, Cottonwood, Idaho*

1972 high School Graduation Photo
Photo by Ladd Arnoti Studio, Cottonwood, Idaho

Joan in the dress Conrad liked. Her escort is her brother's friend Larry Murray.

The man I called Michael O'Neill. Photographer unknown.

1987 family photo. TopRow: Marilyn, Don, Allan, Connie, Larry, Carole. Middle Row: Joan, Bertha, Stan, Theresa. Bottom Row: Karen, Maureen.
Photo by Saborah Studio, Troy, Idaho

Jack Hashian

Joan in 1991 at the time she was manic. Photo by Glamour Shots®

Joan in 2009 Photo by Jeremy Kuhlman

Addendum

Schizoaffective disorder

Schizoaffective disorder is a vague set of symptoms that includes traits from both schizophrenia and mood disorder but does not meet the strict criteria for either one. The disorder was introduced in 1933 by a doctor who determined that many formerly diagnosed schizophrenic patients also possessed some traits of mood disorder.

Symptoms: According to the American Psychiatric Association's Diagnostic and Statistical Manual, 4th edition, a person with the schizoaffective disorder will usually have some, but not all, of the symptoms described below.

Schizophrenia: Symptoms fall into two categories: positive and negative.

Positive symptoms (reflect a *distortion* of normal functions):

- Delusions (false beliefs, includes paranoia)
- Hallucinations—hearing voices
- Disorganized speech
- Grossly disorganized or catatonic behavior

Negative symptoms (reflect a *loss* of normal functions):

- Affective flattening—reduced or inappropriate emotional expression
- Alogia—poverty of speech
- Avolition—inability to initiate and persist in goal-directed activities

A person with the schizoaffective disorder will likely have impairment in interpersonal relations, difficulty keeping a job for a long period of time, diminished social contacts, disrupted educational attempts, challenges with self-care, and increased risk of suicide. However, symptoms appear to be less severe than those in schizophrenia. Those afflicted with this disorder often become frustrated because functioning is below that which had been realized before the onset of symptoms. This may be difficult to accept because the person's intelligence is unimpaired. However, the ability to tolerate stress is impaired, and it is this which hinders future realization of goals. Employment is usually at a lower standard than that of their parents or even siblings. Most (60%-70%) do not marry.

Mood Disorder:

Mania:

- Euphoria or elevated mood
- Irritability
- Inflated self-esteem or grandiosity
- Decreased need for sleep
- Pressure of speech
- Flight of ideas
- Distractibility
- Increased goal-directed activities or psychomotor agitation
- Participation in activities with high potential for detrimental consequences such as reckless driving, spending sprees, foolish business investments and unusual or inappropriate (for the person) sexual behavior

Depression:

- Depressed mood
- Diminished interest in activities or pleasure
- Changes in appetite or weight
- Difficulty falling asleep or staying asleep
- Changes in psychomotor activity
- Decreased energy

- Feelings of worthlessness, hopelessness, helplessness
- Inappropriate guilt
- Difficulty thinking, concentrating or making decisions
- Recurrent thoughts of death or suicide

Other People With Mental Illness:

Abraham Lincoln, Virginia Woolf, Eugene O'Neill, Beethoven, Robert Schumann, Leo Tolstoy, John Keats, Tennessee Williams, Vincent Van Gogh, Isaac Newton, Ernest Hemingway, Sylvia Plath, Michelangelo, Winston Churchill, Vivien Leigh, Emperor Norton I, Patty Duke, Charles Dickens.